T0342246

Stateless Commerce

Stateless Commerce

*The Diamond Network
and the Persistence
of Relational Exchange*

BARAK D. RICHMAN

Harvard University Press

Cambridge, Massachusetts, and London, England   2017

Copyright © 2017 by the President and Fellows of Harvard College
All rights reserved
Printed in the United States of America

First printing

Library of Congress Cataloging-in-Publication Data

Names: Richman, Barak, author.
Title: Stateless commerce : the diamond network and the persistence of
relational exchange / Barak D. Richman.
Description: Cambridge, Massachusetts : Harvard University Press, 2017. |
Includes bibliographical references and index.
Identifiers: LCCN 2016050799 | ISBN 9780674972179 (alk. paper)
Subjects: LCSH: Exchange—New York (State)—New York. | Statelessness. |
Diamond industry and trade—New York (State)—New York. |
Consensual contracts—Social aspects—New York (State)—New York.
Classification: LCC HF1008 .R53 2017 | DDC 381 / .4573623—dc23
LC record available at https://lccn.loc.gov/2016050799

In deepest gratitude for lessons on what makes good scholarship:

> *To Daniel Patrick Moynihan, who taught it had to be important*
> *To Oliver Williamson, who taught it had to be novel*
> *To Steven Shavell, who taught it had to be interesting*
> *To Clark Havighurst, who taught it had to be right*

> *And to my parents, who taught that whatever I do, I have to love doing it*

Contents

Preface

A visitor to midtown Manhattan will likely stroll down Fifth Avenue and witness one of the most cosmopolitan retail centers in the world. That same visitor might stroll down Sixth Avenue and view the Rockefeller Center, international bank offices, and other heights of today's modern commerce. But should that visitor wander from Fifth to Sixth along 47th Street—crossing from high fashion to high finance—she would find herself in what looks like an ancient barter economy.

New York's 47th Street is the epicenter of America's diamond industry and feels like a time bubble. Unlike midtown's stylish shoppers and elegant businesspeople, pedestrians on 47th Street are a cross section of the global economy, a colorful fabric of ethnicities, languages, and energies unfurled in the street. Bustling merchants speak English, Yiddish, Hebrew, Hindi, Bucharan, Marathi, Rajasthani, and assorted Slavic languages. Many march with briefcases handcuffed to their wrists and bark on cellphones; others inspect stones in open storefronts, removing them from carefully folded paper and holding a jeweler's loupe to their eye. And they wear a diversity of hats: ultra-Orthodox Jews wear black fedoras and sport full beards with traditional nineteenth-century black garb; Jewish merchants from across the globe wear yarmulkes—some knitted, most black, some tucked beneath baseball caps; Central Asian merchants wear traditional karakul and papakha hats; old-style Europeans in long overcoats wear ascot caps, flat caps, and an occasional derby. Merchants with similar hats coalesce together in small gaggles, walking briskly or gesturing aggressively to each other, evincing a determined energy that makes this lucrative center feel like an outdoor market in a developing economy.

The diamond industry is unusual in many respects, and 47th Street—which the *New York Times* called "an anachronism, a 17th-century industry smack in the middle of a 21st century city" (Weber 2001)—offers a glimpse into the industry's majesty and mystery. This book explores the diamond industry with an academic agenda, and it does so with two objectives: to understand the roots of the industry's unusual features and to glean lessons that explain the features of the modern economy. In short, it asks, Why does the diamond industry appear so extraordinary, and why doesn't the rest of the economy look the same?

This effort began over a decade ago when I studied under Oliver Williamson, and it closely reflects his approach to research. Williamson impressed on his students to avoid methodological orthodoxy, remain curious, and pursue an interdisciplinary approach—or, as he put it, approach a research project "with multiple arrows in your quiver." Combining the insights of a cultural anthropologist (Roy D'Andrade) and a Nobel Prize–winning economist (Robert Solow), he later wrote,

> D'Andrade (1986) captures the [interdisciplinary] spirit in his contrast between authoritative and inquiring research orientations. Whereas the former is characterized by an advanced state of development, is self-confident, and declares that "This is the law here," the latter is more tentative, pluralist, and exploratory and poses the question, "What is going on here?" ... Witness Solow's (1997) observation that "there is a lot to be said in favor of staring at the piece of reality you are studying and asking, *just what is going on here?*" (Williamson 2007, 14, emphasis added by Williamson)

This book begins with asking *what* is going on, and then proceeds to ask *why* it is going on. I have spent a lot of time, in Solow's words, staring at this piece of reality, and hopefully I offer both an accurate description of that reality and some lessons that accompany it.

"Stateless Commerce"

Forty-Seventh Street and its midtown Manhattan environs are an illustration of a paradox that is common to many of the world's commercial centers: the coexistence of the modern and the primitive. The world's urban centers frequently exhibit shiny skyscrapers that house the most sophisticated and contemporary financial institutions alongside pockets of ethnically homogeneous merchants operating a barter economy just as their ancestors did centuries ago. Conventional understandings of economic, cultural, and technological progress suggest that the old commercial world would be displaced by the new, yet this old world persists.

Ethnic trading networks continue to thrive in each of the globe's richest and most modern cities. They are organized around personal exchange, in which transacting parties either have firsthand familiarity with each other or rely on clan- or ethnic-based connections to acquire personal information about business partners. Transactions are often paperless, usually lawyerless, and disputes are rarely resolved in state courts. Goods and services, frequently of significant value, are regularly sold on unsecured credit. Deals rely on mutual trust, even as distrust of strangers causes these networks to remain insulated from, and often secret to, the outside world.

Why, and how, do ethnic trading networks remain a staple of the modern economy? This book's central argument rests simply on principles of efficiency: for some industries, ethnic-based exchange remains economically superior to all available alternatives. This is remarkable only when one considers how much other industries have come to rely on contemporary alternatives. Modern commerce is associated with complex commercial structures, such as large corporations, banks, and other sophisticated economic entities. Most industries have moved away from "primitive" personal exchange and ethnic networks. Yet in some pockets of modern commerce, premodern forms of organization remain the norm.

I call these pockets "stateless commerce" because they do not rely on the modern state for support. Noted economist Avinash Dixit, one of several prominent scholars who have become interested in commercial networks resting on personal exchange, has described this kind of economic organization as "lawless," but I think "stateless" is a more accurate term. The distinction between this commerce and conventional commerce is not the absence of law, since law is very much present in stateless industries: promises made in personal commercial contexts are legally enforceable, theft is punishable, and parties injured by tortious conduct have a legitimate legal claim. What makes these merchant communities unusual is that members do not enforce these legal claims with state-sponsored instruments. Whereas most industries rely on courts, governmental authorities, and other instruments of the state to enforce contracts, secure property rights, provide regulatory certainty, and preserve the value of financial assets, these industries reject state instruments and instead use private substitutes. Rather than relying on courts and judges to adjudicate disputes, merchants in these industries turn to local and community leaders to resolve disagreements. Rather than relying on state-sponsored public servants—police officers and court marshals—to enforce contracts or deter illegal conduct, merchants in these industries orchestrate and implement their own punishments.

The diamond industry is a paradigmatic stateless industry. It rejects wholesale any use of modern legal instruments to resolve disputes—in fact, diamond merchants who invoke the state by filing suits in court are deemed to have transgressed an important industry norm. It also presents a colorful example of how ethnic trading networks serve the functions that are usually filled by modern state institutions. Taking the diamond industry as a concrete case study offers an opportunity to examine in great detail the social conventions, industry institutions, community forces, and economic pressures that enable stateless commerce.

The Book's Thesis: Comparative Institutional Advantages

The persistence of stateless commerce poses a challenge to the conventional wisdom—shared by policy makers, economic historians, and all shades of academics—that modern legal institutions are a necessary component in the path to prosperity. State-sponsored courts, specifically, play an important role in this standard narrative of economic history. Because public courts can secure transactions between "impersonal" transactors and open markets to new merchants and new ideas, many theories of economic development credit courts for laying an important foundation for economic growth. Conversely, personal exchange is associated with primitive, prelegal societies with a limited capacity to create wealth.

In spite of rejecting the very institutions that receive credit for building modern economic development, stateless commerce continues to thrive in the modern economy, and several stateless networks maintain strangleholds over entire segments of commerce. Their persistence raises two puzzles. The first is the more obvious conundrum: Why do these industries retain premodern modes of organization when the rest of the world has embraced, and relies on, modern state-sponsored instruments to support commercial exchange? If market and evolutionary forces favor instruments that offer more efficient economic institutions, why does this pocket of economic activity continue to rely on premodern instruments that most of the world has long abandoned? The second puzzle is the converse of the first: If these ethnic economic networks thrive in the modern economy, why do they not dominate a larger portion of modern commerce? If their method of economic organization has withstood all economic and evolutionary forces, why has it not dominated other methods of organization?

This book explains both the persistence and the limits of stateless commerce with a very simple argument: For certain kinds of commercial transactions, personal exchange remains superior to court-supported impersonal exchange, and for certain industries, premodern mechanisms remain superior to our modern institutions. This argument piggybacks on the key insight in Ronald Coase's 1937 paper that launched institutional economics. Coase asked why certain transactions are organized inside firms and others within markets; this book asks why certain transactions are governed by personal exchange and others by state-sponsored institutions. Both questions suggest that there are both virtues and limitations to different kinds of economic organization. Therefore, the endurance of commerce that does not require support from public courts—and remains structured much as it was in premodern times—suggests that there are meaningful limitations to what our modern public institutions can do.

Overview of the Book

As was noted previously, this book begins with asking *what* is going on here, and then proceeds to ask *why* it is going on. It thus begins with a framework to understand what statelessness is, proceeds with a detailed empirical examination of the diamond industry, and then inductively extracts theoretical arguments. Chapter 1 reviews the academic literature with an aim to defining statelessness. It distinguishes within the literature an assortment of enforcement mechanisms, identifies important characteristics that vary across those mechanisms, and offers a taxonomy that puts statelessness in context. Chapter 2 then introduces the diamond industry, presenting an overview of the diamond network by tracing a diamond's long, global, and multistep path from its mining from the ground to its purchase by a jewelry manufacturer. It also recounts the long history of Jewish diamond merchants, who have played a leading (but not exclusive) role in the industry for nearly a millennium. Domination by ethnically homogeneous merchant communities is both a salient characteristic of today's industry and a persistent feature of the industry over centuries.

Chapter 3 then elaborates on the industry's structure—its particular rules, its customary norms, and the elaborate mix of commercial and community institutions that organize the industry—and describes how diamond merchants enforce contracts and secure credit sales without relying on state support. It begins by examining the features of a typical diamond transaction and lays the underpinning for one of the book's foundational arguments: The unusual organization of the entire industry is a natural consequence of the particular challenges of a conventional diamond sale. Nearly all of the remainder of the book flows from this microanalytic understanding of the diamond transaction. Chapter 3 then provides an in-depth description of New York's Jewish diamond merchants and focuses on how family, religious, and community institutions support economic exchange. It explains how the industry has managed to remain stateless into the twenty-first century.

These chapters lay the groundwork for Chapter 4, which constitutes the heart of the book's theoretical contribution. This chapter offers a positive theory of statelessness that predicts when industries and merchants will opt for personal exchange and private contract enforcement, even when state-sponsored courts are available. It also explains why the diamond industry is one such industry that relies exclusively on private ordering.

Chapters 5 through 7 then explore the implications of the empirics in Chapters 2 and 3 and the theory articulated in Chapter 4. Chapter 5 describes certain economic downsides to statelessness and, as an illustration, documents both the inefficiencies that plague New York's system of private enforcement, many of which are revealed through antitrust suits, and the current struggles to modernize the diamond industry. Chapter 6 applies the lessons derived from the earlier chapters to explore current debates in Jewish economic history, economic geography, and development policy. Chapter 7 discusses the particular governance challenges presented by stateless industries, using the diamond network to understand how ethnic commercial networks interface with a globalizing economy and how stateless commerce illuminates foundational geopolitical regulatory challenges and governance deficits. Chapter 8 then concludes, observing that the diamond exchanges and many generations-old merchant families find themselves at a crossroads that might lead to significant changes to the industry's millennia-old structure.

This book has been in the making for over a decade, and it is humbling to consider the debts I have accrued during that time.[1] My first thanks goes to those listed in my dedication—Senator Pat Moynihan, Oliver Williamson, Steve Shavell, and Clark Havighurst—who were instrumental in my growth as a scholar and teacher. Thanks as well to Judge Bruce Selya, another intellectual giant who offered mentorship and lessons in the law and in life. My first writings on the diamond industry took place when I was a graduate student, and I benefited enormously from attentive training from Pablo Spiller, Rui de Figueiredo, Einer Elhauge, Louis Kaplow, Christine Jolls, and Andrei Shleifer. Special thanks go to Lisa Bernstein for inspiring me (and many others) with her pioneering work on the diamond industry and for graciously offering timely comments as my early work emerged, and to Marc Galanter, both for his foundational scholarship on which this book relies and for continuing to connect contemporary scholars of legal pluralism. One of those scholars is Manuel Gomez, whom I thank for sharing his research on Indian diamond merchants and a common academic interest.

I cannot convey how deeply indebted I feel to my colleagues at Duke University, who have offered enormous support, collegiality, and community over the years. They have tolerated many iterations of these chapters and created a vibrant intellectual environment in which I could share them. I'll refrain from mentioning names to avoid listing the entire faculty, but I do want to give special thanks to Jennifer Behrens, Michael Hannon, Joy Hanson, and Jean Jentilet for exceptional research support. I also thank colleagues at Columbia and Harvard for hosting me for semesters and providing fruitful feedback on drafts of this manuscript.

My conversations with principals in the diamond industry have been invaluable, and their time and insights give texture and feeling to each chapter. I want to express particular gratitude to and admiration for Chaim

Even-Zohar, whose knowledge, expertise, and wisdom relating to the diamond industry are truly unrivaled. And very special thanks go to the many people at Diacore who have offered insights and given me patient, in-person tutelage in the industry: Shahaf Teichman (in Mumbai and later in Antwerp), Rakesh Ghia (in Mumbai), and Pavlo Protopapa (in Geneva).

Diamonds lend themselves easily to metaphors, and many come to mind when I think of the love, inspiration, warmth, brilliance, and good cheer I've enjoyed from my wife, Laura, and three children, Ariella, Eden, and Izak. The only question is which metaphor works best: A diamond, like family, is forever? A father / husband begins as a rough stone and requires skillful and patient polishing? None quite fits, but I am blessed to have them in my life and to share this work with them.

Stateless Commerce

1

Statelessness in Context

THIS BOOK joins a literature that has attracted widespread interdisciplinary attention. The fascination is due to a number of sources, with each field finding something that caters to its own interests. Economic sociologists and anthropologists are fascinated by the social structures that emerge to organize commercial relationships. Economists aim to understand markets and the structures that enable exchange. Historians study the development of pre-legal institutions, ethnographers observe norms and behaviors in insular communities, and political scientists examine the mobilization of collective power. But perhaps most revealing is the interest of legal scholars since this interest might be motivated by a particular self-criticism. When communities create their own system of law, they reject much of what is taught at law schools. Rejected are the procedural rules that purportedly assure notice and guarantee due process, the substantive rules that we claim promote efficiency and fairness, and the civic obligations we promote to develop a common system. All are spurned in favor of tailored law and a separate system of governance. How are legal scholars to understand a rejection of their trade?

Of course, the world of law can learn from those who reject it, and especially from those who have constructed alternatives. And although the diamond industry offers an extreme case study of rejection—a commercial world that has removed itself from state-sponsored institutions perhaps for longer and more thoroughly than any other industry—it has been noted that "the study of extreme instances often helps to illuminate the essentials of a situation" (Williamson 1985, 35, citing the 1962 Behavioral Sciences Subpanel of the President's Science Advisory Committee). As unusual and unfamiliar as the diamond network might appear, it can reveal core lessons into the world from which it removed itself.

Thus, the law can learn from the extralegal and the state can learn from statelessness. But an important beginning is to be precise in conveying what "statelessness" is. The definition provided in the preface—a reliance on private, rather than state, governance—could use some elaboration, particularly since so much of our economy appears independent from state involvement. This opening chapter pursues precision by beginning with context. It reviews highlights of the abundant literature in private governance, offers some clarifying organization to that literature, and then pinpoints the categories and phenomena within the literature that embody statelessness.

The Many Faces of Private Law

The foundational scholarship that built the literature on private governance has achieved such renown—and has attracted such widespread interest—that it is even familiar to scholars in unrelated fields. Many credit the beginnings of this literature to Stewart Macaulay when, as a young law professor writing in the *American Sociological Review* in 1963, he observed in "Non-contractual Relations in Business: A Preliminary Study" that in business, "disputes are frequently settled without reference to the contract or potential or actual legal sanctions" (61). Although the observation that businesspeople try to avoid the courtroom seems self-evident (perhaps only in retrospect), it marked the start of a growing scholarly fascination with the world of extralegal enforcement. Whereas traditional legal scholarship focused on the substance of positive laws and court rulings, scholars began focusing on how actions outside the contemporary courtroom affect and support commerce.

The outpouring of subsequent scholarship naturally invited a diversity of perspectives: law and society scholars inquired into the social structures that induced cooperation, law and economics scholars examined how extralegal institutions maintained economic governance, law and psychology scholars examined how the interplay between legal and nonlegal norms motivated conduct, and legal historians investigated how commercial agreements were sustained in premodern times in the absence of court ordering. This research has remained widely interdisciplinary, benefiting from ethnographies by sociologists and anthropologists, archival discoveries by historians, data analysis by economists, and case studies by legal scholars. Avinash Dixit has further observed that "these distinct approaches have not developed in isolation from one another," and thus these diverse scholars "have learned from the work of others, and have built on it in their own way" (2004, vii).

One immediate result is that it is now rudimentary to observe that contracts can be enforced, and markets can work, without the intervention of state-sponsored institutions. There is a widespread recognition that state coercion is only one of many mechanisms that guide behavior and create social order; thus, state instruments have both private complements and private substitutes. But another result of this scholarly exuberance is a bit of conceptual confusion. The confusion might have been a consequence of the literature inviting new voices into what previously involved homogeneous legal scholars, or it might have been collateral damage from the richness of the case studies themselves, as fascinating details overshadowed some imprecision in the theoretical questions. But literature's assorted depictions of how private social institutions interact with and supplant state mechanisms have conflated different species of self-governing commercial worlds without identifying important differences among them.

It is critical to understand the different economic challenges that commercial parties confront before explaining how their institutions resolve those challenges. Once we understand the instances in which extralegal mechanisms arise, we can formulate better definitions for the assortment of informal mechanisms that emerge and recognize their economic significance. Identifying important distinctions within the literature's case studies—describing coherent categories and placing the world of diamond merchants within one of them—is a prerequisite to developing a concrete definition of, and theoretical framework for, stateless commerce.

Two Scholarly Threads

The literature has uncovered two prominent, but distinct, species of extralegal mechanisms to resolve disputes between commercial parties. The first category involves parties operating in the "shadow of the law," and the second involves institutions that enable "order without law."

Shadow of the Law

Parties regularly settle disputes within the "shadow of the law," meaning that they anticipate how a court or other legal authority would intervene, if asked, and they accordingly resolve their dispute without expending the costs of litigation. The term "shadow of the law" was originally coined by Martin Shapiro (1975) when he observed a lack of delineation between courts and other systems of adjudication. Although Shapiro used the term to emphasize that the law's "shadow" was distorted from law itself—he intended to observe that nonstate dispute resolution often varied significantly from how state courts actually functioned—the metaphor has come to represent the broad space in which parties understand the possibility of legal coercion.

Marc Galanter, writing in 1981, deserves credit for popularizing the law's proverbial shadow. Galanter used the shadow metaphor to criticize the legal academy's preoccupation with "legal centrism," a "state-centered view of legal phenomena" (1) in which scholars focus only on legal instruments found in public courts, to the exclusion of the broad array of private mechanisms and social forces (perhaps the subsequent onslaught of scholarship exploring private ordering would convince Galanter to temper his criticism). Galanter argued instead that the law's primary impact on human behavior is through its casting of a shadow, and the "principal contribution of courts to dispute resolution is providing a background of norms and procedures against which negotiations and regulation in both private and governmental settings take place" (6).

Under Galanter's view of the law's shadow, parties have a reasonably accurate understanding of their legal rights—specifically, the rights that a state-sponsored court will enforce with the state's coercive powers—and will manage their disputes and efforts at dispute resolution accordingly. Robert Mnookin and Lewis Kornhauser (1979) modeled and explored the parameters of the law's shadow in their seminal analysis of divorce settlements in "Bargaining in the Shadow of the Law: The Case of Divorce." Combining Mnookin's interest in negotiation theory and Kornhauser's expertise in economics, the pair reported that divorce lawyers can create value for their clients by first explaining clearly how a court would divide family property and then encouraging an early resolution that approximates the court's default. George Priest and Benjamin Klein's seminal 1984 model of the litigation process generalized the role of the law's shadow when it explained why so many disputes are resolved out of court. When defined and predictable legal rules cast a discernable shadow over the litigation process, the prospect of collective savings by avoiding litigation induces settlement. And conversely, the cases that do continue to litigation exhibit distinct features, including that they feature issues not clearly determined by existing law. In short, the law's shadow both encourages most cases to settle while also explaining which cases do not.

The "shadow" metaphor also extends to conduct that is upstream to dispute resolution, as it helps explain conduct that prevents disputes altogether. Macaulay's (1963) famous study, which observes that businesspeople invest in relationships precisely to avoid litigation, can be understood as parties maximizing within the law's shadow. Macaulay reported that when disagreements arise, parties recognize not only that litigation itself is costly but that it also damages potentially valuable commercial relations. So when disagreements emerge, they tend either to renegotiate or reconcile with a view toward continuing mutually beneficial commerce. Although Macaulay's study focused on businesspeople who encounter transactional disputes with commercial partners, his insight into how individuals operate for mutual benefit around the law's shadow extends to many different legal entitlements, including for property, tort, and contract law. When the law reduces uncertainty and establishes a well-understood foundation from which parties can pursue cooperation, beyond situations in which parties are embroiled in a potentially litigious dispute, it supports mutually beneficial relations. Ronald Coase's (1960) famous paper, which produced what is now known as the "Coase theorem"—that private parties with well-defined legal entitlements will engage in efficient cooperation regardless of how those rights are allocated—echoes this insight by modeling how bargaining takes place within the shadow of the law. Coasean efficient bargaining can only take place, and externalities will only be accounted for, if legal entitlements are reliably enforced (this is true even as Coase accounted for transaction costs in his analysis; introducing transaction costs might change the optimal allocation of legal entitlements, but productive bargaining still relied on the clear shadow of those entitlements). So long as the law's shadow is well defined, parties can engage in mutually valuable conduct without bearing the costs of state-made legal procedures.[1]

The growing and elaborate world of arbitration also falls neatly within Galanter's shadow. Arbitration and other forms of alternative dispute resolution (commonly referred to as ADR) are creatures of contract, in which parties to a deal agree to resolve their disputes through an alternative process. Typically, arbitration clauses direct disputing parties to turn to preidentified private agents, often an association of arbitrators, and preclude their litigating in a state court before the private arbitration process is complete. Parties include arbitration clauses in their contracts for all the same reasons Macaulay observed that businesspeople avoid litigation in courts. Arbitration is faster and cheaper, and often produces results that are more sensitive to the parties' intent when they entered into the agreement. Detailed arbitration clauses can also articulate the substantive rules and administrative procedures that parties want to resolve any future disputes. Once parties understand the substance and consequences of state substantive law, they can craft alternative rules that are mutually preferable to state-made contract and procedural law. One could think of arbitration clauses and other contract mechanisms as a product of Coasean bargaining from defined contract rules, or alternatively, as the same mutually beneficial bargaining that Macaulay observed, though bargaining that takes place while a contract is still being negotiated rather than after a disagreement has arisen in the course of a contract's performance. Arbitration and dispute-resolution contractual provisions are all efforts by parties to superimpose alternative rules and procedures that better meet their collective needs.

But arbitration clauses would be fruitless if state-sponsored courts either preempted arbitration procedures or were hesitant to enforce arbitration results. If American courts were not eager to encourage arbitration—if they either initiated proceedings before arbitration procedures were complete or were hesitant to enforce arbitration results—then arbitration and other ADR mechanisms would be limited. As it turns out, U.S. law lays a solid foundation for ADR. The Federal Arbitration Act instructs courts to defer to both arbitration procedures and arbitrator fact-finding, and the Supreme Court has issued a series of rulings that aggressively and enthusiastically enforce the act, interpreting it to establish "a liberal federal policy favoring arbitration agreements" (*Moses H. Cone Mem'l Hosp. v. Mercury Constr. Co.*, 460 U.S. 1, 24 (1983)). Accordingly, contracting parties proceed with confidence that arbitration clauses will be enforced in state-sponsored courts. Thus, the substance of arbitration and the mutually beneficial efficiencies that parties create through alternative dispute resolution are consequences of private bargaining, but the force and credibility of arbitration agreements lie in their enjoying the support of state-sponsored enforcement.

These related illustrations reveal that the law's shadow enables many categories of mutually beneficial conduct: economizing on litigation costs while resolving a dispute, navigating mutually beneficial relations so they avoid disputes altogether, bargaining with competing rights holders to internalize externalities, and drafting cost-reducing arbitration agreements. All are instances of cooperative private dispute resolution, and although none directly involve state institutions, they all are enabled by the shadow of state coercion. When state-sponsored courts enforce legal entitlements with reasonable predictability and reliability, parties can privately resolve their disputes through a host of efficiency-enhancing behaviors without direct assistance from the state.

Order without Law

Robert Ellickson's famous *Order without Law* (1991) documented the cooperative norms and behaviors of ranchers in Shasta County, an agrarian county in Northern California where straying cattle are a common source of property damage. Ellickson observed that ranchers do, indeed, ensure that the cattle owners are held responsible for their livestock and compensate neighbors when cattle damage fences or consume grass, but they do not comply with these norms because of the threat of legal coercion. The laws of Shasta County, unlike most other counties in California, held property owners responsible for safeguarding their property, rather than holding cattle owners liable for the damage caused by their livestock. In the language of the Coase theorem, the law bestowed the legal entitlement to the rancher, not the farmer, and thus the theorem would predict that cooperation would have the farmer pay the rancher to tend his cattle. Instead, Ellickson found that both ranchers and farmers rejected the county's substantive property law and in its place articulated alternative substantive rules: "Shasta County Neighbors, it turns out, do not behave as Coase portrays them as behaving in the Farmer-Rancher Parable. Neighbors in fact are strongly inclined to cooperate, but they achieve cooperative outcomes not by bargaining from legally established entitlements, as the parable supposes, but rather by developing and enforcing adaptive norms of neighborliness that trump formal legal entitlements" (Ellickson 1991, 3–4). Thus, Ellickson identified a different category of cooperation, described as "order without law." In Shasta County, ranchers and farmers cooperated—and generated mutual gains—without calculating (indeed, ignoring!) what a court would do. This was cooperation wholly outside the law's shadow, and instead was without legal coercion altogether.

The lack of legal coercion did not mean there were no consequences to misbehavior. Key to Ellickson's observation, and consistent with an economist's view of individual self-interest, was that cooperation relied on the threat of coercion, albeit in the form of private coercion. Ellickson observed, "In Shasta County I found one important type of third-party enforcement—the general circulation of negative gossip about deviants. Procedural norms encourage third parties to transmit this truthful remedial gossip to those in the best position to make use of it. . . . By facilitating the flow of reputational information, these norms deter future uncooperative behavior by increasing an actor's estimates of the probability that informal enforcers would eventually catch up with him" (1991, 232). Shasta County's informal network of gossip and social sanctions induced ranchers to tend to their cattle and penalized ranchers who didn't. Violators of the community's norms and customs suffered from scorn and exclusion, even though they would not be held liable in any formal legal action brought in a state-sponsored court. Ellickson's book earns its title because neither state property law nor its shadow played a role in securing social order. Order and enforcement of community norms arose entirely from indigenous community institutions.

Ellickson's book was part of an explosion of studies of order without law (and it rightfully is credited for subsequently fueling that explosion). Scholars in multiple fields and employing diverse methodologies have devoted growing attention to self-enforcement systems that rely on indigenous institutions. Recent scholarship has included examinations of eleventh-century Mediterranean traders (Greif 1989, 1993), medieval Europe's merchant guilds (Milgrom, North, and Weingast 1990), Mexican Jesuits in 1830s California (Clay 1997), mountain shepherds in Törbel, Switzerland (Ostrom 1990), fishmongers in Congolese villages (Fafchamps 1996a), fishermen off the coast of Monterey (Libecap 1989), and old-style Jewish diamond merchants in the heart of modern New York (Bernstein 1992; Richman 2006).

Common to these case studies is a focus on communities that instituted their own mechanisms for rewarding cooperative behavior and penalizing violations of norms. There is great interest and speculation as to why individuals in communities adhere to certain norms, and of course several motivations are at play. Internal notions of justice and innate motivations of guilt or magnanimity are certainly important, and blind habits and other institutionalized behaviors are relevant as well. But these scholars all adhered to the economist's requirement that community members would comply with commercial norms only if the rewards from doing so (and the punishments avoided) exceed whatever benefits might accrue from defecting from those norms. In short, economist's explanation might simply follow from Niccolò Machiavelli ([1531] 1882, 97): "People cannot make themselves secure except by being powerful." Order-without-law systems rely on coercive mechanisms just as modern commerce relies on state coercion to induce cooperation. But unlike conduct within the law's shadow, order-without-law relies entirely on extralegal rewards and punishments, which are a wholesale alternative to—and not an extension of—formal legal sanctions.

The case studies also illustrate a diversity of coercive instruments, including organized shunning, social disdain, and violence. For example, merchants in medieval Mediterranean societies used families and community members to foreclose future commerce to merchants who failed to keep a commercial promise (Greif 1989, 1993). Similar group sanctions were documented in Ghanaian and Vietnamese merchant communities, where aggrieved parties spread reputational information among their trading partners so any merchant with a checkered history is foreclosed from future commerce (Fafchamps 1996a; McMillan and Woodruff 1999). Many tight-knit communities additionally inflict noneconomic punishments, including social shunning and a reduction of social status. Comedians impose harsh social sanctions on fellow performers deemed to have appropriated another's jokes without permission; infringers not only lose invitations to perform at clubs but are excluded from and ridiculed by the intimate fraternity of stand-up (Oliar and Sprigman 2008). Finally, the mafia and other criminal networks have tended to employ more literal forms of coercion (though they use financial and status incentives too). Because mafia networks profit from transactions that are illegal and thus unenforceable in state courts, self-enforcement mechanisms are necessary to support exchange—Milhaupt and West (2000) euphemistically called the emergence of mafia coercion a "response to inefficiencies in the property rights and enforcement framework supplied by the state" (43). And the colorful world of pirates, whose commercial world was beyond the reach of reliable court enforcement, employed combinations of financial incentives (plunder), social status (skull and bones and other monikers), and physical coercion (the plank) to engineer reliable self-governance and social order (Leeson 2009).

The absence of state coercion is especially stark for some of these communities because, unlike in Shasta County (where a state court would have implemented an alternative rule) or in mafia-controlled illegal markets (where courts refuse to support exchange), state courts are, in theory, available. For many of these merchant communities, the targeted cooperative behavior was to keep one's promises, or comply with one's contractual obligations. Because contract law does, indeed, require one to keep one's promises, what distinguishes the order these communities maintained was not that it was without *law,* but that it was without the *state.* In many cases, a norm violation coincided with a legal violation, but the communities maintained *stateless* order. This category of cooperation is distinct from cooperation supported by legal sanctions, including parties cooperating within the shadow of the law, solely because the sanction that targets the transgressor is created and maintained by private, nonstate actors and institutions. By this nomenclature, Dixit's (2004) masterly work, *Lawlessness and Economics,* which illustrates through formal game theory how several alternative systems of exchange could be sustained through credible promises of reciprocity, perhaps should have been entitled *Statelessness and Economics.* In commercial transactions that involve an exchange of promises, the law is unavoidably present, whereas state coercion often is not.

The Varying Formality of Informal Enforcement

A second area in need of clarification is the use of the term "informal enforcement," a term the law and governance literature has frequently invoked to describe the sort of private enforcement systems that typify those in the order-without-law category. Whereas "formal" is meant to refer to traditional, state-sponsored instruments, "informal" has referred to reputation, social pressure, or other extralegal mechanisms. This is an unfortunate label because formality, in the colloquial sense, varies widely across both order-without-law and shadow-of-the-law mechanisms. Moreover, formality is an important but often misleading dimension of variance. On one hand, mechanisms that vary in their formality exhibit important differences that reflect key elements to their institutional environment. On the other, differences in formality obscure key similarities and often reflect merely cosmetic variation. It would be fruitful to jettison the term "informal enforcement" to describe categories of enforcement and instead consider carefully what role formality plays in alternative enforcement systems.

Dispute resolution mechanisms that lie within the shadow of the law vary significantly in their formality. The businesspeople Macaulay interviewed in his 1963 study, for example, found simple and straightforward solutions. Macaulay noted that, in the event of a breach, "often [parties] will never refer to the agreement but will negotiate a solution when the problem arises." (Macaulay quotes one person expressing a "common business attitude" when he says, "If something comes up, you get the other man on the telephone and deal with the problem. You don't read legalistic contract clauses at each other if you ever want to do business again.") (61) Alternatively, some dispute resolution is highly formal and is often legalistic. The most pervasive instance of modern alternative dispute resolution is the highly formal world of arbitration. The American Arbitration Association (AAA), for example, is a leading collection of arbitrators to help parties resolve commercial, labor, and other complex disputes. Advertising its services for "individuals and organizations who wish to resolve conflicts out of court," AAA arbitrators adhere to a large body of complex rules and procedures, including a comprehensive code of ethics and a due-process protocol (AAA 2016). The complexity and formality of this world of alternative dispute resolution rivals the formality of modern state courts and is a world away from the unstructured strategies employed by Macaulay's businesspeople.

Degrees of formality also vary across extralegal enforcement mechanisms, ranging from what could be called spontaneous mechanisms to structured, or bureaucratic, mechanisms. Just as Friedrich Hayek (1973) credited unregulated markets for providing "spontaneous order," because no deliberate coordination is required to maintain accurate price mechanisms, spontaneous reputation mechanisms similarly require no deliberate coordination. Shasta County cattle ranchers might be a paradigmatic illustration of spontaneous private enforcement. The ranchers relied only on word of mouth and casual gossip to spread reputational information. They never gathered to establish or articulate norms that defined unacceptable behavior and never demanded a collective commitment to inflict a coordinated punishment. Instead, information spread throughout the community without institutional help, and individual ranchers responded to specific conduct according to their personal ethical beliefs and their understanding of customary expectations. Without any centralizing institutions, Shasta County ranchers directed scorn at and denied fruitful relationships to individuals who transgressed customary codes of conduct. Spontaneous reputation mechanisms, therefore, are highly informal: community members respond individually and spontaneously, without explicit coordination, yet their collective response to particular conduct inflicts both economic and psychic costs to those who violate established norms.

Other reputation enforcement mechanisms employ greater degrees of formality. During Vietnam's early stages of economic liberalization, for example, Vietnamese merchants relied on commercial information networks, families, and common trade connections, a moderately formal system of information exchange (McMillan and Woodruff 1999). Vietnamese firms commonly used these informational networks to scrutinize prospective trading partners before commencing business, but the community of merchants did not establish formal or community-wide institutions to collect, scrutinize, or disseminate reputational information. Nineteenth-century traders in Mexican California relied on a similarly semiformal network of abbeys and monasteries as informational conduits to learn and share reputational information (Clay 1997). And Seafax, an Internet company that serves wholesalers of caught fish, serves as an established and structured informational instrument within a commercial reputation mechanism. The company compiles the payment histories of prospective buyers of fish, along with their credit records and other publicly available financial data, to help sellers decide with whom they will transact. It thus creates a formal mechanism of accumulating reputational information on prospective buyers, but sellers use the information without coordinating among themselves and sanctions proceed informally.

Figure 1.1. Alternative private orderings.

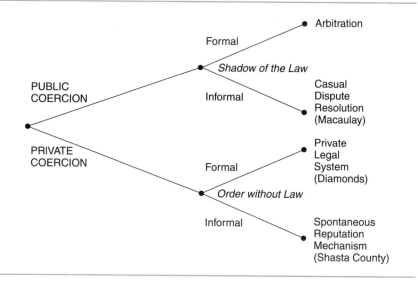

In sum, although the collection of private enforcement systems spans time, geography, and culture, two significant dimensions of variation have emerged in the literature. The first concerns the source of coercion that secures transactional compliance, as some systems rely ultimately on the state, whereas others rely on private power. The second is the degree of formality that characterizes the dispute resolution and adjudicatory mechanisms. The institutional features of these assorted mechanisms of enforcement can thus be summarized with the schema shown in Figure 1.1.

Private Legal Systems and the Law of Diamond Merchants: A Confusing Hybrid

A particular species of private enforcement that has received significant academic attention is industry-wide arbitration systems that use both privately tailored industry law and privately ordered industry sanctions. In these private legal systems, a particular merchant community, which often comprises an entire industry segment and is frequently organized as a trade association, constructs an elaborate system of law and procedure that is responsible for all disputes within the merchant community. Lisa Bernstein is a leader in uncovering such systems, including those supporting the

Diamond Dealers Club of New York (Bernstein 1992), the National Feed and Grain Association (Bernstein 1996), and the assorted trade associations that govern America's cotton merchants (Bernstein 2001). John McMillan and Christopher Woodruff uncovered similarly organized reputation systems that enforce agreements made by America's fresh-fish wholesalers and by New York's dress manufacturers (McMillan and Woodruff 2000), and other scholars have brought this analytical lens more recently to studies of kosher certification, food labeling, and eco-friendly accreditation (Starobin and Weinthal 2010; Lytton 2013).

A number of common features typify these trade-association-led private legal systems. First, the arbitration systems are highly developed and comprehensive, employing fellow merchants as elected arbitrators, relying on specialized law, and using expedited procedures. These systems resemble the formality of the AAA's arbitration procedures but invoke privately crafted substantive and procedural rules that are tailored to the needs and common concerns of disputing merchants, such as requiring industry-provided form contracts or that goods are delivered by certain times and in certain measurements. The National Feed and Grain Association, for example, instructs industry arbitrators to issue rulings in accordance with highly codified trade rules and trade practices rather than the Uniform Commercial Code and other statutes (Bernstein 1996). Second, these arbitration systems tend to assume exclusive authority over all intraindustry disputes. Not only do all merchants have access to arbitrators to resolve any dispute with a fellow merchant, merchants are also prohibited from seeking redress in alternative venues, including state courts. Bernstein (2001) reports, for example, that as a condition of membership in the Memphis Cotton Exchange, members must agree to submit all disputes with other members to the association's arbitration system. And third, failure to comply with an arbitration ruling leads to expulsion from the trade association. And although expulsion in its own right is not associated with penalties or financial loss, it signals untrustworthiness to other merchants, thereby foreclosing future commerce. In other words, an adverse arbitration ruling and expulsion from the trade association triggers a coordinated group boycott.

Because private legal systems develop elaborate systems of arbitration, they have often been conflated with other formal arbitration mechanisms. This is a conceptual mistake that both clouds a proper understanding of different private ordering mechanisms and impedes a precise appreciation of these systems themselves. From appearances, private legal systems look like the world of arbitration that operates within Galanter's shadow of legal entitlements. But because they rely on private coercion to effectuate arbitrator rulings, rather than legal instruments, they squarely belong in the order-without-law category. Accordingly, they are subject to different economic forces and offer different implications for legal institutions than instruments within the law's shadow.

Legal scholarship has played a prominent role in causing this confusion by focusing attention on the adjudication efficiencies generated from industry-tailored law. Scholars have observed that specialized substantive rules reduce the complexity and required time to generate rulings, stream-lined procedures reduce the costs of advancing or defending claims, and expert adjudicators produce more accurate rulings than generalist judges or juries. As such, legal enthusiasts proclaim that private legal systems are more efficient, reliable, and accurate than state courts.

In particular, admiration for private legal systems and their exhibited efficiencies has been part of, and has contributed to, what has been called the "New Formalism," which probably has been the most significant development in contract legal scholarship in the past two decades. David Charny (1999) described New Formalism as more of an "anti-antiformalism," a backlash to Karl Llewellyn's efforts—embodied in the Uniform Commercial Code—to incorporate flexibility into the legal process and encourage judges to issue rulings that liberate merchants' contractual intentions and enforce industry customs. New Formalism, in Charny's words, has been an effort "to discredit and displace Llewellyn's claim to found commercial law in immanent commercial practice" and to displace the norms and standards enshrined in most parts of the Uniform Commercial Code with rigid procedures, bright-line rules, and legal formality. Contracts scholars advancing so-called New Formalism have championed private legal systems as evidence that when merchants design law for themselves, they strongly prefer formalism over the Uniform Commercial Code.

One cannot blame legal scholars for focusing on the features that are naturally of greatest interest to them. If private legal systems were a Rorschach test, legal scholars, who are deeply familiar with the costs of adjudicating disputes in state courts, would remark on the systems' specialized law and procedures to identify administrative efficiencies. This enthusiasm is not just understandable but, in large part, quite justified. Private legal systems indeed generate meaningful administrative efficiencies, and the benefits of industry-wide and industry-made rules offer lessons not just for arbitration law but for commercial law generally.

But this scholarly enthusiasm has led to a causality error. More than merely admiring the adjudication efficiencies, scholars have argued that merchant communities develop private legal systems specifically to capture these savings. Scholars of contract law and civil procedure frequently characterize private legal systems as an "opting out" of state-sponsored dispute resolution, suggesting that state courts are a viable but merely less preferable venue, and that constructing a private legal system reflects a deliberate choice to capture adjudication savings. They view the private enforcement of arbitration rulings as conduct within the shadow of otherwise enforceable law, and thus have conceived private legal systems to be close relatives of more typical arbitration systems.

Despite appearances, private legal systems do not arise to economize on adjudication costs and thus should not be viewed as a generalizable species of arbitration. To the contrary, they arise out of idiosyncratic circumstances, achieve different efficiencies and objectives, and operate under a different theoretical framework from typical arbitration. Charny cautioned against enthusiasm among contracts scholars, noting that "trade association formalism . . . does not counsel formalism in commercial law generally; rather, it reflects, and takes advantage of, the idiosyncratic institutional structures of the associations themselves" (1999, 843). Although there are very good reasons to conclude that Charny was being overcautious, and that, in fact, trade association formalism does offer strong lessons for generally applicable commercial law, he was correct in warning that legal scholars were failing to pay adequate attention to the institutional surroundings of private legal systems. The defining features of these systems are not, as much of the literature suggests, their rigorous use of arbitrators or formulation of tailored law. The key features are how their agreements are enforced and the nature of the coercive mechanisms they employ.

Because private legal systems rely on private sanctions and private enforcement, they are properly characterized as formal—perhaps extremely formal—instances of private ordering. They have much more in common with Ellickson's Shasta County ranchers than they do with arbitrators or other conduct that takes place within the shadow of the law. Legal scholarship has overemphasized the role of adjudication efficiencies and has failed to appreciate private legal systems' other economic attributes that are much more significant in defining their utility and propensity. Accordingly, understanding these systems requires examining not the familiar law-like qualities but instead the social and economic structures that sustain and support cooperation.

Conclusion: What Statelessness Is, What Statelessness Is Not

The outpouring of case studies that document private ordering by merchant communities has at least two achievements: it opened scholars to a rich world of private ordering, illustrating a diversity of commercial exchange that is secured without the direct intervention of public institutions, and it assembled a collection of genuinely interesting case studies, ensuring that this remains a fascinating field of research. What it has not done, however, is provide sufficient theoretical precision to distinguish among the disparate economic challenges that private ordering—and specifically private legal systems—arises to address.

As a result, it is useful to define what statelessness is before proceeding to articulate when statelessness emerges and why it persists into the modern era. First, statelessness is not arbitration. Arbitration occurs within the shadow of the law and relies on the state for ultimate enforcement. It similarly is not the mere avoidance of lawyers or out-of-court resolutions that take place within the law's shadow. Second, private legal systems are not arbitration. Many private legal systems have adopted elements from formal arbitration organizations, and many have adopted their own efficiency-enhancing formalities, but because private legal systems ultimately rely on private coercion, they are beyond the law and its shadow and are instead an embodiment of statelessness.

Third, and most important, statelessness is to be understood as a governance mechanism that is an alternative to state enforcement. Therefore, an assessment of the persistence of statelessness into the modern era requires understanding its governance attributes in comparison with state-sponsored alternatives. It is clear that private legal systems can be more administratively efficient than public legal proceedings. Private legal systems boast expedient procedures, formalist rules, and expert judges that create a dispute resolution system that is faster, cheaper, and more accurate than state courts. But despite the enthusiasm for the *legal* substance of private legal systems, there has been inadequate attention to the *private* element of those systems, namely, the use of private enforcement. The attraction of administrative efficiencies can explain why merchant communities would create private arbitrators to issue rulings, just as it explains the proliferation of arbitration more generally, but it does not explain why they would construct private mechanisms that enforce those rulings. In fact, if administrative efficiencies were the driver of private legal systems, then we would expect them to be no more than systems of arbitration, in which rulings made by private judges would be enforceable in public courts and the merchant community would not be burdened with the heavy duties of self-enforcement. The central question is why those self-enforcement mechanisms arise.

The formality of certain private legal systems is revealing because it illustrates the sophistication of those systems and offers a critique of both substantive contract law and the rules of civil procedure. But the distinction between formal and informal systems is far secondary to the distinction between self-enforcement occurring within the shadow of the law and self-enforcement that creates order without law. Because private legal systems belong squarely in the order-without-law category, their economic significance lies in their institutional foundations and not in the substantive law they offer. The remainder of this book focuses on these institutional foundations of statelessness and their implications. Following this introductory chapter's elaboration on what statelessness is, Chapters 2 and 3 offer an example of how statelessness works and Chapter 4 formulates a theory of when statelessness persists. As this opening chapter illustrates, it is important to be precise in connecting the phenomenon being observed to the economic challenge it addresses. Thus, any theory of statelessness must articulate the economic challenges stateless institutions are designed to mitigate and address the riddle of why these premodern instances of stateless commerce persist into the modern economy.

2

A Case Study in Statelessness
Diamonds, the Diamond Network,
and Diamontaires

GLOBAL SALES of diamond jewelry created a $72 billion market in 2013 (by comparison, the world spent $24 billion on vaccines and $36 billion going to the movies). But before diamonds reach the consumer, they take a fascinating and circuitous path across the globe and along many separate stages of production. This chapter describes the diamond chain that distributes rough diamonds from miners to retailers, and it introduces the network of middlemen that is the focus of this book. It focuses on the relatively stable industry structure that began in the late nineteenth century, when diamonds were discovered in South Africa, and persisted into the early twentieth century to sustain the diamond centers of today.[1]

The manufacturing and distribution process that culminates in diamond jewelry for retail sale consists of three basic stages: (1) exploring and mining rough diamonds from underground and alluvial deposits, (2) sorting and cutting diamonds to produce polished gemstones, and (3) incorporating polished diamonds into manufactured jewelry. Of these three stages, the first generates by far the greatest profit margins, and the second—the network of middlemen that includes diamond dealers (or diamontaires), cutters (or polishers), brokers, and assorted distributors that create the antiquated world that one sees on 47th Street—offers the smallest (see Figure 2.1).

Diamond Origins and the Upstream Monopoly

In order to examine the network of middlemen, it is first important to understand the earliest stages of diamond production, along with the economic challenges and colorful history of the upstream segment of the market.

Figure 2.1. Profit margins for different stages of the diamond chain. Diamond jewelry retail and mining account for the majority of the diamond industry profit pool. *Source:* Bain & Company 2014, 6. Used with permission from Bain & Company, www.bain.com.

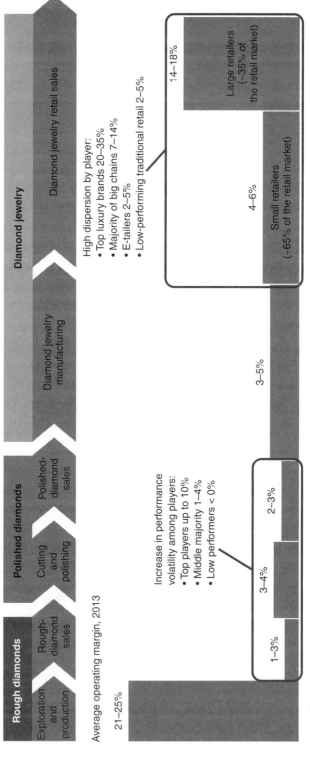

The journey for most diamonds currently begins in Africa (which produced 54 percent of rough diamonds in 2013), Russia (29 percent), Australia (9 percent), or Canada (8 percent), with nearly all production coming from large mines owned by vast industrial interests. This diversity of geographic sources for diamonds, however, is a relatively recent development. For nearly two and a half millennia, from the first discoveries in 800 B.C. to the mid-nineteenth century, the riverbeds of the Indian subcontinent were the world's only known source of diamonds. In the early eighteenth century, just as Indian mines were depleting, diamonds were found and mined in the jungles of Brazil. Even so, diamonds remained extremely rare, and their natural scarcity sustained the extreme value they commanded in the marketplace.

In 1867, however, huge diamond deposits were discovered near the Orange River in South Africa, and diamonds were soon being scooped out by the ton. It took the mines of Brazil two hundred years to equal India's production over the previous two thousand; it took the South African mines just fifteen years, and production continued at an accelerated pace well into the twentieth century. Edward Jay Epstein, in a well-known 1982 article for the *Atlantic*, wrote, "Suddenly, the market was deluged with diamonds. The British financiers who had organized the South African mines quickly realized that their investment was endangered; diamonds had little intrinsic value—and their price depended almost entirely on their scarcity. The financiers feared that when new mines were developed in South Africa, diamonds would become at best only semiprecious gems." The assorted mining interests responded with a twofold strategy: restrict supply and manufacture demand.

To restrict supply, the owners of the early African diamond interests consolidated their mines to form a single entity that could control output and maintain diamonds' scarcity. In the first decade of South Africa's diamond rush, production was very unconsolidated, in part because of local rules prohibiting the amalgamation of claims, and the nation's mines consisted of a patchwork of 1,600 individual holdings. When prohibitions against consolidation were removed in 1876, small entrepreneurs—including an Englishman named Cecil Rhodes, who first came to South Africa at age seventeen—began purchasing claims. Rhodes saw an opportunity as mining interests started consolidating, and he convinced European investors to finance him to purchase all South Africa's available mines and control supply through a London-based venture, which became known as "the Syndicate." The process culminated when Rhodes engineered a merger of the two primary diamond holding companies in 1888—producing De Beers Consolidated Mines—that promptly became the predominant supplier of rough diamonds (Rhodes converted his extraordinary wealth into immortality when his will endowed the famous scholarship to Oxford in 1902). De Beers proceeded to enjoy monopoly control of rough diamonds for much of the next century, and from 1929, when Ernest Oppenheimer took control of the company, through the end of the twentieth century, De Beers regularly controlled over 80 percent— and often closer to 90 percent—of global production.

Perhaps to hide its dominance, De Beers has assumed many faces. In London, it operated under the innocuous title of the Central Selling Organization, and later the Diamond Trading Company, each of which was the arm that distributed rough diamonds. De Beers has been discussed in reference to Anglo American plc, one of its primary holding companies, and it also continues to be known somewhat mysteriously as the Syndicate. In Africa, it has masked its colonial past by creating assorted subsidiaries with names like Diamond Development Corporation and Mining Services, Inc., and more recently, De Beers has tried to emphasize and celebrate its African origins, forming ventures with African governments with names such as Debswana (in Botswana) and Namdeb (in Namibia). Despite these many maneuverings and corporate facades, interlocking ownership arrangements and overlapping boards have ensured that the Oppenheimer family controlled the entire network. In 1934, Ernest's son Harry became chairman of De Beers, and in 1999, Harry's son Nicky became chairman. Known as "the diamond cartel," the De Beers network is best understood as a monopolist entity controlled by a single family.

Through its many incarnations and corporate arms, De Beers has enjoyed remarkable success constraining the supply of diamonds through monopolistic controls. The strategy from the beginning was rather simple. Whenever any entity discovered a new source of rough diamonds, De Beers would either buy them out or enter into exclusive purchasing and distribution agreements. Whenever there was a surge in production, De Beers would stockpile the new finds and maintain a steady supply to the market. And whenever an independent distribution channel emerged, working around the monopoly and posing a threat of competition, De Beers' agents employed combinations of coercion and persuasion to reassert its market control.

Sometimes this strategy required extreme measures. When a huge diamond field was discovered in Siberia in the 1950s, De Beers cut a secret deal with the Soviet Union to purchase 95 percent of all the diamonds it could produce (to avoid a political scandal, which would be expected given the mutual animosity between colonial South Africa and the communist USSR, a UK merchant bank set up offices across the street from the Central Selling Organization and secretly channeled Soviet diamonds through London). When Zaire tried to sell its diamonds outside the Syndicate, De Beers released a large stockpile to reduce the market price, making Zaire's sales unprofitable, and Zaire swiftly returned to selling exclusively through De Beers, accepting significantly worse terms than before. When Angola's diamond-rich riverbeds dried up in 1992, prompting individual miners to swarm the area and gather small bundles of alluvial diamonds, De Beers spent an estimated half billion dollars to purchase all of the new finds. And when alluvial gems were being smuggled from Sierra Leone in caravans to Liberia and thereafter into the global market, De Beers retained a former chief of the MI-5 to organize a paramilitary outfit called the Diamond Security Organization to ambush the caravans. There is even a tale of Ernest Oppenheimer conspiring with financiers at J. P. Morgan in 1921 to shut down a potential diamond mine at an Arkansas hog farm, which has since been converted into Crater of Diamonds State Park and a tourist attraction.

In 2000, James Surowiecki summarized De Beers' market dominance in the *New Yorker*, writing, "The Syndicate outlasted colonialism and it outlasted Communism, and throughout that time it has—with few exceptions—kept diamond prices stable and rising. For the better part of a century, in short, DeBeers beat back the market." Milton Friedman, whom the *Economist* described as possibly the most influential economist of the twentieth century, identified De Beers (along with the pre-1934 New York Stock Exchange) as the only monopolist he could think of that sustained its market leadership for a long period of time without a government's grant to monopoly ("I don't understand it," he quips with what looks like genuine admiration in a popular YouTube video) (Malthus0 2011).

De Beers has met equal success manufacturing demand. In what Epstein called "The Diamond Invention," De Beers collaborated with Madison Avenue's most talented agencies to, remarkably, synthesize traditions that turned diamonds into a necessary feature of betrothal. Advertising firm N. W. Ayer coined the now famous "A Diamond Is Forever" campaign in 1947, which *Advertising Age* hailed as the twentieth century's top advertising slogan and its sixth most successful advertising campaign. Merely two decades after launching the marketing effort, which included opening an office in Hollywood and bedecking its top female stars with assorted diamond jewelry, N. W. Ayer reported to De Beers its success in the American market: "To this new generation a diamond ring is considered a necessity to engagements by virtually everyone" (Epstein 1982).

One key motivation behind the "Forever" campaign was the acute recognition that diamonds are durable and do not depreciate over time, and so demand for new diamonds would always be vulnerable to a resale market. Thus, De Beers aimed its campaign at convincing recipients of diamond gifts that regifting or reselling their jewelry would amount to a betrayal of romance. Advertisers portrayed diamonds as family heirlooms that should never be resold, and so each newlywed would have to purchase a new stone. The advertising campaign also capitalized on other life cycle moments to foster new sources of demand, and De Beers supplemented the diamond engagement ring with the diamond anniversary band and the twenty-fifth anniversary diamond. A De Beers promotional video, designed to help jewelry manufacturers and retailers craft their sales strategy, pledged, "Our goal is to make diamonds a cultural imperative for all these important occasions in a woman's life. That's why we are continuing to support these segments, so that your products, like the diamond anniversary band and the 25th anniversary diamond, will become as obligatory as the diamond engagement ring, bringing your customers back again and again" (*Frontline* 1994).

De Beers also sought to develop new geographic markets for its diamond, and its marketing campaign proved equally adept at changing centuries-old marriage traditions in European and Asian societies as it did in the United States. In Japan in 1967, when De Beers began its international advertising campaign, less than 5 percent of engaged Japanese women received a diamond engagement ring, and by 1978 it was half. After two decades of advertising in West Germany, where brides traditionally had received a wedding ring of two gold bands, that nation became the world's third-largest consumer of diamonds. De Beers also cleverly tailored its advertising campaign to market stones that sat in its reserves. When it purchased tons of Soviet diamonds in the 1950s and learned that they included a large proportion of

Figure 2.2. Price fluctuations of diamonds versus other commodities, 1980–1998. *Source:* Spar 2006.

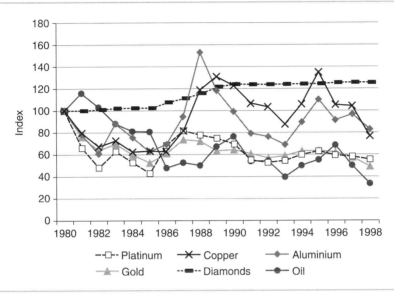

small stones, De Beers came up with a new product—the "eternity ring"—that utilized this large supply of low-size stones. (Thomas Helsby, a longtime investigator of the diamond industry, remarked, "It is perhaps amusing to think that, at the height of the cold war, the eternity ring that was being so successfully marketed in America was filled with stones from Siberia.")

The sum of these many distribution and advertising successes meant that for nearly all of the past century—until about 2000, when the diamond industry began exhibiting a seismic restructuring (discussed in concluding Chapter 8)—De Beers sat as an upstream monopoly atop the diamond industry's distribution chain. De Beers alone determined total output and, in turn, was the chief investor in maintaining demand by paying for the bulk of industry-wide advertising. Its control of the marketplace across political and technological upheaval was nothing short of masterful. As then–Harvard Business School professor Deborah Spar sharply illustrated in a comparison of commodity prices, De Beers was able to maintain remarkable stability in how diamonds were valued in the market, in spite of the market turbulence that other commodities experienced (see Figure 2.2).

While De Beers enjoyed monopoly dominance in production of rough diamonds, it limited its role to mining and did not enter the downstream processes of cutting, polishing, and sorting diamonds. Instead, it left the intermediate distribution chain—the steps that transformed rough diamonds into polished stones and brought them to jewelry manufacturers—to a web of intermediaries.

Sorting and Cutting Middlemen: From Sightholders to Ethnic Networks

Upon mining and gathering tons of rough diamonds from its many mines, De Beers collects its rough stones in London, at the Diamond Trading Company (or DTC, formally known as the Central Selling Organisation, or CSO), located at 17 Charterhouse Street. It then sells its rough diamonds through an unusual mechanism: De Beers invites a select group of diamond merchants known as "sightholders" to its Charterhouse offices and, through a secret process, sorts tailored bundles of its stones in small cardboard boxes, arranged according to size and color, for each particular sightholder. It then presents the sightholder with a take-it-or-leave-it price for the entire box. Negotiating over price or purchasing only a subset of the diamonds is not permitted.

Despite participating in an arrangement that sounds like a Hobson's choice, sightholders—the number of whom has ranged over time from about fifty to two hundred—occupy an attractive position in the diamond distribution chain. They are handpicked by De Beers to have exclusive access to rough diamonds and can parlay their position atop the distribution chain into swift profits. Sightholders are selected chiefly because De Beers has assurances both that they can finance their purchases (a typical sight involves several hundred million dollars of rough diamonds) and, more importantly, that these diamontaires know how to create value from these stones. While sightholders generally have a stable clientele—and some even sell sighted boxes in their entirety for a small margin—De Beers urges sightholders to find new distribution avenues and expand the reach of De Beers' supply. For these reasons, only well-entrenched and highly knowledgeable diamontaires are invited to transact directly with De Beers. One longtime diamontaire, when asked who becomes a sightholder, told a documentary film team, "If you can come up with a huge sum of money, it . . . certainly would not qualify you to be a sight-holder. It's rather the man that started twenty-five years ago with very little, with one or two cutters, who has fifteen or twenty now here and who is constantly on the scene, buying and—and who—and he's the man who means to stay here, with his children to follow him. He's the man that qualifies to be a sightholder. It's like being admitted to a club" (*Frontline* 1994).

Despite the honored position sightholders enjoy, De Beers is clearly in control, and sightholders are expected to purchase the cache of diamonds at the stated price. Stefan Kanfer, in *The Last Empire: De Beers, Diamonds, and the World*, recounts what happened when a renowned diamontaire refused a sight: "Harry Winston, the biggest name in jewellery until his death in 1978, . . . disliked this high-handed manner of diamond disposal (after all, didn't his clients include the Duke and Duchess of Windsor? the Arab emirates?). At one sight he handed back his box, walked out, and attempted to go around the syndicate, negotiating to buy rough diamonds from an independent firm in Angola, then a Portuguese possession. One phone call was made, from a British Cabinet member to a high official in Portugal. The Crown, the member said drily, would regard a deal between the colony and Mr. Winston as 'an unfriendly act.' Winston got the message. He never refused a box again" (Kanfer 1993, 3–4).

Economists have explained De Beers' unusual sales practices as an effort to economize on the costs of inspecting and appraising individual diamonds. Yoram Barzel (1977) explained, "Had the contents of a particular bag been available for appraisal by all buyers, each probably would have spent resources to determine the properties of the diamonds. . . . The incentive for DeBeers to engage in this peculiar form of trade seems to be that buyers are now in a position to spend on the actual purchase of the diamonds the amount they otherwise might have spent on collecting information" (304–305). Roy Kenney and Benjamin Klein (1983), in a famous paper on "block booking," articulated a similar reason for De Beers' bundling, and they further argued that the same efficiency forces explained why movie distributors sold movies in bundles rather than individually: because there was little way of predicting which movies would be more popular—and profitable—than others. Rather than investigating and estimating the value of each, they were sold in a bundle at an approximated average price.[2] I revisit and critique these explanations in Chapter 8, reexamining them in light of recent changes to De Beers' distribution strategy. But regardless of the accuracy of the explanations, these scholarly inquiries of sightholders and the diamond chain are indications of how unusual De Beers' distribution strategy has been, and they reflect the steady academic fascination with the economics of diamonds.

From this small collection of sightholders, diamonds descend into a thick web of intermediaries and slowly make their way down the supply chain to jewelry manufacturers (rough diamonds not controlled by De Beers, and sold either directly from mines or through other channels, descend into the same distribution network). Approximately 80 percent of the rough stones distributed by the DTC find themselves in Antwerp at its four large diamond bourses, where sorting becomes the primary activity in diamond distribution. Sightholders and other players atop the distribution pyramid sell parcels of their rough diamonds to individual dealers, who in turn sell smaller parcels to other dealers. As the parcels shrink in size, the number of players in the distribution chain increases, and caches of stones get increasingly individualized attention.

Antwerp serves as little more than a weigh station for these rough stones, and, following the large-scale sales and sorts, distribution scatters globally. The sorting process then goes hand in hand with the process of cutting, or polishing, which converts opaque rough diamonds into gem-quality diamonds for retail. The vast majority of rough stones from Antwerp go to India, where most of the world's polishing takes place, while many others go for cutting to East Asia, Africa, and Central Europe. Larger stones stay in Western Europe or head to Israel or the United States, where they come under the care of master diamond cutters. After each stage of cutting, diamonds are again sorted by quality, so merchants can sell a large cache of homogenous gems together, and many are then polished and repackaged again. Some then return to Antwerp for more sorting and repackaging, others instead head to the large diamond center in Israel, and eventually polished diamonds head to the United States, Dubai, Hong Kong, or other gateways to affluent markets. Parcels are sold and resold, stones are cut and recut, and gradually they make their way to jewelry manufacturers for commercial sale.

The sorting and cutting of diamonds is enormously important to their attaining value, and the total value of polished diamonds is approximately 50 to 75 percent more than the value of mined stones. This is not just because consumers demand only polished diamonds, but also because diamonds are not standardized commodities, and there are many ways to cut and produce a rough stone. Unlike refining oil into usable gasoline, it is as much an art as it is a science to bring maximum value from an unpolished stone, and thus skilled cutting is a critical value-added process. Depending on the size, rough stones can be cut in multiple ways, and cutters can pursue different strategies to bring out the color, facets, and quality of a finished product. Nearly all cutting factories and master cutters use lasers and computer software to evaluate alternative cutting strategies, but there remains a role for discretion and expertise. Moreover, cutters vary significantly in their skills. Very small stones can be cut in large quantities through an industrial process, but most diamond cutting is done by hand, with a cutter sitting before a spinning grinding wheel and carefully applying the stone to the abrasive surface.[3] Many diamond cutters, especially master cutters who deal only with large stones, learn their craft from their fathers and uncles (though there are a growing number of cutting schools in several diamond centers throughout the world), and their skills are used exclusively on the most precious stones. Accordingly, cutting factories vary significantly in the prices they charge, the labor they employ, and the wages they pay.

Another reason the sorting process significantly determines a diamond's ultimate value is that different end consumers place very different values on a given stone, depending both on an intended use for a diamond and on subjective judgments. No matter how a stone is prepared, it can command different prices from different jewelry manufacturers, and thus finding the optimal buyer for a specific stone is a very profitable enterprise. Diamonds, especially high-end stones, feature subtle differences—beyond the standard qualities reflected in grading for the four Cs: color, cut, carat, and clarity—that translate into significant variation in manufacturers' willingness to pay. Most diamontaires therefore insist on inspecting and sorting their diamonds by hand, as there are few reliable ways to codify a diamond's features. Because in-person inspection remains a standard practice, the valuation process is time consuming and labor intensive.

These market features offer important profit opportunities for middlemen. The primary objective in this distribution chain is to find the optimal buyer for each individual stone, and the middlemen who facilitate this matching process secure attractive profits or commissions. The process requires synthesizing market information with inventory availability, or, in other words, hustling to know what sellers have and what buyers want. Many merchants also use brokers, who work on small commissions, to assist these sales and find the best price for a given stone. Consequently, the industry is home to many middlemen who create value and collect revenues through the nuanced process of matching individual stones with the manufacturers and retailers who value them highly. In one day, a diamond can move from one end of New York's 47th Street diamond center to the other, doubling in value after passing through seven or eight hands.

Accordingly, a diamond will pass through many transactions before it reaches a consumer. These frequent transactions also showcase a unique zeal that diamond merchants have for their trades. One insider shared the following parable:

> One diamond dealer said to another, "The most magnificent diamond has come into my hands—you simply have to buy it." The other inspects the diamond, agrees that it is exceptional, and the two negotiate a price. A few days later the first dealer finds the second and says, "Do you still have that diamond? I've never seen such beauty, and I hope you'll let me buy it back from you." They agree on a price 15% above the original purchase price. More days pass, and the second dealer approaches the first and says "You know, I've done nothing but think about that diamond, and I simply must repurchase it." They agree on a price with another 15% mark-up. One more time the first dealer finds the second and says, "That diamond was so perfect—I would love to buy again." The second apologizes and informs the first that he sold it to a jewelry manufacturer, to which the first responds, "But why? We were doing such wonderful business!"[4]

Diamontaires exert similar fervor and intensity negotiating the financial details of their deals, both in the bourses of the diamond trading centers and along the surrounding streets. Price, quantity, delivery method, payment schedule, method of payment, and credit security are all variables that enter into a deal. Different proposals shoot back and forth, sometimes with brokers consulting on a cell phone with the dealer they represent, and vibrant gesticulations are a communication staple. The frenzy reminds one of the pit of a commodities exchange, and in many respects, diamond trading centers are indeed exchanges that facilitate matches between buyers and sellers, but with a cloak of the old-world bazaar.

Diamond Sales and the Implicit Credit Market

Despite the steady stream of diamond transactions, neither the flow of diamond supply nor the pace of demand is steady. For starters, rough diamonds are supplied into the distribution network in discrete bundles. There are ten DTC sights each year, one held approximately every five weeks, and each sight brings a significant supply of new rough stones into the market. Sightholders are required to pay the CSO in full within seven days of the sight, but it can take as many as three months for a manufacturer to sort, polish, and sell all of the diamonds in the bundle. Other dealers who are not sightholders purchase their supply of diamonds on a cycle that follows, but lags behind, the schedule of sights, and they too are forced to balance the need to pay suppliers promptly while taking the required time to sort, cut, and then sell their cache of diamonds. Meanwhile, the pace of manufacturing, particularly diamond cutting and polishing, is constant since the cutting process involves one cutter and one stone at a time. But since these diamontaires are intermediaries, they must capitalize on the discrete opportunities to purchase rough supply while taking the time necessary to transform their goods into more valuable products. They are thus pressed between the schedule De Beers imposes from above and the deliberateness required to polish and sell the stones in lucrative bundles.[5]

In addition, demand for diamond jewelry is highly seasonal and requires diamontaires to extend themselves between the time they must purchase stones and the opportunity to sell them. For example, 30–40 percent of all U.S. retail sales occur in November and December, and many jewelers, and thus the dealers who supply them with diamonds, must wait for the holiday season before consumer cash becomes available. While efficient utilization of diamond cutters and jewelry manufacturers requires polishing and setting stones throughout the year, diamontaires must navigate the irregularity of supply and demand.

Consequently, selling diamonds on credit is far preferable to simultaneous exchange. In fact, buying and selling on credit is essential for the production chain to operate efficiently. Credit sales allow merchants to balance their inventories and manufacturing schedules in accordance with the ebbs and flows of supply and demand. Moreover, liquidity constraints are very tight for merchants since most merchants work for themselves as individuals, not for heavily capitalized corporations, and many dealers concede that they can get a better price if they extend credit to their buyers.[6] These economic forces mean that time-inconsistent exchange, where a buyer pays for a diamond some time after taking possession (that is, there is a separation of the quid from the quo), is the industry norm. The terms of future payment often become a principal element of negotiations in a transaction, often subject to extreme detail (certified check or bank check? Thirty days or sixty days?), but the structure of diamond production and distribution necessitates purchasing on and extending credit. The role of credit in diamond transactions is so central that Lisa Bernstein (1992) called the market for diamonds "an implicit capital market" (131).

In sum, the middlemen that constitute the intermediary stage of the diamond distribution chain collect uncut stones in London and Antwerp and match them with high-valuing jewelry manufacturers throughout the world. In the process, a stone passes through the hands of several layers of middlemen—cutters, brokers, and dealers—who polish the stone and find an attractive buyer while minimizing the costs of cutting and sorting.

The diamond industry's pyramidal distribution system, with monopolist De Beers sitting at the top, has been in place and remained largely unchanged since Cecil Rhodes founded the company in 1888. And for centuries, including long before De Beers controlled global supply, diamonds relied on an army of middlemen to reach the world's buyers. Until the entry of relative newcomers in the 1980s, this distribution system was dominated by Jewish merchants.

Jews and the Diamond Industry

One of the most salient features of the diamond network is the pervasiveness of ethnic trading networks and family businesses, and especially the presence of Jewish merchants. Because the role of ethnic trading networks, discussed in detail in Chapter 3, is so critical to understanding the industry's structure, and because Jewish merchants have had such an impact on the industry's rules and operations, some background on Jews and the diamond industry is constructive before examining the mechanisms that support the industry's statelessness.[7]

Jewish predominance has deep historical roots. Throughout the Middle Ages, when India was the world's leading source of raw diamonds, Jewish communities along the Indian Ocean trade routes—in Egypt, Maghreb, and the shores of Southern Europe—were home to diamond traders and cutters. In the eleventh century, two Jewish brothers living in Cairo as prominent bankers and diamond merchants supplied the Fatimid Caliph Empire with precious stones. The earliest concentrations of diamond merchants and cutters were in small Jewish ghettos in Venice and Bruges in the thirteenth century, and Jews brought the trade to Antwerp shortly afterward. Jewish merchants escaping the Inquisition in Spain and Portugal in the late fifteenth century set up the world's largest diamond market in Amsterdam, and after Jewish diamond merchants helped finance the Dutch East India Company in the sixteenth century, they controlled diamonds' entry point from India into Europe for several centuries. A sizable Jewish community in Hamburg dominated the diamond trade to the courts of Europe in seventeenth- and eighteenth-century Germany, while Jewish merchants emigrating from Amsterdam helped build England's diamond trade with India, organizing diamond imports with the British East India Company and making London a lucrative diamond trade center.

Jewish predominance in diamond production persisted into the industry's modern era. At upstream levels of production, the Jewish presence has been felt since the Oppenheimers took control of the De Beers syndicate in the early twentieth century, and now several billionaire Israeli diamontaires are among the elite few who mine and supply rough diamonds in competition with De Beers. Jewish merchants are also disproportionately represented in the world's diamond centers of Antwerp, Tel Aviv, and New York. Interestingly, the modern-day Jewish presence in these diamond centers reaches deeply and most categorically into the supporting occupations of diamond cutting and diamond brokering. In the early twentieth century, 80 percent of all of Amsterdam's thirty thousand cutters were Jewish and one-third of Antwerp's cutters and three-fourths of its brokers were Jewish. Similar percentages have been maintained in today's diamond centers of New York, Antwerp, and, more obviously, Israel. In New York's diamond industry, the Jewish presence is most profound at the ground level, as the industry's brokers and cutters are disproportionately ultra-Orthodox Jews, adherents to an insular and highly ritualistic version of Jewish practice. The many shops on 47th Street and the trading halls of its offices are filled with merchants wearing long, untrimmed beards, speaking Yiddish, and dressed in black suits, overcoats, and black hats or caftans. And daily buses carry scores of workers directly from Boro Park, Monsey, and Williamsburg—all homes to concentrated ultra-Orthodox Jewish communities—to the diamond district in Manhattan.

The Jewish presence in the diamond industry has also shaped many of the industry's norms, behaviors, and practices. The industry's system of arbitration and dispute resolution, described in detail in Chapter 3, has arbitrators who periodically rely on Talmudic and Jewish legal principles in adjudicating disputes. Negotiations and deal making on the floors of the diamond bourses frequently display an intensity that has been likened to the typical fervor of heated Talmudic debates in yeshivas (traditional houses of learning). When leading diamond journalist Russell Shor (1993) wrote *Connections*, which profiles "diamond people and their history," he began with a *Fiddler on the Roof* invocation of "Tradition." And whenever diamond dealers arrive at an agreement, they shake hands and say together, "Mazel," which is the word for "luck" in Hebrew (sometimes they say, "Mazel u'Vracha," which is "luck and blessing"). In fact, according to the New York Diamond Dealers Club bylaws, no agreement between diamond dealers, regardless of heritage or language, is official or enforceable if it is not sealed with a "Mazel." (I once witnessed a transaction in Mumbai, involving several Indian merchants, in which animated negotiations took place in Hindi, Gujarati, Marathi, and occasional English, and when a deal was reached, the parties collectively said, "Mazel.") Jewish customs have infused the industry, and the industry has embraced its Jewish flavors, even as it has globalized and watched 47th Street merchants represent an increasingly diverse slice of the world.

Not only have Jewish merchants deeply shaped the diamond industry, but, as ethnographer Renée Rose Shield (2002) argues, the diamond industry has shaped important elements of the Jewish experience. Shield writes, "The story of Jews working in the diamond industry in New York tells how they mix in and stay apart, how they are open in important ways to mainstream American 'culture,' and how they also adapt to new times in ways that are both modern and traditional, indeed ancient. . . . The diamond . . . has allowed Jews to transform themselves from rejected refugees of one country to respected businessmen of another. Time after time, they have occupied an important but vulnerable niche in a process that has repeated itself over and over throughout the centuries" (ix). As Chapter 3 describes, Jewish predominance in the industry is no coincidence. The way Jewish merchants have excelled in peddling diamonds reveals important institutional features of the industry. Chapter 6 additionally connects Jewish success in the diamond trade to other hallmarks of Jewish economic history, so today's diamond industry might also suggest how Jewish merchants have thrived over centuries despite lacking political power. An examination of the economic demands of the diamond industry and the economic features of the Jewish community might explain why many Jewish communities and the diamond trade share a deeply entwined narrative.

Conclusion

New York Times columnist Thomas Friedman (2005), in describing how globalization has woven together the political and economic activities of nations, has said, "The world is flat." Perhaps the diamond industry is a paradigmatic example of the world's flatness, as the path of a single stone one might purchase on 47th Street in New York commonly takes it from Africa to London, Antwerp, Mumbai, Gujarat, back to Antwerp, then Israel and perhaps Hong Kong, and finally to New York. Along the way, it passes through the hands of multiple dealers and brokers; it is polished by multiple cutters, examined by people of many different races and cultures, and eventually is set carefully and artistically in a piece of jewelry.

Most buyers of diamond jewelry are blissfully unaware of a diamond's origins and path, and this is no accident. Diamond marketing relies on demarking a particular life moment—an engagement, an anniversary, a romantic surprise—and owners of jewelry are induced to associate their gems with personal memories, not the gem's origins. In fact, De Beers' early advertising campaigns in Hollywood intentionally promoted *surprise* as part of a diamond's allure, encouraging male diamond purchasers to devise a dramatic staging for a jewelry gift to their female companion (obviously much better for diamond sales than encouraging a laborious coshopping for the perfect stone), and one intentional consequence is that thoughts of the stone are recalled to that moment of presentation rather than to the background industry.

In truth, the industry would have it no other way, as it would be a liability if consumers were to think about a diamond's origins and path more than they currently do. Working conditions in Africa's mines and India's cutting factories are representative (at best) of those typically found in developing economies, which is to say that they are difficult to square with the sensibilities of many who purchase expensive diamonds. De Beers and other mining interests have shady histories with several African governments, which include allegations of bribery, corruption, paramilitary enterprises, and supporting kleptocracies. And the emergence of conflict diamonds had the potential to freeze demand for new stones entirely. Alternatively called "blood diamonds," "hot diamonds," or "war diamonds," conflict diamonds are sold by militarized groups to fuel armed conflict and civil war. The industry is acutely aware of the precipice it abuts, and it has supported regulations to rid the market of conflict diamonds (the Kimberley Process, the international regulatory regime designed to ensure that conflict diamonds do not enter the global market, is discussed in Chapter 7). But industry leaders recognize that demand for diamonds depends heavily on how diamonds are perceived, which in turn depends heavily on what thoughts are associated with the diamond gift. It thus continues to invest heavily in "the diamond invention."

Diamond consumers are not the only ones who might be accused of being selectively blind to diamonds' origins. Diamond dealers, as Chapter 3 discusses in detail, rely heavily on the integrity of their reputations to thrive in the market. Diamontaires on 47th Street and worldwide speak of core industry values of honesty, good dealing, and trust. These values supposedly embody what they do, their relationships to each other, and their generations-old devotion to the trade. The dominance of religious and ethnic networks in the industry causes religious principles to become a part of the diamontaire's vernacular, and it is common to invoke religious values—most frequently Jewish but increasingly Hindu, Buddhist, and Christian—to describe the motivations underlying business practices. There is much to admire in how these diamontaires conduct themselves and describe what they hold dear—indeed, several ethnographies (*Diamond Stories* by Shield [2002] and *Precious Objects* by Otulski [2011], for example) beautifully capture these values and the personalities that lead the industry. But there also is much to learn from the diamond production chain, the industry's modern history, and the reason that these topics are kept so removed from consumers and from the diamontaires themselves.

3

The Mechanics of Statelessness

The economic importance of personal and especially family relationships, though declining, is by no means trivial in the most advanced
economies; it is based on non-market relations that create guarantees of
behavior which would otherwise be afflicted with excessive uncertainty.

—*Kenneth Arrow, 1972 Nobel laureate in Economics*

Nothing is more fundamental in setting our research agenda and in-
forming our research methods than our view of the nature of the
human beings whose behavior we are studying.

—*Herbert Simon, 1978 Nobel laureate in Economics*

MUCH OF THIS BOOK, especially the theoretical model described in
Chapter 4, relies heavily on transaction cost economics, a subfield of
institutional economics that has been, in part, responsible for several Nobel
Prizes in Economics. Its origins are traced to a seminal 1937 article by
Ronald Coase (who received the Nobel in 1991), it relies on seminal work by
Kenneth Arrow (recipient in 1972), Herbert Simon (1978), Douglas North
(1993), Oliver Hart and Bengt Holmstrom (both in 2016), among others,
and it was fully formulated by Oliver Williamson (2009). True to its name,
transaction cost economics begins its analysis with the underlying transaction, so explaining the diamond industry's seemingly anachronistic and exotic
features and the forces that shape them—*what* is going on, and *why*—begins
with examining the mechanics of the typical diamond transaction. As it
turns out, the structure of nearly the entire industry can be explained by
understanding the unusual challenges generated by a typical diamond sale.

Diamonds, like many expensive and valuable goods, are most efficiently
purchased on credit. But while purchasing on credit is valuable—so much
so that only those who can purchase on credit can thrive in the industry—

selling diamonds on credit, of course, exposes the seller to opportunistic cheating. After all, diamonds are easily portable and concealable, yet they command extreme value throughout the world. A diamond thief encounters little difficulty hiding unpaid-for or stolen diamonds from law enforcement officials, fleeing a country's jurisdiction, and selling the valuable diamonds to black-market buyers. Diamonds remain the currency of choice among fugitives and are a wildly attractive target for thieves.[1] In fact, stolen diamonds are often unwittingly repurchased by the very merchants from whom they were stolen. Most of the haul from the Antwerp Diamond Center's largest diamond heist, when over $100 million in diamonds and other jewelry was stolen from a subterranean vault, was expected to find its way back into Antwerp's regular flow of gem sales (Selby and Campbell 2010).

Traditional law enforcement is generally helpless in restoring lost diamonds to the victims of theft. Even when diamond thieves are found, which they often are not, their spoils are long gone and are rarely retrieved. State authorities can neither trace to where diamonds have been transported nor detect when or to whom they are sold and resold. Thus, as one country music hit instructs, once they're gone, they're gone forever. And just as law enforcement cannot return stolen diamonds to their original owner, it cannot return diamonds bought on credit but left unpaid to their original seller. This is a critical premise of this book: *modern courts and state-sponsored law enforcement, which we rely on to secure contract and property rights, can do virtually nothing to secure a diamond executory contract.* Each diamond sold on credit places a would-be purchaser in a very tempting position and puts a seller in a very vulnerable one.[2]

This is a distinguishing feature of the diamond industry: trade in diamonds invites extraordinarily lucrative opportunities to cheat, namely, to take another's diamonds on credit and later renege on a promise to pay. Purchasing goods on credit is useful to any market, and has been for centuries, and jurists have suggested that the very heart of contracts and contract law is "to facilitate exchanges that are not simultaneous by preventing either party from taking advantage of the vulnerabilities to which sequential performance may rise" (*Wisconsin Knife Works v. National Metal Crafters*, 781 F.2d 1280, 1285 (7th Cir. 1986) [J. Posner]). For that reason, modern commerce has developed many mechanisms to secure credit sales, such as attaching liens or assigning collateral to purchased goods. Banks, businesses, and consumers alike take advantage of these legal instruments routinely. Homes are purchased with mortgages, cars are purchased with loans, lines of credit are extended against collateral, and transactions can take place, at lower risk and thus at lower prices, on a scale that was unavailable to earlier generations. But because such modern instruments are ineffective for today's diamond dealers, the industry has needed to construct alternative instruments to secure credit sales.

This chapter, building off of the mechanics and unique challenges of the diamond credit sale, describes the institutions built by and surrounding the diamond industry that enable the industry to enforce executory contracts. It focuses, aiming to be as specific as possible, on New York's diamond dealers and the New York Diamond Dealers Club (DDC), the diamond district's bourse and the industry's epicenter. This community of diamontaires is responsible for making the diamond industry work and for giving it its unique features.

Many disciplines can offer explanations for the behavior and organization of a group like the diamond merchants, one with intimate relations, a web of social and religious institutional connections, and distinct industry and commercial norms. This chapter examines the diamond market through an economist's lens. It poses the rudimentary economic question, *Why do diamond merchants comply with their contractual obligations, when breaching is so lucrative?* And it offers an answer that rests on economic logic and complies with the economist's assumption of maximizing rational agents. The economist's explanation is by no means the only one that works, nor is it entirely satisfying by itself, but it would be hard to imagine an industry that has been largely unchanged for centuries, particularly one that is so vulnerable to theft and market failures, that is not consistent with economic theory. Through the economist's lens, this chapter explains how the DDC creates an institutional environment that disseminates information so merchants can reliably use reputations to support exchange. It then describes how intergenerational family businesses and tightly knit ethnic communities enable cooperation. The complementary industry and community institutions enable the diamond industry to secure transactions that are beyond the reach of courts. These institutions also explain why certain ethnic communities have a comparative advantage in the industry, and thus why the world of diamond merchants looks so different from modern industries that rely on court enforcement.

"Trust-Based Exchange"

The conventional narrative states that diamond merchants shun legal instruments and formal dealings and instead rely on trust. Mutual trust among merchants—which the *New York Times* has called "the real treasure of 47th Street" (Starr 1984)—assures dealers that by maintaining a trustworthy reputation, they will remain in good community standing and preserve the opportunity to engage in future lucrative transactions. Through this mutual trust, dealers comfortably engage in executory contracts outside state courts. Indeed, the narrative continues, this is part of the industry's charm, and its clinging to mutual trust is a hallmark of its anachronism and its old-world flavors.

"Trust," however, is a vague descriptor, or an "elusive notion," as Diego Gambetta (1988) observes in his writings about Italian mafia networks. It raises more questions than it answers. What makes people trust others and what sustains that trust? Social scientists have rested heavily on notions of trust to explain certain economic phenomena without fully answering these questions. Assorted scholars have used trust-based explanations to explain the organization of national industry (Dore 1983; 1989, chap. 9), the bonds that secure ethnic trading networks (Carr and Landa 1983; Landa 1981), the success of certain credit associations (Geertz 1962; Ardener 1964; Velez-Ibanez 1983), and regional and national economic performance (Putnam 1993; Fukuyama 1995). These studies usefully examine important economic activity that takes place within particular social environments, and they laudably recognize that behaviors they observe are deeply shaped and constrained by their surroundings.

However, "trust" can too easily be a convenient explanation for too wide a variety of vexing phenomena. This has motivated some prominent thinkers to develop simplified conceptions of trust that are consistent with economic models of self-interested behavior. James Coleman (1990), for example, translates "relations of trust" that are popular in the sociology literature into a rational choice formulation, and Russell Hardin (2002) advances an "encapsulated interest" theory that states that individuals trust those persons whom they believe will act to advance their well-being. Similar accounts by game theorists explain mutual trust with utility-maximizing models that rest on rational and calculative actors (Dasgupta 1988; Kreps

1990). And Williamson offers a "hyphenated trust" that, while adhering to the economist's taste for utility maximization, recognizes that since "man, after all, is a 'social animal,' . . . socialization and social approvals and sanctions are also pertinent" (1993, 475).

Rather than relying on a vague or ineffable notion of "trust" to explain cooperative behavior in the diamond industry, this chapter explores in detail the industry's mechanisms that reward trustworthy behavior (namely, keeping promises) and punish breaches of trust. And rather than describing transactions as taking place within "trust-based exchange," it uses the concept of "personal exchange"—or, alternatively, reputation-based exchange or private ordering—to describe diamond transactions. The point of emphasis is not what induces individuals to enter into transactions that leave them vulnerable, but instead the consequences to those who act opportunistically. "Personal exchange" characterizes commerce between individuals who use private, nonstate mechanisms to punish individuals who breach promises. When public courts are unavailable, inaccessible, unreliable, or too costly to support impersonal exchange, merchants might find personal exchange to be a viable alternative.

Contrary to the label, personal exchange can take place between two individuals who do not know each other well. In fact, for personal exchange to support a lucrative industry, it *must* develop mechanisms that can enforce contracts between large numbers of merchants even though familiarity inevitably declines as the number of merchants rises. If private mechanisms can credibly threaten to impose sanctions on a large number of merchants and thus induce them to comply with their commercial obligations, the merchant community can achieve levels of competition, volume, and scale economies that can sustain a viable market. In short, if a merchant community can create what could be called "impersonal personal exchange," then it might be adequately efficient to sustain itself into the era of modern courts. Creating such a system, however, requires a robust collection of institutions.

The New York Diamond Dealers Club

Nearly half of the world's $72 billion diamond jewelry sales are in the United States, and merchants in Manhattan's crowded 47th Street diamond district handle over 95 percent of the diamonds imported into the United States. At the epicenter of 47th Street's diamond district lies the New York Diamond Dealers Club, known colloquially as the DDC.

The New York Diamond Dealers Club formally began in 1931 and modeled itself after the diamond bourses that served Europe's older and larger diamond centers. It began with twelve founding incorporators and 50 original members, grew substantially toward the end of World War II when many European dealers immigrated to the United States,[3] and steadily consisted of between 1,800 and 2,000 members for much of the late twentieth century. As in Europe, New York's diamond industry is heavily populated by Jewish merchants, and the DDC's culture and operations reflect its approximately 85 percent Jewish membership.[4] The DDC includes a kosher restaurant and prayer hall, is closed for Jewish holidays, and invokes Jewish law to resolve disputes.

The DDC also operates as a sophisticated trading exchange. It serves as the trade association for New York's diamond dealers and, among other activities, engages with local and state governments to redevelop 47th Street and improve the local business climate. It offers members a properly lit trading hall, equipped with special florescent lights and natural light from the north, precise industry scales for official measurements, and intense security that keeps out nonmembers and uninvited guests. But more important than its physical infrastructure, the DDC supplies a legal infrastructure for diamond transactions. The DDC issues trade rules that govern diamond sales and provides a mandatory private arbitration system to resolve all disputes between merchants.

This private system replaces any opportunity to seek redress from a state court, and any member who does attempt to adjudicate in state courts will be fined or suspended from the club. Through an election, select DDC members are chosen to serve as arbitrators, and only members held in the highest esteem win election. Although arbitration panels deliberate in strict secrecy, it is known that arbitrators may question parties, rely on either secular or Jewish law or mere common sense to reach rulings, and are not bound to adhere to previous rulings or any form of precedent. Arbitrators are therefore intended not to be legalistic jurists but rather compatriots who understand business pressures, common dangers, and industry customs. Panels pass down rulings without issuing written justifications or creating case law, and the only evidence that an arbitration hearing took place is its highly publicized ruling, which only identifies the wrongdoing party and announces a judgment amount. All arbitration rulings are final, and although a state court may be asked to help enforce an arbitration ruling, those who ask a state court to review an arbitration ruling will, like those who bring a suit in state court, be suspended or expelled.

The private arbitration system has been hailed as an efficient and highly effective enforcement mechanism. Because DDC arbitrators are highly familiar with the diamond industry and archetypal diamond transactions, they are credited for issuing rulings that are more prompt and accurate than any public judge or state court. Arbitrators are familiar with the process of identifying diamonds,[5] so the evidentiary process of recognizing stolen goods is possible and far less costly than it would be if it were handled by a state court. Plus, DDC arbitration procedures and remedies are tailored for typical disputes, so litigation costs are lower and penalties can match the true costs of misconduct. In a mysterious world that peddles unique and hard-to-measure goods and relies on extending credit, DDC arbitration has been remarkably effective in maintaining credibility among so many merchants.

However, the perceived authority and respect attributed to the DDC's arbitration system belies its toothlessness. DDC arbitrators are incapable of enforcing agreements on their own and do not have the power to punish diamond theft. The DDC's arbitration board can issue fines or revoke an individual's club membership, but these sanctions are only effective if the party intends to continue transacting in diamonds and utilize the benefits of DDC membership. These sanctions are meaningless if that merchant decides never to transact again.

The arbitrators' powerlessness echoes the inability of state courts to enforce its own rulings. While decisions by the DDC's arbitration committee are theoretically enforceable in New York's state courts, state courts are no more capable of deterring theft than the arbitrators.[6] Diamonds' portability and universal and extraordinary value make them a thief's best friend, and any property abandoned by a fleeing thief is unlikely to compensate a stiffed diamond seller.[7] Despite the enormous value of the goods being sold and traded, there is a common recognition that neither public courts nor private arbitration panels can recover adequate damages from a person who has squandered or stolen another's diamonds and is either unable or unwilling to pay. One diamond dealer conceded, "The truth is that if someone owes you money, there's no real way to get it from him if he doesn't want to pay you."

Consequently, despite its accolades, the DDC arbitration board is not capable of recovering stolen or squandered goods, and compensation is not its primary mission. Instead, its power is limited only to cooperating parties who hope to remain members of the diamond community, and its remedies—the ability to expel, to fine, or to order damages—are meaningful only against merchants hoping to maintain a long-term, profitable diamond business. Merchants therefore *only* cooperate with the DDC arbitration board, and cooperate with each other, to preserve good reputations and protect the opportunity to engage in future diamond transactions. Accordingly, the true power of the DDC's dispute resolution system rests on the degree to which it supports reputation-based exchange and can foreclose future transactions to merchants who have previously failed to fulfill their contractual obligations. The DDC fulfills this role by serving primarily as an information device, publicizing individual wrongdoing and thereby serving as a guardian to individual reputations.[8]

The Power and Purpose of Reputational Information

A typical game-theoretic formulation of how reputations can sustain long-term cooperation states that individual players will cooperate so long as the present value of continued cooperation will exceed the potential profits from cheating once.[9] Both the intuition and the underlying math to prove the possibility of sustained cooperation are rather simple. The burdensome features of enabling reputation-based exchange are almost exclusively mechanical: How can reputational information be sufficiently widespread and accurate so individuals will know who has breached agreements in the past? How can merchants who are tempted to cheat be assured of being foreclosed to commerce if they commit wrongdoing?[10]

Historically, the foremost function of all diamond bourses and their formal predecessors has always been to facilitate a flow of information about market participants and business opportunities. Diamond clubs in fact sprang from cafés and other informal meeting places where dealers congregated to exchange information and create business. Many merchant groups originally met at private houses, which were additionally attractive because they provided a safe place for conducting business over valuable items. In fact, the very origin of the word "bourse," which now colloquially refers to any trading exchange, is traced back to the city of Bruges, Belgium, in the fifteenth century, where international diamond dealers met in the house of a nobleman named Van der Beurse.

Like their informal predecessors, today's bourses provide an infrastructure that organizes a network of dealers. Bourses now serve as vital sources of information that enable merchants to become familiar with potential business partners. Lisa Bernstein (1992) observed, "The bourse is an information exchange as much as it is a commodities exchange. As one author put it, 'the bourse grapevine is the best in the world. It has been going for years and moves with the efficiency of a satellite communications network. . . . Bourses are the fountainhead of this information and from them it is passed out along the tentacles that stretch around the world'" (121, quoting Berquem [1988]).

The DDC supports information exchange through several mechanisms. First, the floor of the trading hall is bustling with information about parties and market conditions, and some traders spend time on the trading floor just to keep abreast of available information. Traders on the floor will ask others about potential business partners and get references, and supplementary credit reports about diamond buyers float through the trading community.[11] Many spend their time with colleagues sharing meals in the dining room, praying in the synagogue, or casually socializing on the trading floor and keeping a proverbial ear to the ground, alert to profitable opportunities and market developments. Thus, the club creates both a physical and a relational infrastructure that facilitates information sharing between members.

A second mechanism is the wall of the trading floor. The wall posts the pictures, background, and references of any visitor to the club, providing easy referral for potential business dealings (most visitors are required to be sponsored by a member, who is cited as a reference next to the visitor's picture). The wall also announces the nomination of potential new members and invites current members to comment on the candidate's reputation. Most importantly, the wall publicizes the judgments from recent disputes before the arbitration board and posts a picture, not unlike a sheriff's office's

"Wanted" poster, of any party who is responsible for an outstanding debt. This information is shared with all of the world's bourses, and pictures of delinquent debtors from around the world are prominently broadcasted in the DDC trading hall. The DDC's arbitration committee uses the wall to promptly and prominently announce its rulings, identifying to the community the individuals against whom there are unpaid judgments and subjecting those individuals to the inevitable shame that accompanies the proclamation.

A third device—the simplest and perhaps the most significant—that disseminates information on reputations is DDC membership itself. Maintaining DDC membership in good standing signals to potential trading partners a clean past and the absence of an outstanding judgment. Thus, the social gatherings and business dealings in the trading hall, the formal arbitration judgments, and the visual representations on the DDC wall enable any member to swiftly research the past of a potential business partner and learn who has failed to comply with their obligations.

With so much reputational information available to members, and with so much at stake in maintaining a good reputation, the credibility of the entire enforcement system depends on the accuracy of the reputation information it disseminates. Some very interesting mechanisms and norms help police the reliability of the reputational information that spreads throughout the trade. One source is the DDC's arbitration board itself. The arbitration board is composed of insiders who are familiar with the nature of the industry and the difficulties involved in entering diamond contracts. Their expertise helps arbitrators understand the context within which disputes arise, distinguish meritorious from nonmeritorious claims, verify the veracity of proffered evidence, and, when appropriate, estimate the appropriate damages. Additionally, DDC bylaws empower the arbitration board to act on its own initiative to respond to misinformation and punish any party responsible for spreading inaccurate information. In one case, a dealer falsely accused another of stealing his stone. He later realized that he actually misplaced the stone and apologized to the dealer, but the accusation had already become common knowledge. The second dealer then brought the first before the arbitration committee for impugning his reputation, and the board ordered the false accuser to publicly apologize and donate $50,000 to a Jewish charity.

Certain sources of Jewish law and tradition also enhance the accuracy of shared reputation information by discouraging the dissemination of certain rumors. Consider the following tale imparted by the prominent nineteenth-century scholar Rabbi Israel Meir HaKohen, popularly known as the *Chafetz Chayyim* (1873): "A man goes before his Rabbi and admits to having spread harmful information about his neighbor. He asks the Rabbi what he should do to repent. The Rabbi says 'Find a feather pillow, cut it open and release the feathers into the wind.' The man follows the Rabbi's instructions and returns the next day. The Rabbi then says, 'Now, to gain forgiveness, you must go back to your home and retrieve all of the feathers. Because you can remove the damage of your words only as much as you can recollect the feathers.'" This parable encapsulates Jewish law's prohibition of *lashon harah,* or "the evil tongue," which forbids the spreading of unflattering information about another individual, even if that information is accurate. Jewish law also forbids individuals from knowingly disseminating false and damaging information about others,[12] but it does not place excessive barriers to communicating reputation information when that information is necessary to sustain one's livelihood. To the contrary, Jewish law mandates the sharing of damaging yet truthful reputation information if the information would be of substantial use to the recipient, is shared only because it would aid the recipient, and is shared only to the degree necessary to assist the recipient. These religious rules deter the spread of misinformation and unnecessary reputation information, help filter communications to increase their accuracy, and ensure that merchants share the information required to support the market's functioning.

These religious rules have a pervasive effect on how merchants share information, as merchants are careful before sharing either flattering or damaging reputational information. For example, when one dealer asked a colleague about the reputation of an unfamiliar buyer in the DDC trading hall, the second dealer replied, "I hear he is good. I hear he is very good. But don't take my word. Be sure to ask for his references and talk to members who have dealt with him." Another dealer, after sharing in an interview that he had some difficulty securing payment from a certain merchant (while not naming the merchant), admitted, "That frustrating experience—that is the kind of information I would share with my close colleagues and relatives. If they asked me about what kind of businessman this individual is, I'd tell them that he has given me some trouble. But truthfully, I would only share the information if I were asked—I wouldn't spread it around on my own initiative. Also, I think I'd only share the information with people I knew well. If a colleague that I don't know so well asked me about this person, I'd probably just say that I don't know anything." Accordingly, reliable information is available upon request from colleagues, but it does not float around without purpose. In a world where good reputations are so critical to commercial success, and where gossip can be so damaging, these filters are necessary to discourage the aimless spreading of information of questionable veracity.

The DDC's system of arbitration and information exchange thus sets the stage for other family- and community-based institutions that enforce the industry's executory contracts; if the DDC announces the verdict, then these complementary institutions are the sheriffs that enforce it. These community and family institutions play central economic roles in sustaining New York's diamond industry, and they illuminate many of the fascinating and unusual features of the world of diamonds.

The Parties

The driving force behind diamond merchants' ability to participate in reputation-based exchange is their membership in intimate communities. *Who* the merchants are is what enables them to make credible contractual promises—to commit to an obligation that state courts cannot enforce—and this in turn gives them a competitive advantage over outsiders. They can purchase goods on credit, whereas competitors who cannot make similarly credible commitments are forced to purchase on less favorable terms.

Each established diamond merchant can be placed in one of two "identity" categories. One category might be labeled the "family" category, which includes merchants who have family connections to the industry and usually have a proprietary stake in a family-run business. These merchants gain entry into the industry through the sponsorship of a family elder, and they later employ younger family members to whom they eventually bequeath the business. Thus, they are inducted into an intergenerational family business, work in this business for their entire career, and then pass on the same business to their descendants. The merchants in this category could also be described as "long-term players" because they inherit a preceding relative's reputation and work hard to bequeath a good reputation to their progeny. They both benefit from and invest in long-term reputations that maintain a family business for generations.

The second group consists of religious community members and could be labeled a "community" category. Most of New York's diamond workers in this category belong to ultra-Orthodox Jewish communities and adhere to a zealously religious life that rejects most aspects of the modern world. They live in concentrated ultra-Orthodox Jewish neighborhoods, speak Yiddish, which is a lost language in most parts of the globe, dress in the same clothing as their sixteenth-century ancestors, and, even while they are frequently in possession of enormously valuable caches of diamonds, they are committed to the austere lifestyles of ultra-Orthodoxy. The pervasiveness of this second group—the industry's "diamond-studded paupers"—is one of the most distinctive and striking features of the diamond industry. When these merchants fill the DDC trading halls, their clothes, language, and intense demeanor make observers feel they are watching commerce in Europe's old bazaar markets. But instead of trinkets or small crafts, these paupers peddle caches of precious diamonds.

Thus, the industry is home to two distinct categories of players. Although these two categories sometimes overlap, as when members of a family business are part of an ultra-Orthodox community, merchants from these different categories are motivated and constrained by dramatically different forces. Whereas long-term players work to build up profitable businesses (and profitable reputations) that they can bequeath to their descendants, paupers instead hope that their sons commit their lives to religious study and avoid commercial endeavors altogether. They therefore assume assorted contractor roles, chiefly as brokers (who search for a buyer and retain a small sales commission) and cutters (who cut or polish a diamond for a fixed fee), in which they can secure a steady income without being tethered to a business or inventory. In stark contrast to family merchants, contractors hope to accumulate sufficient resources for themselves only so they and their families can leave the business and devote their time to their religious lifestyle. They are committed to the industry for anything but the long run.

Like family merchants who purchase diamonds on credit, both brokers and cutters assume possession of diamonds that they do not own, nor do they offer payment or collateral to diamond owners when they take possession. Therefore, even though these two categories of middlemen are from different groups, are connected to different community institutions, are constrained by different individuals or institutions, and have different business incentives and life preferences, they are both in a position in which it is easy to steal lucrative caches of diamonds. Consequently, distinct mechanisms are required to induce the two types of parties to comply with their contractual obligations. What induces one group to cooperate does not necessarily control the behavior of the other.

Long-Term Players

Oliver Wendell Holmes Jr. (1897, 462) famously said, "The duty to keep a contract at common law means a prediction that you must pay damages if you do not keep it—and nothing else." It might be similarly said that the duty to keep a contract within a private system of reputation-based exchange amounts to a prediction that your reputation will suffer if you do not keep it. Private enforcement systems secure commercial obligations by threatening breaching parties with a soiled reputation and thus the inability to earn the trust of merchants for future transactions.

The paramount requirement in making a reputation mechanism work, therefore, is to impose costs on individuals who tarnish their reputation. Although it might be obvious that a party who has cheated in the past is less likely to earn the trust of future business partners, it is less apparent that the expected benefits of cooperation will exceed the expected benefits from cheating; or, put otherwise, that a cheater will be sufficiently punished so that cheating is less attractive than cooperating indefinitely. Wouldn't a cheater be able to reenter the industry and offer a premium to future partners that is enough to attract new business yet is less than the profits from cheating in an earlier transaction?

Aware of the benefits of cheating even once, diamond dealers are collectively committed to exacting coordinated punishment, where all merchants refuse to do business with a merchant who has failed to comply with a contractual obligation in the past. A merchant who has failed to pay a debt or refused to comply with an arbitration ruling will be expelled from the DDC and will be unable to obtain business from dealers in good standing. Moreover, merchants known to do business with bad-standing members see their reputation suffer as well, thus the industry sustains what could be called a secondary boycott: not only do merchants boycott wrongdoers, but they also boycott those who do business with wrongdoers.

Even so, the value of sustaining a good reputation is not infinite, and just as the common law must create a law of damages to adequately induce parties to comply with their obligations, so must a private reputation-based system create punishments that deter wrongdoing. For merchants dealing in diamonds, where the size and value of typical diamond sales offer enormously lucrative opportunities to cheat, this is a tall order. From a simple game-theoretic perspective, the value of continued compliance for diamond sales must exceed the extraordinary value of a one-time theft. Even the prospect of being banned from all future diamond transactions might not be enough to force compliance. Moreover, in the long run we're all dead, so an end-game problem arises as individuals approach their inevitable end. It becomes increasingly difficult to induce cooperation with the prospect of future lucrative transactions as that future becomes increasingly finite.

The diamond industry solves this interesting end-game problem primarily through the pervasiveness of family-based firms. The intergenerational nature of the family firms extends the time horizon for cooperation beyond the limited life span of an individual dealer. A leader of a family business can bequeath his good reputation to several descendants so those descendants can enjoy the valuable trust of potential business partners. Accordingly, the elder merchant—so long as he is motivated to improve the well-being of his heirs—is continually incentivized to enhance the value of his reputation through his last dealings, and an imminent retirement is no cause for an end-game problem. In fact, the opposite may be true: when a dealer nears the end of his career, he knows that his reputation will influence the transactions of several relatives, and he will continue to cooperate even if he plans to retire soon.[13] Conversely, if a merchant commits wrongdoing, he is punishing not just himself but his progeny as well.

The possibility of bequeathing valuable family reputations has some important economic implications. First, the family-based nature of businesses secures future riches for relatives who currently hold entry-level positions. Young relative employees who handle their elder's diamonds have the very reasonable expectation that they will inherit the business. This is enough to make their individual time horizons very long and increases the value of each decision to cooperate. And second, aspiring merchants benefit significantly from a family-sponsored reputation, whereas new and unknown merchants will have significant trouble convincing diamond sellers to sell on credit. For many, the only way to feel comfortable trusting an individual is to know his family.

A third interesting consequence is that sometimes the reputation mechanism shows leniency for what might be called the industry's extended family. Although sanctions for failing to comply with credit obligations are severe, there are instances where an individual fails to pay his debts yet is rescued by an elder merchant who is motivated as much by compassion as by profit. One dealer described the process as follows: "There are a lot of pressures in the trade. A dealer often has many transactions he has to be aware of, and sometimes he just doesn't make the right calculation and he is left short of cash when a payment is due. These actions are not condonable—all of us need to keep track of our finances—but they are understandable. And when it happens to someone you think is basically a good person, sometimes one of the senior Club members will try to help him out and let him recover." The elder enters into an agreement with the fallen dealer as a way to allow him to recover and rebuild a reputation. These generosities are usually undertaken by a senior leader who commands respect from other dealers and whose judgment is a sufficient signal to convince others that the recovering dealer is worth a second chance.

This element of forgiveness also adds a human dimension to the otherwise strict rules that reputation games require. It reflects the balance between the serious need to deter cheating with the compassionate recognition that individuals have human frailties. The critical challenge is to distinguish between individuals who are either untrustworthy or unreliable and those who made a mistake they are unlikely to repeat.[14] The reputation system empowers the individuals who have the most information about a merchant in question and who have the most experience in judging character to make the ultimate determination.

Thus, the role of family reputations makes it possible for the industry to sustain long-term cooperation. But it also imposes a lock on both sides of the industry's door. Entrants have enormous difficulty breaking into the industry, whereas low-level family workers wear golden handcuffs in which the prospect of inheriting a valuable business induces them to learn and remain in the trade. The combined result is that the industry's profile is highly ossified, with family businesses remaining enmeshed in the business for generations while aspiring entrepreneurs largely stay away.[15]

"Diamond-Studded Paupers"

The ultra-Orthodox brokers and cutters, who constitute the second category of diamond merchants, provide important value-added services and are critical in making the diamond industry profitable. However, since they are much less likely to bring their descendants into the diamond trade, the prospects of future exchange are insufficient to induce them to cooperate. In fact, because of their commitment to ultra-Orthodox Judaism and love for traditional religious learning, many would like nothing more than to stop working and engage in full-time study. Their incentives to cooperate must take effect within a much shorter time horizon.

An observer would instantly recognize that, unlike successful diamond dealers from family-run businesses, these brokers and cutters are not wealthy people. This is remarkable given the industry in which they work—they have lots of diamonds, but no money. Moreover, although some diamond brokers are sophisticated matchers of buyers with sellers, many brokers are rudimentary holders of sellers' diamonds, waiting in the DDC for inquiring buyers to enter and look for available stones. They do not possess hard-to-replicate skills. Cutters, similarly, usually fill rudimentary jobs and, aside from cutters who shape large stones, including "master cutters" who often learn their skills from their families, they have skills that are learned fairly easily. Thus, even though most of the labor comes from the same community, the labor markets for brokers and cutters are very competitive and their incomes remain rather low. The consequence is striking to the observer: workers with very modest appearances, often with tattered clothes, drop scores of diamonds from their fingertips.[16]

These workers therefore pose an interesting challenge to basic economic theory: Why do they persist in low-wage jobs when a fantastically valuable theft—with diamonds that could start a new life anywhere—would be so easy? To be sure, some economic elements make theft additionally costly for these individuals. Most members of the ultra-Orthodox community do not have marketable skills that would make alternative employment easily available to them, and many lack the modern-world capabilities to survive outside the insular community, especially to lead a life as a fugitive. In addition, ultra-Orthodox norms encourage certain behaviors that cause members to be fully embedded in, and largely dependent on, their community before they are financially independent or otherwise capable of leaving. One interesting mechanism that binds young individuals to the community is a by-product of the conflicting pressures to commit many years to study while also marrying young and having many children to fulfill the biblical commandment to "be fruitful and multiply." Males will often remain full-time students deep into adulthood, yet will marry and have several children long before those studies conclude. A young couple with children therefore will frequently live with their in-laws for years or receive community stipends until the male completes his religious study, which can continue until he is forty years old. By the time the male assumes economic responsibilities, he, his spouse, and his children are thoroughly entrenched within the community. Many ultra-Orthodox communities also entangle personal and community property, which prevents a community member from leaving the community with his assets. These patterns of communal life and religious structure make exit from the community uncommonly difficult, and they accentuate members' reliance on whatever employment the community makes available to them.[17]

Nonetheless, sustained cooperation by ultra-Orthodox diamond workers, despite the attractiveness and ease of theft, belies a simple wealth maximization model and demands a more complicated utility theory. One useful model developed by economists studying religious communities—one that can explain seemingly noneconomic behavior in language that an economist can appreciate—is a "club good" model (Iannaccone 1992; Berman 2000). Members of "clubs" have preferences not just for standard consumption goods, which everyone desires, but also for goods and services that are unique to the club.[18] Only the club can produce club goods and only club members can enjoy these club goods. Moreover, club members also derive additional utility from the group's collective club goods consumption. So members desire to remain in a particular community both where certain club goods are available and where they can live with like-minded individuals who have a similar taste for those same club goods.

Although a club could be anything that offers unique enjoyment to members when similar individuals come together, the paradigmatic "club" is an ethnic or religious community that has intersecting institutions—educational, religious, social, and the like—that bind community members together. Club good models are designed precisely to explain why individuals desire to remain members of a community even though better economic opportunities exist elsewhere, and they recognize a trade-off between consuming economic goods and consuming club goods. Although other social scientists offer their own theories to explain the same seemingly uneconomic behavior, the club good model is a concrete way to explain behaviors and community structures using formal economic tools that are more nuanced than the traditional profit-maximizing homo economicus.

The club good model is especially effective in elucidating the unusually strong fidelity that ultra-Orthodox Jews show for their communities. Specifically, it can explain why ultra-Orthodox Jewish brokers are so unlikely to flee with stolen diamonds. Even though such a theft would significantly enhance their consumption of economic goods, it would foreclose consumption of club goods, which for the ultra-Orthodox community member is a trade-off that decreases utility and thus is not preferred. Members remain in their community simply because that is where club goods are offered and available for consumption. A representative conversation proceeded as follows:

> *Author:* So none of these diamonds before you belong to you?
> *Cutter:* That's right. I polish them and then I return them to the owner.
> *Author:* Why don't you just take them?
> *Cutter:* What?
> *Author:* These are worth a tremendous amount of money. They could support you and your family probably forever. Why don't you just take them?
> *Cutter:* [*smiling*] Where would I go?

More interesting, the club good model explains more than just the lack of flight. It also explains why the structure of the ultra-Orthodox community is so helpful in supporting cooperation in the diamond industry. Because community members want their fellow community members to share and exhibit common values (or, in the language of the club good model, to consume common club goods), the entire ultra-Orthodox community is motivated to police members' behavior and punish undesirable conduct. Consequently, the community will establish certain norms and institutions—primarily by doling out or withholding community goods and services—that, in the economist's language, will incentivize the behavior that appeals to community members. In other words, because community members care not just about their own behavior but also about the behavior of their peers, they are motivated to build institutions and develop community rules that will encourage desirable conduct.

For starters, desirable conduct includes ethical behavior in business. It might be said that ethical business conduct—and especially keeping one's business promises—is one club good that is enjoyed by merchants, and therefore enjoyed by the community when practiced by individual merchants in the community. Interestingly, the source of the desire for ethical business conduct is not an appetite for ethical conduct generally, but rather comes from Jewish law. Even though Hellenistic and early Muslim scholars made progress in the early study of positive economics, ancient and medieval Jewish scholarship is surprisingly lacking in works on economics. Instead, early Jewish authorities focused on legal and philosophical studies, and Jewish texts offered only normative examinations of economic life (historian Salo Baron [1975] remarked that "the emphasis upon ethics and psychology far outweighed a realistic conceptualism" [48]). Though Jewish law commands certain behaviors that have clear economic consequences, such as protecting private property and mandating crop rotation, and though these mandates arguably have efficient consequences, the principles underlying such directives rested on purely ethical and religious justifications, not economic reasoning.[19]

Accordingly, Jewish teachings infuse discussions of economics with moralistic overtones, and adherents to Jewish law engage in market behavior believing they must act in accordance with the ethical precepts of religious law. One such obligation is to keep promises made to others, so fulfilling contractual responsibilities upholds a divinely inspired commandment.[20] Relatedly, the doctrine of the "just price" requires strict rules for accurate weights and measures because the lack of enforceable standards would damage human relations.[21] And the theory of "misrepresentation" prohibits a merchant from overcharging (or even undercharging) for a certain good—and permits an injured party to nullify any sale—because such distortion is akin to breaking an oath before the divine. The central message, reaffirmed in many sources of Jewish law, is that merchants are not permitted to exploit or mislead their business partners.[22]

These ethical principles are very much alive in today's ultra-Orthodox community, as brokers and cutters draw a direct relationship between contractual performance and ethical behavior. The most common instance occurs when one is asked with whom they do business. The answer goes beyond whether the individual is considered reliable and always assumes an undertone of moral judgment, such as, "Who do I do business with? Well, who do I trust? Is the person a good, reliable, trustworthy individual? Is he an honest and decent human being? Does he come from a good family and a good community?" Similarly, ultra-Orthodox merchants view their commercial actions as a part of a moral example they assume as observant Jews and as providers for their families. Another common response when merchants are asked why they do not pursue obvious wealth by shirking contractual duties is, "That's not what I want to teach my kids."

Importantly, not all policing of ethical behavior is self-directed, and the ultra-Orthodox community has ways to punish behavior that transgresses Jewish law, including behavior that is deemed unethical business conduct. One blunt enforcement instrument is to use rabbinic courts to excommunicate an offender. Although excommunication is a severe and rare sanction, proceedings are not unprecedented, and the mere power to excommunicate, even if rarely invoked, is a powerful tool to induce community members to comport with religious precepts. The DDC arbitration committee itself can initiate a proceeding in a rabbinic court, and the close connection between the two forums illustrates the diamond industry's reliance on community institutions to help enforce contracts.[23] Indeed, the cooperation between industry institutions that identify misconduct and community mechanisms that sanction it is one of the central features of Jewish involvement in the diamond industry, and it enables Jewish merchants to credibly commit to diamond transactions that most outsiders cannot.

Since excommunication is appropriate only in the event of severe misconduct, policing merchants also requires more moderate sanctions that are appropriate for business dealings that are unbecoming yet fall far short of theft or outright cheating. Again illustrating how the ultra-Orthodox community institutions play critical roles in sustaining cooperation in the diamond industry, rabbinic courts and other authorities in the ultra-Orthodox community are well suited to address other sorts of misconduct. Rabbinic courts, for example, can impose sanctions such as stripping an individual of a community honor or requiring contributions to a community charity. Less formal institutions also play a role in sanctioning misconduct, and community leaders are regularly in a position to reward community members—with leadership roles in daily prayer, recognition during life-cycle ceremonies, and access to teachers or schools that are in limited supply—who have behaved honorably, and withhold those same honors from those who have not. And, in what might be akin to gold at the end of a rainbow, community members are highly motivated to pair their children with desirable marriage partners. Arranged marriage is the norm in many ultra-Orthodox communities, and a family's community status remains a leading factor determining with whom their children are paired.[24]

Importantly, Orthodox Judaism is replete with concrete, identifiable community goods that have subtle hierarchies. Small distinctions can translate into either valued honors or disappointing slights, and the large number of religious goods offers community leaders a broad menu of punishment options with varying degrees of severity, including distinctions that would go unnoticed or unappreciated by an outsider. Consider one diamond merchant's remarks: "It really doesn't happen very often, but sometimes an individual has poor judgment and is unable to deliver on a business promise. Usually his business partners and he are able to renegotiate something fair and little damage is done, or maybe someone else comes to his aid and, for a small price, helps him out. But there's no avoiding that we knew he made a mistake and that we are disappointed. We don't try to punish him—you have to understand the financial pressures that come with the business and with the burdens of raising a large family. But we remember. So he probably doesn't get shishi." *Shishi*, which means "sixth" in Hebrew, refers to the sixth aliyah, or Torah reading, during the Sabbath services.

Being asked to say the blessings for any aliyah is an honor, and some ultra-Orthodox communities consider the sixth aliyah to bestow an honor greater than those associated with the other aliyot since human beings (Adam and Eve) were created on the sixth day. Accordingly, community leaders who allocate these and other ritualistic roles can make deliberate distinctions that give honor to respected individuals while withholding respect from others. By tailoring the punishments to match the severity of the harm done, these distinctions have an appropriately substantial deterrent effect.

The passage also illustrates another nice feature of this form of community disciplining: it is done with compassion. Although there are inevitable interconnections between an individual's commercial behavior and the community respect he subsequently receives, the community generally responds with a forgiving overtone. Community members understand the temptations of ambitious deals, the difficulties of managing liquidity constraints, and the costs of inexperience. Punishments, when invoked, are accompanied with sympathy and, sometimes, even financial assistance. But the goals of deterring misconduct are still sufficiently important to trigger an appropriate punishment, and a breach in trust, whether intentional or careless, remains in community members' memories. Although the community avoids draconian or debilitating punishments, it follows through with small punishments for even minor breaches, and these are certain to impact behavior.

The remarkable feature of these community enforcement mechanisms is not that they work perfectly. No enforcement system is perfect, and the Orthodox community experiences theft like all others. Instead, it is that they are intimately woven into the natural community fabric. Ethical business behavior is, simply, ethical behavior, and an honorable businessman is an honorable community member. There appears to be nothing inherently Jewish about these values, nor anything inherently religious, but Jewish law and the community's system of disbursing excludable religious goods has become enmeshed with the enforcement needs of the business world. Such a combination of institutional complementarities has created a remarkably effective system. While diamond dealers concede that there have been and will continue to be merchants who cheat, make mistakes, or somehow deviate from their contractual obligations, these occurrences are extremely infrequent given the quantity of transactions and the amount of credit in which merchants engage.[25]

This success, however, cannot explain—nor should it be construed to explain—the religious commitments of the ultra-Orthodox. To the contrary, the diamond industry found the ultra-Orthodox and not vice versa. Even as the ultra-Orthodox have instituted remarkably effective mechanisms for policing the community's diamond merchants, these rules and norms were not designed with the diamond industry in mind. Perhaps wealth from the diamond industry has enabled ultra-Orthodox communities to maintain many anachronistic features of their lifestyle, but the club good model is intended as a general theory of human behavior. It captures essential human qualities, such as a desire to be engaged with likeminded people and an appetite for recognition within an intimate community, that humans exhibit around the globe. Thus, while the club good model might accurately describe the preferences of ultra-Orthodox community members, and while those preferences might be critical in sustaining cooperation in the diamond industry, those preferences come from human origins and not economic expedience. In short, these preferences come first and the economic consequences follow—the old Latin maxim *De gustibus non est disputandum*[26] comes to mind—and Jewish predominance in the diamond industry ought to be understood as an incidental complementarity between a particular community's unusual mobilization of its members and the idiosyncratic demands of a particular industry.

Conclusions and Implications

To summarize, New York's diamond merchants can be divided into two groups. Long-term players enter the industry through family connections and cooperate because maintaining a good reputation ensures they will inherit a lucrative family business they can later bequeath to their descendants. Other diamond workers who do not have family legacies overwhelmingly come from the ultra-Orthodox community. They comply with their contractual obligations because failing to do so would prompt the denial of excludable community goods. This two-pronged system of family-based reputation mechanisms and community-based enforcement institutions allows New York's diamond merchants to organize reliable time-inconsistent exchange. It works because all players who are entrusted with another's diamonds belong to one of the two categories and thus are subject to one of the two punishment devices. The system embodies what Yoram Ben-Porath (1980) called "the F-connection," where trade networks organized around families and friends (that is, community members) can execute implicit contracts that enjoy efficiencies unavailable to formal, arm's-length transactions.

As Chapter 8 discusses, this system of cooperation has started breaking down in recent years. Structural changes to the diamond industry, introduced by geopolitics, technology, and natural market dynamics, have changed the economic calculus for diamond middlemen. The rewards of long-term cooperation for many merchants now are simply inadequate to overcome the temptation of short-term strategies. Importantly, the deterioration of trust only reinforces the explanations articulated in this chapter for how cooperation was sustained for generations. Although social, psychological, and cultural forces surely are at work as well, cooperation was sustained so long as its economic rewards exceeded the possibilities of defection. And when the economic calculus changed, so did the behavior of the industry's middlemen.

The recent deterioration of trust also reinforces what should be evident after reading this chapter: sustaining an industry-wide reputation mechanism demands a rigorous set of institutions. Reputation mechanisms do not arise easily and do not persist for long without institutional support. Scholars can too easily have a Panglossian view of reputation mechanisms, thinking that reputational sanctions will readily discipline misbehavior. This chapter illustrates that mobilizing reputational sanctions, particularly to support impersonal trade for a global industry, requires a reliable informational infrastructure, a robust menu of acute sanctions, and a deeply interconnected merchant community that is committed to long-term exchange.

Even if trust is no longer the prevailing norm in the industry, there is much to admire in how these merchants collectively invested in and implemented a system that for so long had sustained cooperative exchange. It might be additionally admirable because holding individuals to their promises, by rewarding good reputations while punishing those who have transgressed, contributes to popular notions of business honor and integrity. To be sure, diamond merchants for decades had been very proud of how their industry rewarded trust and integrity. But examining the social and industry institutions that undergird the trade reveals that much more than business integrity has been at work. The industry and, critically, the communities that engage in the trade have assembled forceful institutions that enable exchange. Merchants are able to credibly commit to credit purchases not (necessarily) because they have accumulated goodwill and an unblemished reputation, but because it is known that they will be punished if they break their promise, and that in the long run, they will be better off keeping their promises.

It might be said that the *New York Times,* in declaring that "trust" is "the real treasure of 47th Street," got it entirely wrong. The institutions that surround the diamond industry enable exchange, and those institutions are effective because they institute a reliable system of rewards and punishments. To the economist, this might sound like trust—hyphenated trust, or calculated trust—but to many, cooperation that relies on financial rewards and threatened punishments sounds like the *opposite* of trust. In fact, diamond dealers are quite untrusting. They strongly favor familiar business partners, investigate the backgrounds of potential new partners with fastidiousness and skepticism, and are very hesitant to outsiders. Contrary to the popular narrative, they exhibit a healthy reluctance to trust, one that appropriately recognizes the transactional dangers of the trade. But they ultimately do trust—or show confidence in—the institutions that support the trade, and for that reason have been able to sustain a remarkably vibrant market.

4

A Theory of Statelessness

CHAPTER 1 DETAILS THE RICH, diverse, and interdisciplinary literature on privately ordered transactions, or what I am calling stateless
commerce. The literature includes a wealth of case studies on how merchants,
spanning centuries and continents, have been able to enforce contracts and
secure exchange without the assistance of state-sponsored courts.

Yet despite its rich empirical success, the literature on self-enforced contracts and stateless exchange remains undertheorized. Even as researchers
from a diversity of perspectives have observed and documented how social
and institutional arrangements can support private cooperation and exchange,
there have been few efforts to develop a theory to address when and under
what circumstances a private ordering regime will emerge. Put another way,
the literature has done remarkably well in explaining *what* stateless commerce
is (including showing that it is quite pervasive), and it has made significant advances in explaining *how* stateless commerce works. It has not, however, made
much headway in explaining *why* it arises and persists. Why are mechanisms
that were relied on by eleventh-century Mediterranean traders still being
used in the twenty-first-century New York diamond center? Why do premodern modes of organization remain when much of the world has embraced, and relies on, modern state-sponsored instruments to support
commercial exchange? The field's wealth of empirics and lack of theoretical
foundation conjures the self-critical and commonly invoked image of two
legal scholars looking at a car's engine and asking, "But does it work in theory?"

Empirical Answers That Beg Theoretical Questions

Research on stateless commerce has been deemed a success in large part
because of the consistency of its findings. There is agreement that contracts

must be reliably enforced for a merchant community or region to achieve commercial success, and despite the diversity of methodologies and the exotic mix of subjects and locales, the accumulated research has identified similar mechanisms that sustain exchange in each of these communities: parties benefit from ongoing transactions with their colleagues; in each transaction, parties have an opportunity to cheat their counterparts; if a party cheats any other party, that party's misconduct becomes known throughout the community; and no one will transact with any individual known to have cheated in the past. Thus, a party's good reputation ensures the opportunity to benefit from future transactions, and, conversely, the prospect of future beneficial transactions induces cooperative behavior. In game-theoretic language, the assurance of ex post sanctions against cheaters induces trustworthy conduct and, reciprocally, allows transactors to commit credibly to fellow merchants that they will fulfill their contractual duties.

However, Chapter 1 also reveals that there is a significant and largely unappreciated divide within the separate studies. Many studies observe private ordering in environments where state-sponsored contract enforcement is unavailable. Merchant communities that fall into this first category include those in early commercial societies, which predated modern state institutions and reliable state courts (Clay 1997; Greif 1993; Milgrom, North, and Weingast 1990), modern-day communities in third-world societies where contract enforcement and independent judiciaries are not yet well developed (Fafchamps 1996b; McMillan and Woodruff 1999, 2002), and members of mafia or other criminal networks whose transactions involve illegal activity, which state courts deliberately refuse to enforce (Milhaupt and West 2000; Gambetta 1993). These commercial networks resort to self-enforcement because state contractual enforcement is not a reliable option, if it is even an option at all. This first category of communities reveals insights into the ancestors of commercial societies and the utility of modern courts, and most scholars characterize these enforcement mechanisms as prelaw orders that are supplanted when reliable public ordering emerges (Greif 2004b).

A second category of reputation-based enforcement mechanisms raises more difficult and underexplored questions. These instances of private ordering take place in a modern economy where reliable state-sponsored contract enforcement is available, and yet the merchant community deliberately chooses instead to rely on private ordering to enforce agreements (Bernstein 1992, 1996, 2001; McMillan and Woodruff 2000; Richman 2006). The persistence of what is essentially a premodern market structure in a modern economy challenges much of the conventional wisdom in economics. Institutional economics, for example, has taught that states with institutions that reliably enforce contracts and property rights exhibit superior economic performance over time (North 1990; North and Weingast 1989). Development economics routinely includes legal reform in its prescription for economic growth, particularly recommending strengthening contract enforcement through public sector reform (Sen 1999; World Bank 2004; Greif and Kandel 1995). Cross-national studies in political economy have also shown that nations with strong state enforcement of contract and property rights outperform those with weak or unpredictable enforcement (World Bank 2004; Levine, Loayza, and Beck 2000; Rodrik 2003). Legal scholars have also adopted the popular hypothesis concerning "underdeveloped" legal systems that relational contracting and private ordering would inevitably succumb to public courts (Salmond and Fitzgerald 1966; Cooter 1994).

The mere existence of this second category begs for a richer theory. If early systems of private ordering arose because of the absence of reliable courts, why do some systems of private ordering persist into modern societies? One answer is suggested by Lisa Bernstein's work (1992, 1996, 2001), which carefully articulates many efficiencies that private legal systems enjoy over public courts. As is discussed in Chapter 3, many of these efficiencies are due to the development of dispute resolution rules that are tailored to an industry's needs and to the use of industry experts as adjudicators. But administrative efficiencies would explain the use of private arbitrators that issue rulings, not private mechanisms that enforce those rulings. In fact, if administrative efficiencies were the driver of private legal systems, then we would expect them to be no more than systems of arbitration, in which the arbitrators' rules would be enforceable in public courts and the merchant community would not be burdened with the heavy duties and associated costs of self-enforcement. Similarly, if private legal systems offered overwhelming efficiencies, why do so few of today's merchants employ them? And if organizing commerce around private enforcement is more efficient, why does economic research overwhelmingly indicate that reliable public courts are central to facilitating economic growth? Correspondingly, why did most instances of private ordering dissolve with the emergence of public courts?

Given the diversity of systems used in the modern state to resolve disputes and enforce contracts, a question arises that is analogous to Ronald Coase's famous 1937 query in "The Nature of the Firm." Coase wondered why some economic transactions were organized inside a firm, whereas others were between firms. We similarly might ask, why are some transactions governed by public legal systems, whereas others are governed by private self-enforcement? Coase's answer to his own question was, "The limit to the size of the firm would be set when the scope of its operations had expanded to the point at which the costs of organizing additional transactions within the firm exceeded the costs of carrying out the same transactions through the market or in another firm." In other words, transactions that are more efficiently organized inside the firm than elsewhere will remain inside the firm. Although Coase's answer was clearly a tautology, for which he was playfully unapologetic,[1] it opened institutional economics to comparative assessments that began articulating when transactions were superiorly organized within firms versus markets. My analogous challenge is to devise a theory that can explain why some merchant communities choose to rely on stateless commerce even after encountering modernity and obtaining access to reliable public courts and other valuable state instruments, and why so many do not.

The interdisciplinary nature of the literature suggests that a meaningful theory able to explain these emerging tensions is also likely to invoke multiple disciplines. A helpful start is to return to the antecedents that gave rise to this recent scholarship and to look to basic principles of institutional and legal economics: When and for what purposes are certain systems of organization comparatively more efficient than others?

The Antecedents: Transaction Cost Economics, Legal Realism, and the Attributes of Organizational Alternatives

Scholarship on private legal systems might have exhibited a recent resurgence, but its beginnings lie squarely in institutional economics and legal realism. These two bodies of scholarship set the stage for understanding the literature's origins, and their interaction paves the way toward developing a

theory of stateless commerce. They therefore provide foundations and in-
spire points of departure for a new theory.

Transaction Cost Economics

Several economists have previously recognized that private mechanisms
arise to enforce contracts where public instruments are ineffective. In modeling how a repeat purchase context creates a market-based contract enforcement mechanism, Benjamin Klein and Keith Leffler (1981, 615–616)
challenged the "implicit assumption . . . of the legal-philosophical tradition
upon which the economic model is built [that] without some third-party en-
forcer to sanction stealing and reneging, market exchange would be impossible." (See also Telser [1980].) Oliver Williamson (1996b, 122–123) put the
relationship directly, writing that "the incentives of private parties to devise
bilateral contractual safeguards [are] a function of the efficacy of court adjudication." The notion that transactors can successfully operate outside the
law—and frequently choose to operate outside the law when the legal system
is unhelpful or costly—is not new.

Economists were naturally drawn to use market forces to explain extrajudicial enforcement, and one category of models described how consumers
can attribute reputations to sellers and thereby extrajudicially compel sellers
to comply with their assurances for high quality (Klein and Leffler 1981;
Kreps and Wilson 1982; Milgrom and Roberts 1982; C. Shapiro 1983). Other
approaches, however, describe self-enforced agreements in the bilateral
context, in which parties create a contractual relationship that they, by design, choose to enforce extrajudicially. One model offered two contracting
parties that elect to provide each other with the capacity to impose severe
ex post sanctions should either one breach (Williamson 1983). Labeled a
"hostage exchange," this model resembles a simplistic portrayal of self-
enforced contracts, in which one party's capacity to inflict harm on the other
party in the event of a breach, and vice versa, allows both parties ex ante to
commit credibly to fulfill their obligations.

Another self-enforcement approach, perhaps a mix of the stark bilateral
"hostage" model and the unilateral consumer-driven reputation models, is
so-called "administered contracts" (Williamson 1976; Goldberg 1976; Klein
1980). These are situations, such as public utility investments or franchisor-
franchisee relationships, in which one contracting party needs to make

significant up-front investments, yet because certain promised conduct is hard to either monitor or verify, or because both parties know that circumstances will inevitably change and force coordinated adaptations, the other transacting partner cannot credibly commit to a specific arrangement. The result is a "hold up" problem that, without reliable assurance, will cause parties to avoid the transaction altogether, and common solutions involve complex arrangements that include cross-ownership and heavily administered procedures to govern disputes and necessary changes. The common feature of these "administered solutions" is that contracting parties develop an intimate framework that enables self-enforced resolutions rather than court-driven solutions.

It was from within this perspective that Williamson, building on Coase's 1937 query, proposed that vertical integration is yet another solution to persistent contractual problems. When parties to a transaction are cooperating within a single economic entity, hold-up problems, monitoring difficulties, and challenges in coordinated adjustment are solved administratively by intervention from a single proprietor. The firm, in short, is a self-enforcement mechanism and a form of extralegal adjustment to contract failures.

This is the literature that, in large part, paved the way for Williamson's transaction cost economics (TCE). Although the paradigmatic issue in transaction cost economics is Coase's "make-or-buy" question (alternatively coined "the question of vertical integration"), which asks whether a particular transaction will occur inside or outside the boundaries of a firm, TCE is a broader theory to explain the choice of instrument—whether a spot market, complex contract, hostage exchange, administered contract, or vertical ownership—to govern a particular transaction. The inquiry begins by articulating the structural attributes of firms, markets, and other alternative forms of economic organization, in which each enjoys strengths and drawbacks. TCE-motivated hypotheses posit that certain transactions are more efficiently organized within one structure rather than alternatives. An automobile manufacturing firm, for example, might decide to manufacture the car's fuel tank yet would purchase the gas cap from a supplier.[2] The underlying idea is that no organizational arrangement is ideal, and any arrangement that is superior for one transaction might be inferior for others. Parties choose between distinct organizational alternatives based on the inherent efficiency tradeoffs. (See generally, Williamson [1975, 1996b]; for a survey of empirical studies relying on transaction cost economics, see Shelanski and Klein [1995], Macher and Richman [2008].)

Precisely because it articulates the economic strengths and drawbacks of alternative modes of economic organization, TCE offers a useful beginning to understand how merchants will organize their transactions. According to transaction cost theory, firms enjoy strong administrative controls that can assure the security of exchange and therefore can arise to resolve transactional difficulties. For this reason, the firm is an effective self-enforcement solution to a contracting failure. But firms also insulate parties from the economic benefits of transacting in market environments. Specifically, markets exhibit what Friedrich Hayek described as "spontaneous governance," where incentives are in place "to provide inducements which will make the individuals do the desirable things without anyone having to tell them what to do" (1945, 527).[3] This intensity of incentives and the ability to adapt in market environments supplies an important efficiency to market-based organizations that provides a comparative advantage over hierarchical forms, such as the firm. Thus, agents acting inside a firm are less sensitive to market incentives and less responsive to market information, such as changes in price or demand, than are autonomous market actors.[4] Consequently, internalizing a transaction inside a firm involves trading high-powered incentives and the capacity for spontaneous adjustment for transactional assurance. Transactions where agreements are particularly difficult to secure are more likely to occur inside firms, but transactions that do not present enforcement difficulties are more efficiently organized in markets where information is freely disseminated and high-powered incentives are not diluted.

The key lesson from transaction cost theory, as it applies to understanding when private ordering systems emerge, is that firm-based organizations are also a solution to unreliable contract enforcement, and thus any discussion regarding transactional security and any evaluation of alternative economic organizations must consider the firm as a feasible alternative. A related lesson is that in considering the firm as an alternative to contracts, transaction cost theory reveals the economic tradeoffs between contract-based exchange and firms: even though firm-based exchange can offer more transactional security, contracting systems operate with autonomous economic agents and thus benefit from greater incentive intensity and spontaneous adaptation. Although firms are useful self-enforcement mechanisms, they introduce certain inefficiencies that merchants prefer to avoid.

Public versus Private Ordering

Although legal scholarship has been a broad participant of late in interdisciplinary examinations of stateless commerce, its origins in this area are quite distinct. Emerging from the "law and society" movement that aimed to understand, generally, how the law both reflected and structured human relations, the first legal scholars interested in extralegal enforcement were contract scholars who pushed beyond legal formalities to understand how contracts were actually enforced. As Chapter 1 describes, Stewart Macaulay (1963) launched this inquiry when he famously observed that much contract enforcement occurs outside courtrooms—instead of, in anticipation of, and to avoid formal legal action. And Macaulay's colleague at Wisconsin Law School, Marc Galanter, similarly criticized what he called "legal centralism," when he urged attention to the "shadow of the law" (Galanter 1981). These law and society pioneers encouraged contract scholarship to focus on how parties settled disputes, or self-enforced their agreements, with the law as a backdrop rather than a featured player.

A related legal literature explored "relational contracts"—contracts that are embedded within a relationship or social network that surrounds the commercial transaction—and whether formal contract law should adjust to different economic and social contexts. Ian Macneil (1974), heralded as the pioneer who identified the important distinction between discrete and relational transactions, argued that prevalence of "relational patterns" in modern economic society "justifies examination of the many futures of contracts in relations and their contrast with the singular future of contract in discrete transactions" (695–696). He later (Macneil 1978) argued that discrete and relational contracts have contrasting legal needs, and neoclassical law appropriately recognized those differences and afforded each the distinct treatment it needed. Charles Goetz and Robert Scott (1981), in a valuable refinement, argued that relational contracts arise as a response to predictable problems from uncertainty and complexity that arm's-length contracts—and courts—cannot efficiently anticipate or resolve. Their work echoed what

Yoram Ben-Porath (1980) called the "F-connection," wherein family and friendship relations serve useful economic functions in governing long-term or necessarily incomplete contracts. In focusing on the social context that surrounds many commercial transactions and the role that social relations can play in creating commercial value, these scholars recognized that formal law and state-sponsored courts are often alternatives, and sometimes complements, to private mechanisms that sustain valuable commerce.

These works paved the way for the scholarship in the 1990s that introduced the colorful case studies discussed in Chapter 1. One can see how this literature relied on its predecessors' observations that a great deal of commercial activity takes place both within the "shadow" of formal legal enforcement and also within the "relational" context in which commerce takes place. But the research focusing on case studies of merchant organizations also brought the lens of shadow bargaining and relational contracting to communities, not dyads, and to systems of commerce, not just bilateral individual transactions. Since most of the economics literature also focused on bilateral exchange rather than multilateral organizations, evaluating private legal regimes requires a tool kit different from the analytical lens used to evaluate individual transactions.

The primary scholarly objective in examining the private ordering case studies was to contrast these private systems with public alternatives through state-sponsored courts. In this sense, these studies suffered from a variation of Galanter's "legal centrism": they compared only contract-based mechanisms to secure exchange and ignored vertical integration as an alternative. Accordingly, their analyses were limited to explaining why private enforcement was preferred to state enforcement, and they did not provide a comprehensive theory.[5] Nonetheless, the literature has collectively generated a substantial list of features of private law that can inform a comparative institutional analysis.

Specialization, Expertise, and Administrative Efficiency. Private legal systems have been heralded for generating administrative efficiencies by designing specialized arbitration processes. Disputing parties are obligated to resolve their disputes before industry arbitrators who possess industry expertise and specialized knowledge regarding industry transactions, and arbitration procedures are designed to act swiftly and at lower costs than overloaded and procedure-laden public courts. Industry rules can also anticipate likely sources of disputes and require fellow merchants to adhere to prescribed business practices—using form contracts, for example —that both facilitate easy adjudication and reduce the costs of executing transactions. These three advantages of private law—specialized judges, specialized procedures, and specialized substantive law—lead to faster, more accurate, and more predictable legal outcomes.

Extralegal Enforcement. Contract law is only as good as the degree to which litigants comply with its rulings. Public courts provide forceful tools to implement their judgments, including the ability to seize a losing party's assets or to impose alternative sanctions such as jail and other equitable measures. But even these coercive measures are helpless to secure certain kinds of agreements. The basic inadequacy of public courts for these particular agreements reveals a critical additional advantage that some private systems enjoy.

Public courts are especially ineffective at enforcing certain categories of transactions. The archetypal category, embodied in credit purchases for diamonds, is the sale of goods in which one party can easily escape any state court sanction. Other categories include transactions in which courts suffer from informational deficiencies or encounter monitoring difficulties (for example, Libecap 1989), certain time-sensitive agreements (for example, Joskow 1987; Richman 2004),[6] and transactions requiring substantial upfront investments and complicated performance demands (for example, Klein, Crawford, and Alchian 1978).

Private legal systems, resting on reputation mechanisms, can secure transactions that are beyond the reach of public courts, and their successes illustrate how private ordering employs enforcement tools unavailable to public courts. First, public courts are largely constrained by substantive contract law to impose remedial awards only equal to the damage done by the breaching party, which frequently are inadequate to credibly induce compliance. When a merchant's success is predicated on a good reputation, however, the entirety of future dealings is at stake.

More significant, reputation mechanisms have the capacity to employ nonpecuniary incentives to compel merchants to adhere to their contractual obligations. Chapter 3, using a "club good" model (Iannaccone 1992), describes how the diamond industry induces cooperation by awarding or withholding community benefits to the ultra-Orthodox merchants who crave them.[7] Bernstein (1996) similarly reports that cotton mill operators and cotton brokers secure transactions, in part, because those merchants enjoy membership to intimate communities that organize social events, wives clubs, debutante balls, and other institutionalized occasions for recognition and participation. Galanter (1981) observed that such private sanctions are most feasible in intimate communities, where community leaders hold leverage over members that state courts do not hold over citizens, noting that "community standing, seniority, reputation for integrity or formidability may confer capability in the indigenous setting that does not translate into capability in the official setting" (24). This is precisely why there is a tendency to see ethnically homogeneous merchants associated with trading networks governed by private law (Landa 1981). Ethnic groups can mobilize social and community networks, in addition to the merchants themselves, to affect sectors of a merchant's life that public courts cannot reach.

In short, private ordering mechanisms induce cooperation by exacting coordinated punishments. Many rely on community organizations to supply rewards and punishments, and therefore can implement incentives to cooperate that are more powerful and effective than traditional state sanctions. These extralegal mechanisms can provide transactional security beyond what state courts can offer, and thus can fulfill economic functions that actors in more heterogeneous and less intimate communities cannot.

Entry Barriers and Exclusivity. A significant shortcoming to private ordering, however, is that it can only reach those who subscribe to it—reputation mechanisms can only police those who place value in maintaining a good reputation. Galanter (1981) remarked that although "indigenous communities" enjoy powers that are unavailable to public courts, "the indigenous tribunal faces the problem of obtaining leverage over those who are impervious to community opinion, getting them to submit to its jurisdiction or to comply with its decisions" (26). Thus, the reach of private law is limited to long-term players who are assured of, and who credibly are committed to pursuing, a long horizon of transactions.

This leads to a critical limitation to private ordering: reputation-based private enforcement erects sizable entry barriers. Because only participating long-term players have incentives to cooperate, newcomers who have not yet established a good reputation are unable to commit credibly to uphold their contractual promises. McMillan and Woodruff (2000) accordingly noted, "The corollary of ongoing relationships is a reluctance to deal with firms outside the relationship" (2454). Even an honest merchant who has yet to demonstrate a good reputation will not be able to transact with other merchants.

Entry barriers impose many well-known inefficiencies, especially dynamic inefficiencies, to an economic system. They limit the threat of superior competitors—those with lower costs, superior skill, or new technologies—and shelter inefficient incumbents. For example, some observers of the international diamond industry have lamented the impact of entry barriers on the trade, noting that diamond firms have felt the need to employ trustworthy nephews and neighbors rather than recruit at the top business schools (Richman 2009a). The exclusivity demanded of privately ordered reputation mechanisms also sustains economic homogeneity and conformity, precluding entrants with innovative business models and insulating ossified merchant leaders from new sources of competition. Moreover, a closed community composed of traders who are linked by intimate relations and common channels of information is prone to collude on price or mobilize collective boycotts that target entrants or other competitive threats.[8] These inefficiencies are discussed in greater detail in Chapter 5, and Chapter 8 illustrates how the accumulated costs of some inefficiencies are forcing structural changes to several segments of the global trade.

In sum, systems of private ordering enjoy an assortment of administrative efficiencies over the public courts, including savings in arriving at and implementing accurate adjudications. Private ordering can also secure some contracts that public courts cannot, thus adding transactional credibility. Yet reputation-based private ordering also exhibits some significant inefficiencies. Its reliance on familiarity restricts entry to outsiders, thus limiting innovation and inviting collusive conduct. These significant dynamic costs are tradeoffs with the also significant benefits of greater transactional security and low-cost adjudication.

A Synthesis: Firms, Courts, and Reputation Mechanisms

I aim to synthesize these two parallel literatures into a new model, one that is a composite of well-established theories in economics and law yet also leads to a theoretical advance of its own. The aim is to develop a theory that explains the persistence of relational exchange, such as in the diamond industry, in certain pockets of the modern economy.

First, incorporating transaction cost theory into the legal literature on private contract enforcement introduces the vertically integrated firm as an alternative self-enforcement mechanism. When a public court fails to secure exchange, a theory of statelessness must explain why a merchant community would create a private ordering system rather than resorting to vertically integrated firms.

And second, studying private legal systems introduces community-wide systems of adjudication and enforcement. These systems are multilateral in nature, and they depart from the standard bilateral paradigm in transaction cost economics and contract theory. They therefore require a distinctly different application of the transaction cost model that considers entry barriers, or exclusivity, as an attribute exhibited by multilateral reputation mechanisms. The multilateral setting is longitudinal and dynamic, and the existence of entry barriers can be very costly.

The importance of entry barriers in the multilateral context, and their absence in the bilateral context, requires a revision to the unidimensional transaction cost market-firm spectrum. In the unidimensional model, there is a single tradeoff between market incentives and transactional security—markets provide the first, hierarchies provide the second—and bilateral private ordering negotiates a certain balance between the two considerations. Incorporating the additional variable of entry barriers into the multilateral setting introduces an entirely new tradeoff between entry availability and transactional security—public courts provide the first and private ordering provides the second. Adding a second tradeoff to the transaction cost paradigm requires altering the predictive template in a substantial way. Private ordering does not merely occupy an intermediate location between markets and firms but is instead *a distinct system of economic organization* that requires independent comparisons with markets and firms. The analysis therefore requires use of three variables—market incentives, transactional security, and entry barriers—to evaluate three separate governance mechanisms—firms, markets, and private ordering. Depending on the needs of the underlying transaction, the model's analysis can then predict which one mechanism will excel above the others.

Put simply, moving from the bilateral to the multilateral context requires the introduction of an additional institutional attribute, nonexclusivity, that in turn requires consideration of a second tradeoff, entry versus transactional security. Incorporating the second tradeoff into the transaction cost model therefore requires revising the unidimensional model into the three-by-three chart depicted in Table 4.1. The result is a more nuanced and more complicated model that must account for more variables. But it also represents an extension of transaction cost theory into new territory, even while the model retains transaction cost theory's parsimonious methodology and fundamental principles.

Table 4.1 formulates a positive theory of private ordering and contains refutable hypotheses with which to test that theory. The model predicts that private ordering is comparatively superior to both firms and public courts for industries that confront difficult-to-enforce transactions, are particularly sensitive to high-powered incentives, and do not prohibitively suffer when entry is limited.

Preliminary Evidence

The theory proposed here, building off the literatures in transaction cost economics and private legal systems, is that stateless commerce emerges and

Table 4.1 Institutional alternatives and associated attributes

	Public courts, arm's-length exchange	Private ordering, reputation mechanisms	Vertically integrated firm
Transactional security; low-cost enforcement	−	+	+
Nonexclusivity	+	−	+
High-powered incentives	+	+	−

persists when courts cannot adequately secure transactions but when the efficiencies of market organization (or the inefficiencies of vertical integration) overcome the costs of exclusivity. This section briefly examines some instances of stateless commerce, including the diamond industry, to illustrate how the theory plays out.

Intimate Brokerages: Diamonds and Cotton

As is described in detail in previous chapters, the enigmatic diamond industry has systematically rejected public courts and instead privately polices its merchants through reputation mechanisms and nonlegal sanctions. Consistent with the model, the industry's arrival at private ordering is explained by the difficulty of enforcing diamond credit sales, the particular importance of high-powered market incentives, and the relatively low costs of entry barriers.

First, as discussed in Chapter 3, the diamond sale is an extreme instance of a hazardous transaction. Courts cannot reliably impose sanctions to adequately compensate a jilted diamond seller or to sufficiently deter a thief.

Second, the diamond industry creates enormous value from a market-structured distribution chain. Adding value in diamond sales is a process that is largely dependent on collecting market information, exposure to market pressures, and the capacity for spontaneous adaptation. The broad assortment of possible cuts, polishing techniques, jewelry settings, and subjective judgments means that finding an optimal buyer for a specific stone is a very profitable enterprise. This matching process—the search for the "right" buyer—is very sensitive to effort and speed, as sellers and brokers must gather market information regarding buyer demand and quickly pair their idiosyncratic needs with the distinct qualities of available stones. The trading floor of the Diamond Dealers Club reveals this effort and speed in a sea of high-powered incentives, with brokers determining what's available for sale and communicating with prospective buyers. Fervor, intensity, and zeal characterize the DDC's swirl of trading activity.

These industry characteristics—hard-to-enforce transactions and value creation from market incentives—make the diamond industry a paradigmatic illustration of the efficiencies of stateless commerce. The flip side to this organization, of course, is the costs of exclusivity. But there are reasons to believe that the diamond industry's very significant entry barriers, where participation is limited to family members of current merchants and to members of ethnically homogeneous communities, do not impose crippling costs. Since technological innovation has played a relatively small role in the industry's history (diamond cutting employs essentially the same processes—the manual application of a stone to a grinding wheel—that sixteenth-century cutters used), there is limited value that the innovator, maverick, or outsider can bring.[9] Additionally, the numbers of merchants in various diamond centers approach levels where collusion or coordination would be difficult, and to the degree that entry has occurred, it has been by ethnic groups who have been able to mimic or adopt the private ordering mechanisms employed by Jewish merchants. The continued predominance, over several centuries, of Jewish and ethnic networks suggests that the survival of those networks is a function of their superiority over, not their insulation from, market challengers.

This model can be applied to other industries as well. America's cotton industry, for example, features many of the same characteristics as the diamond industry. Cotton merchants belong to trade associations that, like the diamond bourses, disseminate arbitration rules with industry arbitrators, and like the diamond industry's arbitration system, the arbitration rulings merely provide a framework for a reputation mechanism. Arbitration panels determine and publicize the identities of parties who breach their agreements, and wrongdoers are rejected as members of the merchant associations, precluded from future industry business, and subjected to nonlegal sanctions. Although the social sanctions assume different flavors—Jewish diamond dealers deny wrongdoers religious privileges, whereas cotton brokers exclude wrongdoers from Memphis's Old South community—the targeted deterrence is the same.

The theory applies in likewise fashion to the cotton industry. Like diamond transactions, sales of cotton are difficult to enforce and rely on high-powered incentives. Cotton mills operate best when they are in continuous operation, and so mill operators rely on a steady influx of cotton. However, since cotton is costly to store, mill operators supervise a just-in-time system of supply contracts where new quantities of cotton are scheduled to arrive just as the previous shipment is depleted. In addition, cotton mills, depending on their customer orders, require particular grades and qualities of cotton that are difficult to predict in advance. While previewing samples may be helpful, buyers are generally required to rely on the characterizations they receive from merchants. A late shipment or a shipment of the wrong quantity, grade, or quality can be costly to the mill operator, making precise contractual compliance extremely important.

Also, like middlemen in the diamond network, a cotton broker's effectiveness is very sensitive to effort. The supply chain for cotton mills involves a matching process, much like searching for the optimal diamond buyer, where brokers search for specific kinds of cotton to meet a mill's particularized needs. Brokers need to gather market information to discover buyers' needs and determine which sources can meet those needs. For these reasons, the cotton industry maintains a market organization and avoids the substantial bureaucratic costs of vertical integration.

In sum, the diamond and cotton industries fit the theory's prediction with their need for extralegal contractual enforcement and their significant benefits from high-powered market incentives. They both also suffer limited harm from entry barriers chiefly because brokers dominate both distribution chains; the costs of limiting entry are small so long as the number of brokers is sufficiently large to make collusion difficult. In fact, the distinguishing commonality of both industries' distribution chains is that they are essentially brokerages that match buyers with sellers. Other trade associations that function as brokerages, including the New York Stock Exchange, exhibit self-governance traits and might fit the theory's prediction as well. Brokerages, exchange houses, bourses, and other mechanisms that prospective buyers and sellers use to find each other exhibit many of the same economic traits as stateless commerce, and it is no surprise that stateless features frequently appear in each.

Global Middlemen: California's Mexican Merchants, Eleventh-Century Maghribi Traders, and Malaysia's Chinese Networks

The matching, or brokerage, system that is prominent in the diamond and cotton industries appears throughout case studies of stateless industries. Karen Clay's (1997) examination of California's Mexican merchants living in the 1830s and 1840s uncovers a system in which Mexican middlemen structured a nexus of trade in a remote frontier for distant merchants. Using a reputation mechanism to police their colleagues, the Mexican intermediaries brokered purchases and sales for ships that brought goods from Boston,

Mexico, the Hawaiian Islands, and South America. Similarly, Avner Greif's (1989, 1993) seminal work on the eleventh-century Maghribi traders reports a system of intermediaries in which the Maghribis used their cross-Mediterranean connections with each other to broker sales of goods to distant markets. And Janet Landa's (1981) exploration of the commercial networks in Southeast Asia describes ethnic communities of intermediaries who facilitate transactions for distant merchants. These traders rely on reputation mechanisms and community sanctions to ensure that their members resist the significant temptation to steal the goods they are brokering.

The theory developed here can explain not just the predominance of brokerage systems in modern trade associations but also the more general phenomenon of self-policing among commercial middlemen. Middlemen operating distribution networks, including those in stateless commerce case studies, create value by gathering market information so as to match optimally available goods with buyers' demands. Their value creation is driven by the efficient dissemination and collection of information, a process best organized within a market structure with Hayekian qualities. In addition, the duties of an intermediary typically include taking possession of valuable goods that he or she does not own. And even though their systems of private enforcement erect barriers to others who would otherwise serve as brokers, their merchant community suffers few costs from restricting entry so long as a critical mass of merchants remains. The model suggests that these are the merchant communities that are among the most likely to create self-enforcement mechanisms and sustain stateless commerce.

The similarities among these different merchant networks lend additional support to Landa's (1981) broad "ethnically homogeneous middleman group" theory, which describes how ethnic groups can operate distribution networks at lower transaction costs than less homogeneous groups. One important element that is surprisingly missing from Landa's theory, however, is an explanation for why these ethnic networks assume the roles of middlemen—brokers who create value through a process of matching a buyer with a seller—rather than other roles in the economy. The model described here offers an explanation. The matching process in brokerage systems presents severe transactional hazards, but it relies on the incentive intensities and information availability that typify market organization. Consequently, an ethnic group's capacity to self-enforce contracts is put to optimal use when group members act as intermediaries. In short, ethnic networks excel at providing brokerage systems for the same reason that the diamond and cotton industries have turned to private ordering.

Social Norms and Professional Norms

In *Order Without Law*, Robert Ellickson (1991) articulated a "hypothesis of welfare-maximizing norms," which argued that "members of a tight-knit group develop and maintain norms whose content serves to maximize the aggregate welfare that members obtain in their workaday affairs with one another" (167). Ellickson argued that these norms maintain a system of social control similar to how contracts enable a promisee to induce certain behavior from a promisor, and the substantive norms that emerge bring mutual gain to all community members. Why, then, did the residents of Shasta County employ social norms and self-policing (or, in Ellickson's vocabulary, self-help) to maximize their social welfare rather than entering into a multilateral contract, enforceable by the public courts? The immediate answer is that the coordination, negotiation, and administrative costs necessary to form such a contract would be prohibitive compared to the individual gains from the maximizing norms. This explanation evaporates, though, if a social norm is viewed as the product of an implicit multilateral contract—after all, a norm is effective only if it is supported by a collective commitment. Viewing Shasta County norms through what Williamson calls "the lens of contract" (2002) reveals how the implications from this theory might apply to a larger set of social and professional norms.

A wealth-maximizing norm can be characterized as a tacit agreement to engage in mutually beneficial wealth-maximizing behavior—an implicit quid pro quo. The difference between wealth-maximizing norms and wealth-maximizing contracts lies not in the substance of the underlying agreements (since both outline the contours of maximizing behavior) but instead in how the agreements are enforced—contracts are traditionally enforced by courts, whereas norms are policed, if at all, by social sanctions. Accordingly, a tight-knit community's enforcement of its norms parallels a merchant community's development of a private legal system with privately enforced sanctions.

The next question is, why does Shasta County use self-enforced norms to sanction behavior, rather than public courts or vertical integration? Although the question seems absurd on its face, the answer reveals some of the organizational efficiencies of social norms. Gossip and neighborly consternation are less costly than lawyers and courts, and ownership of land by individual families is more efficient than integration that puts the county's land under a single owner. In short, private ordering reflects the market efficiencies of land ownership and avoids the enforcement inefficiencies of courts. Viewing social norms through "the lens of contract" reveals both that social norms amount to agreements among community members to engage in mutually beneficial reciprocal behavior and that this cooperation is most efficiently organized through private ordering.

The same could be said of professional communities that disseminate wealth-enhancing norms. Some observers of high-technology growth (Saxenian 1994; Hyde 2003) have remarked that Silicon Valley engineers developed mutually beneficial norms, including sharing information and cooperating with competitors, even though research-intensive firms are normally inclined to resist openness in order to protect their intellectual property. Firms that punished employees for sharing firm information with outsiders, protected intellectual property rights through aggressive litigation, or restricted employees' ability to pursue outside opportunities were sanctioned by professional engineers, who refused to work for firms that were not committed to collaborative norms. Even the employees of uncollaborative firms were sanctioned by being excluded from professional and social networks.

Champions of these professional norms argue that the engineers' collaborative norms contributed both to their collective wealth and to Silicon Valley's economic growth.[10] The commitment to openness generated positive spillovers from innovation, a more efficient labor market, and a reduced time-to-market period for new technologies. In contrast, Massachusetts's technology corridor along Route 128, the valley's chief competitor, was home to a professional culture that was more supportive of closed firms and resistant of collaboration, and some argue that Route 128's lack of openness made it unable to match Silicon Valley's growth. Other enthusiasts of collaborative norms have cited software programmers who created an open software movement without demanding compensation (those who do demand compensation suffer social sanctions from fellow programmers) and consequently developed socially beneficial products, including Linux (Benkler 2003). Professional norms, these scholars argue, arise when there are benefits from collaborative behavior among competing professionals, yet contracting for such collaboration is too costly either to draft or to enforce.

Critically, many of these scholars do not recognize the potential downside of privately enforced collaborative norms. The American Medical Association famously invoked professional norms—in the form of a code of ethics—that prohibited its member doctors from doing business for low-cost HMOs. Although those norms unquestionably brought financial benefit to the doctors by fighting off cost restraints and maintaining fee-for-service medicine, they harmed those who had to pay for rising health care costs. Lawyers similarly have used canons of ethics to prohibit low-cost lawyering and aggressive advertising. Many of these restraints might have protected unsuspecting clients from misleading promises and economic harm, but many others promoted conduct—including naked price fixing—that unquestionably harmed consumers. America's rabbis also promulgate professional ethics that inflate rabbinic wages and prevent the congregations employing them from exercising free choice.

These are among the harms that the model attributes to merchant communities that police themselves. The danger of nonexclusivity and the power to exclude competitors enables the promulgation of privately beneficial but socially costly conduct. Often characterized as "professional ethics" or "industry standards," norms that can exclude competitors often target innovators or economic mavericks who seek aggressive competition. Such norms can enable productive collaboration, as they did in Silicon Valley, but they also can enable cartels to create rents, stifle competition, and resist valuable change. Understanding professional norms as reciprocal behavior, akin to stateless commerce, reveals both the efficiencies and the costs of privately enforced reputation mechanisms. Chapter 5 expands on these costs of statelessness and discusses how self-enforced norms can foster socially harmful cooperation. From the positive perspective taken in this chapter, these costs are a counterforce to the attractiveness of statelessness and are one meaningful reason why it is not more widespread in the modern economy. From a normative perspective, pursued in Chapter 5, the law—and antitrust law in particular—should develop mechanisms to distinguish between desirable and undesirable forms of cooperation.

Conclusion: A Theory of Stateless Commerce

This chapter has three objectives. First, following Chapter 3's illustration of *how* the diamond industry sustains a system of stateless commerce, this chapter aims to explain *why* the industry does so into the modern era. Relying on prior scholarship in transaction cost economics and the economics of private legal systems, it synthesizes a theory that explains why a privately enforced reputation mechanism is more efficient for the diamond network than either vertical integration or state courts. The second objective is to illustrate that this generalizable theory also applies to other settings. It can explain the persistence of ethnic commercial networks as middlemen in different industries, why middlemen in open exchanges so regularly organize themselves around private ordering and reputational sanctions, and why social norms rather than formal instruments are utilized for disparate cooperative arrangements. Perhaps most important, it highlights why a unique set of circumstances make self-enforced reputational sanctions a more preferable governance mechanism to modern alternatives, and why only some industries, in contrast to most, reject public courts even after the emergence of a modern legal system.

The third objective is to join parallel literatures and bring some coherence to a literature with a diverse collection of empirical studies. This discussion intends to add vertical integration to a legal literature that previously focused on administering and enforcing contracts, and it applies transaction cost theory to multilateral systems of exchange that traditionally have been of interest to legal scholars. The synthesis illustrates how this field continues to benefit from interdisciplinary analysis and the cross-fertilization of theories. Moreover, understanding the circumstances under which merchants in the diamond industry and elsewhere reject state courts can reveal some insights into the shortcomings of today's public institutions. Perhaps understanding those shortcomings can plant the seeds for a constructive agenda for institutional reform.

The theory offered here is perhaps in tension with enthusiasts of private ordering systems that trumpet the efficiencies and freedoms of constructing private legal systems. That enthusiasm tends to overlook the significant drawbacks of private systems. My theory recognizes that public courts impose substantial administrative costs, and that transacting parties regularly construct alternative mechanisms to avoid those costs when possible. But it also observes that there are unappreciated costs—the costs of exclusivity—that accompany the use of networks of reputation-based commerce. My theory is also in tension with development economists who argue that creating public courts and breaking up relational exchange are necessary ingredients to economic development (see Chapter 6). Although I agree that impersonal exchange is necessary to introduce valuable innovations and avoid cartel behavior, I also recognize that relational networks can facilitate commerce in circumstances where public courts cannot. Such a middle-ground theory might not produce exciting policy prescriptions, but it highlights the importance of understanding the inherent trade-offs in comparing alternative organizational arrangements. In evaluating the efficiency of any economic system, one must ask, "efficient compared to what?"

Still, I should emphasize that I offer here *a* theory of stateless commerce, not *the* theory. The objective is to offer another tool in one's toolkit to understand the world's varied economic institutions, not to replace one's current tools. As one sage interdisciplinarian wrote, a theory of the firm "is going to be pretty empty if it is to explain all firms," just as "a theory of the state that applies equally to the United States, Luxemburg, and Belize will either be so unwieldy as to be unworkable or so superficial as to be uninformative" (Goldberg 2013, 85). All the more so for a theory that aims to explain when firms, markets, and state institutions supplant each other.

5

The Costs of Statelessness

Cartel Behavior and Resistance to Change

IN 1942, TWO YEARS after the German invasion of Belgium devastated Antwerp's diamond industry, and following the Nazis' deportment of many Jewish diamontaires to concentration camps, the New York Diamond Dealers Club (DDC) passed a resolution that prohibited admission to all individuals associated with Nazi organizations and business interests. In 1949, when more than 80 percent of DDC members either had family members perish in the Holocaust or were refugees themselves, the DDC passed a more sweeping resolution: "The Board of Directors condemns the action of any member, who manufactures either directly in Germany or who deals in German goods. The names of said members, who are found guilty of manufacturing or dealing in or with Germany or German goods will be posted on the bulletin board and displayed in a conspicuous place in the Clubrooms."[1]

On June 23, 1952, in response to this resolution and its implementation, the Department of Justice's Antitrust Division filed a complaint against the DDC for "engag[ing] in an unlawful combination and conspiracy to restrict and prevent the importation of diamonds from and the exportation of diamonds to Germany" (*United States v. Diamond Dealers Club*, No. 76-343 (S.D.N.Y. June 23, 1952) Complaint, ¶ 11). This was the DDC's first encounter with the U.S. antitrust laws, and the Club found itself in the Sherman Act's crosshairs several additional times in the decades that followed. This is because the Sherman Act scrutinizes cooperation among competitors, and the DDC relies on cooperation among competitors to sustain its agreements.

The Sherman Act

The Sherman Act, 15 U.S.C. §§1–7, is intended to protect free enterprise and promote efficient markets. Its primary components are its first two sections. Section 1, prohibiting certain contracts, combinations, or conspiracies "in restraint of trade," targets price-fixing cartels and other illegal coordinated conduct. Section 2, aimed at "every person who shall monopolize, or attempt to monopolize, or combine or conspire with any other person or persons, to monopolize," targets exploitive unilateral conduct.

The diamond industry has a history littered with both Section 1 and Section 2 prosecutions. The lead character in the industry's trials under Section 2 is De Beers, whose strategy from the company's founding in the late nineteenth century was to secure a monopoly over the world's supply of rough diamonds. As is detailed in Chapter 2, De Beers would move quickly after a new source of diamonds was found in Africa, either to acquire the mine or to secure an exclusive purchasing agreement with its owners (and De Beers often relied on coercive and unseemly measures to secure these deals). Consequently, through its Central Selling Organization, the De Beers "syndicate" became, and remained for nearly a century, the monopolist that sits atop the global distribution chain.

De Beers' monopolistic success earned it frequent scrutiny from American antitrust regulators. The Justice Department sued De Beers under the antitrust laws in 1945, 1957, and 1974, ultimately convincing De Beers that it should stay out of the United States altogether (thereafter, De Beers sold diamonds only in London, with sightholders and other middlemen bringing stones to the U.S. market). The Justice Department brought another suit in 1994, this time accusing De Beers of conspiring with General Electric to fix the prices of industrial diamonds. And a series of private class actions began in 2001 accusing De Beers of manipulating the price of diamonds for sixty years. De Beers decided in 2004 to plead guilty to the government charges so it could reenter the U.S. market and have its officers travel to the United States without arrest, and it similarly settled the class action in 2006, trying to—as a De Beers spokesperson said—"normalize" the company's business in America. Only after these suits were settled could longtime De Beers chairman Nicky Oppenheimer enter into the United States without being arrested.

Antitrust scrutiny of the Diamond Dealer's Club, in contrast, falls under Section 1's prohibition of concerted restraints of trade. After all, the very power and essence of the club is its coordination of diamond dealers who otherwise compete for the same business. As the earlier chapters have detailed, the club's dealers have collaborated to assemble rules and procedures to adjudicate disputes, mechanisms that share information on individual reputations, and, most importantly, coordinated punishments that exclude merchants who have cheated in the past. The very foundation of *Stateless Commerce* is collaboration among competitors.

Yet competitors that institute collective punishments can impose serious economic harm. When the Justice Department sued the DDC in 1952 under the antitrust laws, it accused the DDC of engineering a concerted group boycott, in which competitors in a market join forces to refuse to do business with a particular party. The competitive motivations for a concerted group boycott vary. They could aggregate market power to demand better terms from a seller or a buyer, punish parties who do business with a targeted competitor, or promote or resist a certain technology or business practice. Regardless of the motive, group boycotts are invariably viewed by antitrust policy makers with extreme suspicion. Accordingly, concerted boycotts have traditionally been per se illegal under the Sherman Act, which is a level of condemnation reserved for only the most egregiously harmful conduct. In other words, the Justice Department deemed the DDC's decision to expel those who do business with Nazis to be categorically unlawful. The coordinated punishments that exemplify the industry's signature achievement closely resemble conduct that the Sherman Act vigorously rebukes.

Yet the Sherman Act prohibits only anticompetitive collusion that imposes economic costs, and conversely, it is expected to permit procompetitive collaborations that increase economic welfare. And since the DDC's collaboration among its competitors clearly enables the industry to enforce contracts and provide an institutional infrastructure that supports a $60 billion industry, even the most aggressive antitrust enforcer would (should!) recognize the virtues of the DDC's coordinated punishments. The close resemblance of commendable collaboration with condemnable collusion is one reason antitrust law can be notoriously confounding. (Edwin Rockefeller, an author with a wry sense of humor and former chairman of the American Bar Association's Section of Antitrust Law, once remarked, "The reason why antitrust-as-faith endures is not because it has a fixed basis in science or reason but because it does not" [2001, 282].) But Chapter 4 offers a concrete theory and economic rationale to believe that the diamond industry's system of multilateral private ordering is, indeed, an efficient boycott—a mechanism that exhibits more efficiencies than any institutional alternatives. If this logic is to be believed, then the diamond industry's use of coordinated boycotts should be permitted under the Sherman Act.

Recognizing efficiencies in the diamond industry's coordinated boycotts reveals the merits of incorporating institutional economics into antitrust law. At the same time, antitrust law's historic suspicion of coordinated group boycotts should reciprocally highlight the significant costs of multilateral private ordering. The remainder of this chapter offers a historical context for how institutional economics has informed antitrust law, and it then offers illustrations of where antitrust should reignite its scrutiny of the diamond dealers' coordinated punishments. Balancing the lessons of institutional economics with the wisdom of antitrust law, the chapter tries to make some sense of how to apply antitrust law to an assortment of specific DDC-coordinated boycotts and, more generally, how to understand the potential harms inherent in stateless commerce.

Antitrust and Institutional Economics

The Supreme Court has repeatedly affirmed that antitrust law condemns collusion under the per se rule that "that would always or almost always tend to restrict competition and decrease output" (*Broadcast Music, Inc. v. Columbia Broadcasting System, Inc.*, 441 U.S. 1, 19–20). If coordinated group boycotts in the diamond industry promote consumer welfare, then the per se rule—or even heightened antitrust scrutiny—would seem to be inappropriate for the horizontal restraints that solidify the industry.

Yet antitrust analysis, consistent with the Supreme Court's dictate, has historically focused on how certain collaborations affect prices and output. The typical question is whether a particular concerted action increases efficiencies and reduces costs or whether it mimics a monopoly by increasing prices and reducing output. In contrast, an antitrust analysis of the diamond industry must focus on the economic performance of institutions. It begins with the basic observation that the industry relies on coordinated boycotts because public courts are unable to enforce diamond credit sales. Therefore, while most antitrust analyses of collaborations ask whether the collaboration generates economic outcomes that outperform unfettered competition, an antitrust analysis of the diamond industry's concerted boycotts must ask whether the industry's concerted boycotts outperform reliance on typical state-sponsored enforcement mechanisms. In other words, while typical antitrust analysis asks whether the collaboration corrects a "market failure," an institutional antitrust analysis must ask whether the collaboration corrects a "court failure."

Institutional economics, and specifically transaction cost economics (TCE), has had a long, fairly rocky, but ultimately influential history in antitrust policy. When institutional economics was in its infancy in the 1960s and 1970s, neoclassical price theory dominated antitrust policy making. Policy makers, led by Donald Turner, then head of the Antitrust Division of the Department of Justice, were adherents of Joe Bain's structure-performance-conduct approach to industrial organization. The foundation of this neoclassical approach was motivated by Bain's emphasis on market structure, which held that unusual restraints were often evidence of monopolists aiming to expand monopoly power. Vertical restraints especially were presumed to be anticompetitive expansions of market power, and enforcement agencies regularly condemned categories of vertical agreements such as tying arrangements, exclusive dealing contracts, territorial agreements, and vertical mergers. Under Turner's reign, antitrust enforcement in these areas reached its zenith. It was at around this time that Justice Potter Stewart remarked, "The sole consistency that I can find . . . in [merger] litigation under § 7, is that the Government always wins" (*United States v. Von's Grocery Co.*, 384 U.S. 270, 301), and Oliver Williamson described antitrust enforcement during this period as "overconfident and even shrill" (Williamson 1996b, 306). Turner himself appeared at ease disclosing his predisposition to being skeptical to unusual institutional arrangements, and was famously quoted as having said, "I approach territorial and customer restrictions not hospitably in the common law tradition, but inhospitably in the tradition of antitrust law" (Turner 1966, 1–2). Thus the "inhospitality tradition" to both vertical restraints and TCE-based justifications for such restraints was born.[2]

The inhospitality tradition thrived for many years in both economics and antitrust law, but over time, this hostility could not withstand growing skepticism. Ronald Coase in 1972 lamented the myopia in contemporary economic theory, saying, "When an economist finds something—a business practice of one sort or another—that he does not understand, he looks for a monopoly explanation. . . . And as in this field we are very ignorant, the number of ununderstandable practices tends to be rather large, and the reliance on a monopoly explanation, frequent" (67). In addition, institutional economics began generating attractive justifications for vertical restraints, especially for vertical mergers. Williamson's 1975 *Markets and Hierarchies*, which perhaps marked the official launch of transaction cost economics and led scholars and antitrust policy makers toward a "new institutional economics," pressed that "the policy implications of [institutional economics] that are of principal concern are those having to do with antitrust" (Williamson 1975, 258). To the degree that policy makers consult institutional economics for matters spanning vertical integration, conglomerate organization, dominant firms, and oligopoly, Williamson predicted that "antitrust enforcement will proceed more selectively in the future" (258). The transaction cost approach soon made its way into the world of legal scholars. Robert Bork adopted an institutional orientation in scrutinizing vertical mergers, remarking that "what antitrust law perceives as vertical merger, and therefore as a suspect and probably traumatic event, is merely an instance of replacing a market transaction with administrative direction because the latter is believed to be a more efficient method of coordination" (1978, 227). And Frank Easterbrook, shortly before his appointment to the bench, also embraced the TCE template when he asserted that "the dichotomy between cooperation inside a 'firm' and competition in a 'market' is just a convenient shorthand for a far more complicated continuum" (1984, 1).

By the early 1980s, criticism of the applied price theory approach, coupled with the success of TCE and other institutional approaches, led to some significant reforms in antitrust policy. Because institutional economics largely focused on mechanisms that governed specific transactions, and thus was most applicable to buyer-seller relationships, the most natural application of its lessons was to antitrust policy on vertical restraints. Thus, in 1982, the Department of Justice substantially revised its guidelines for non-horizontal mergers to expressly reflect transaction cost reasoning by removing a presumption of anticompetitiveness for nonstandard forms of organization.[3] Further revisions to the guidelines in 1984 made antitrust policy even more permissive toward vertical mergers, holding that vertical mergers are problematic only where the market structure would permit strategic behavior, such as when a merger would deter entry into one of the affected markets. The Department of Justice has not revised its nonhorizontal merger guidelines since.

Contemporary antitrust factions no longer line up neatly between neoclassical and institutional camps. Instead, many current antitrust debates are characterized as disputes between the purported "Chicago school" and "post–Chicago school," in which the post–Chicago school relies on more contextual and complex economic analysis than parsimonious Chicago school formulations. The role of institutional economics in this debate is contested. Paul Joskow has warned that post–Chicago school theorists threaten to undermine the valuable contributions made by transaction cost economics, saying, "At the present time TCE and [the post–Chicago school] are like passing ships in the night. The development of sound antitrust legal rules and remedies would benefit from integrating these approaches and recognizing that they are compliments rather than substitutes. Otherwise [the post–Chicago school] runs the risk of returning us to the 1960s" (Joskow 2002, 105). But most, like former Federal Trade Commission (FTC) chairman Timothy Muris, indicate that TCE and related organizational perspectives remain central to antitrust policy making. Accordingly, Muris described his personal approach as "neither Chicago School nor Post-Chicago, but rather 'New Institutional Economics.'" Like many others, he commends institutional economics for being "a welcome relief for [moving away from] the very stale Chicago / Post-Chicago debate over economic ideology" (Stockum 2002, 60).

Regardless of the contours of the current schools, there is a general consensus that institutional economics has had a major influence in changing antitrust policy toward vertical mergers and nonstandard vertical contractual arrangements. Institutional economics, however, has not had a comparable impact on antitrust law governing horizontal restraints. On one hand, this is understandable given that transaction cost economics focuses on buyer-seller transactions. But on the other, this is lamentable since horizontal restraints are at the core of antitrust law, as horizontal collusion remains the paradigmatic threat to competition.

Examining the diamond industry and its coordinated boycotts through the institutional lens articulated in Chapter 4 can extend institutional economics into antitrust. The agreements that bind competing diamond dealers are quintessentially horizontal, thus any antitrust lessons drawn from the diamond industry can inform a more general antitrust approach toward horizontal restraints. Moreover, since collusion in the diamond industry is designed to solve a contracting problem, and since TCE is principally an effort to understand contracting problems, transaction cost logic readily offers a template with which to evaluate the efficiencies of the industry's reputation mechanism.

Properly understanding the efficiencies and legalities of the diamond industry therefore offers another chapter to the influence of institutional economics on antitrust policy. Institutional economics explains why the diamond industry's coordinated boycotts are superior to state-sponsored courts and other governance mechanisms. Thus, we learn that horizontal coordinated boycotts are an efficient response to the failures of courts and do not deserve the per se condemnation that is reserved for restraints that are always or almost always anticompetitive. This recent teaching from institutional economics follows its lessons in the 1970s and 1980s that convinced antitrust policy makers to be slower to condemn assorted categories of vertical restraints. The diamond industry's coordinated boycotts therefore deserve a more careful analysis—what antitrust calls a "prolonged look"—in determining its efficiencies and legalities, rather than being presumptively illegal.

The Costs of Concerted Boycotts

Like all prolonged looks, an antitrust analysis of the diamond dealers' coordinated boycotts requires a nuanced conclusion. Institutional economics and the recognition of a "court failure" reveal that, by and large, the industry's concerted refusals to deal are procompetitive, but they also exhibit costs. Accordingly, some particular exercises of the industry's coordinated boycotts run the risk of imposing costs that exceed the general benefits. This section discusses some species of concerted refusals in the diamond industry that are not mere side effects of an otherwise efficient collective organization, which should be permissible under the Sherman Act, but instead are anti-competitive group boycotts, which should not.

This approach illustrates that both transaction cost economics and antitrust analysis pursue almost identical balancing methodologies. TCE teaches that governance mechanisms introduce trade-offs and that the costs of certain institutional arrangements should be recognized alongside their benefits; antitrust's prolonged look recognizes both the benefits and the drawbacks of various multilateral enforcement mechanisms. This approach therefore avoids both categorical condemnation (which is reflected in the per se rule) and categorical approval (which is expressed by some enthusiasts of private legal systems).

In addition, prior antitrust actions against the DDC are revealing. While the DDC's collective action to implement its reputation mechanism is by and large economically desirable, past antitrust actions reveal that reliance on coordinated punishments introduce genuine dangers as well. This chapter discusses three specific legal actions that involved the DDC and its leadership, each one revealing a particular cost of stateless commerce: when industry leaders use boycott mechanisms to advance noneconomic purposes, to target innovators or industry nonconformists who might un-settle the current economic hierarchy, and to obtain preferential treatment for purely personal gain.

United States v. Diamond Center, Inc. (S.D.N.Y. 1953)

The Justice Department's suit in 1952 left no defendant untouched. It iden-tified both the DDC and the Diamond Center, a companion but now-defunct trade association, as defendants, and it listed the members of both associa-tions (1,500 in the DDC, 900 in the Diamond Center), as well as the umbrella organization World Federation of Diamond Bourses, as coconspirators. It alleged that the association and its members agreed that "no member . . . shall deal, directly or indirectly, with any member of the German diamond industry or in its services or products" and "that each defendant shall take steps to expel from its membership or otherwise discipline any dealer violating the terms of the agreement" (*U.S. v. Diamond Dealers Club*, No.76-343, Complaint, ¶ 12, 5). The complaint also notes that "membership in either club is essential to the business of dealing in diamonds since all trading is done in the meeting rooms of the two associations. . . . Suspension or expulsion from either association results in suspension or expulsion from all associations which are members of the World Federation" (¶ 10).

The DDC, with its codefendants, asserted an affirmative defense. It argued that the "Club's opposition to dealing in products of the German diamond industry is an expression of its members' horror and indignation on broad moral grounds at intercourse with a nation and with individuals guilty of waging aggressive war and of genocide, and of murder, rape, arson, robbery and similar crimes. Over ninety-nine percent of Club's members are Jews who themselves, or whose friends, families and associates, were particular victims of the criminal policies pursued by Germany and by Germans" (*U.S. v. Diamond Dealers Club*, No. 76-343 (S.D.N.Y. Nov. 17, 1952), Answer, ¶ 9).[4] This defense did not move the Department of Justice. Indeed, targets of antitrust prosecutions have frequently offered "worthy defenses" that purport to excuse anticompetitive conduct with noneconomic, often moralistic justifications. During the Great Depression, coal mining companies and other large industrial players claimed that colluding to increase prices and reduce output was the only way to recover from depressed commodities markets. In the 1950s, the American Medical Association claimed that group boycotts targeting early HMOs were necessary to preserve physician autonomy. And in the 1990s, the Ivy League universities and MIT jointly fixed undergraduate financial aid, arguing that collusion was necessary to create diverse student bodies and sustain educational quality. Although courts sometimes have been receptive to these noneconomic justifications for collusion, they are more commonly rejected, and the Justice Department in 1953 was unswayed. The DDC thus commenced negotiations with antitrust policy makers in Washington and New York, and it ultimately decided to change its not-guilty plea to a plea of nolo contendere (literally: I do not wish to contend). The DDC thereafter pledged to cooperate with antitrust enforcers and adopted a provision in the DDC bylaws that prohibited all restraints of trade.

The plea agreement between the DDC and the Department of Justice, however, only was a prelude to the suit's dramatic culmination, which occurred in a confrontation in Judge Gregory Noonan's courtroom. John Leddy, a special assistant to the United States Attorney General, reiterated the government's case: that the DDC and the Diamond Center had organized an agreement among all diamond dealers "to refrain from any and all dealings with the German diamond industry" and that "they carried out the resolutions to the detriment of the international trade and commerce of the United States" (*U.S. v. Diamond Dealers Club,* No. 76-343 (S.D.N.Y. Aug. 26, 1953), hearing transcript, 4). Leddy then announced to the court that the government had agreed to a settlement that included only a nominal fine of $1,000 (less than $9,000 in 2016 dollars), in large part because "the Government has given very serious consideration [to] this: That the membership of this defendant is composed almost entirely of Jewish people, a great number of whom, if not a majority, came to this country in recent years, and that they and the members of their families had at one time been directly or indirectly persecuted by the one-time Hitler regime of Germany" (5). Judge Noonan, a former prosecutor and the child of Irish immigrants, was less sympathetic. He first remarked that the defendant families were not persecuted "as much as they say they were" and that "they all seem to end up in the business here with a lot of money" (6).[5] Judge Noonan ultimately imposed an even more modest fine of $250, but he first elaborated on his reservations in offering leniency. He explained to one of the DDC's attorneys, Harry Torczyner, "I can appreciate feelings, counselor. You see, in this country we try to forget the past and to forgive. You cannot permit a cancerous growth to commence and grow in this country which will revive and revivify and continue the ancient feuds and hatreds which these people have in their hearts quite justly and which they brought with them from abroad when they first came to our shores." Torczyner, a native of Antwerp who had fled the Nazis himself, responded, "It is easy to forget the past when all the past consists of the newspaper of yesterday. . . . [But if one] were to appear here in this Court and describe to you in his own version of what happened to him, you would forget that it is only one man speaking, but then you would remember what has happened to thousands of them."

This confrontation—the Jewish diamontaires' attorney speaking truth to power—served later as a source of pride among DDC leaders. As one subsequent chairman of the DDC put it many years later, "Despite that plea [of nolo contendere], the Diamond Dealers Club did not want the terrible facts, which precipitated its actions, to go unrecited. At the sentencing, Nathan Math [the lead DDC attorney] eloquently defended the Club and the action of its members, bringing forth all the pain suffered at the hands of the Nazis. When he had finished, he had accomplished his purpose. . . . The two clubs were fined $250. . . . But the words of Nathan Math, and their impact on those who heard him, gave the Club the victory it sought" (Lubin 1982, 15).

Current antitrust law, with its focus on enhancing economic surplus, would agree that group boycotts are not sanitized when they seek to advance noneconomic justifications. The Supreme Court remarked in 1990, when confronted with a boycott of public defenders claiming a need for additional resources to properly administer justice, that "a rule that requires courts to apply the antitrust laws 'prudently and with sensitivity' whenever an economic boycott has an 'expressive component' would create a gaping hole in the fabric of those laws" (FTC v. Superior Court Trial Lawyers Assn., 493 U.S. 411, 431 (1990)). The DDC's targeted boycott, like the public defenders' four decades later, would still be condemned as a naked restraint.

Antitrust law has very good reason for restraining its sympathy. The DDC's confrontation with the Antitrust Division in 1952 offers a poignant story of a historically disenfranchised immigrant community asserting some political autonomy. But it also illustrates the temptation to abuse a procompetitive multilateral system of private ordering to pursue noneconomic objectives and cause anticompetitive harm. However sympathetic the dealers' motives following World War II, it takes little imagination to alter the facts to present the same legal issue but with far less sympathy. For example, a 1984 case presented a diamond dealer who legitimately feared that DDC arbitrators would be irreversibly biased against him because of his reported connections with the Palestinian Liberation Organization (see Rabinowtz v. Olewski, 473 N.Y.S.2d 232 (N.Y. App. Div. 1984)). The temptation to hijack the power to exclude easily extends into less compelling situations, and political ideology—especially since the Justice Department's scrutiny in the 1950s is viewed retrospectively as a proud instance of vindication—remains a threat to interfere with the DDC's policies and procedures.

Rapaport v. Diamond Dealers Club, Inc. (N.Y. Sup. Ct. 1983)

Martin Rapaport is a successful and ambitious diamond dealer who in 1978 started publishing the *Rapaport Prices List,* a weekly newsletter that published the prices of diamonds of assorted carats and cuts that were sold in the DDC during the preceding week. The newsletter, which soon grew into the *Rapaport Diamond Report* and now covers all matters of interest to the diamond industry, brought much-needed transparency to diamond market prices. Although subscriptions spread throughout the DDC and the entire diamond industry, many dealers complained that prices quoted in the *Report* were frustratingly low.[6] Certain prominent DDC members mounted opposition to Rapaport's growing influence within New York's diamond circles, complaining both that the *Report* generated more benefit to Rapaport than to his subscribers, and that Rapaport was bringing instability to a market and merchant community that craved order and self-control. Rapaport, embracing his label as an industry maverick, coolly responded that the dealers were struggling to adapt to shrinking margins and more competition. A 1984 front-page *New York Times* article described the confrontation succinctly: "The directors of the Diamond Dealers Club . . . complain that the Rapaport report is, in effect, setting prices. Mr. Rapaport says that he is merely reflecting the marketplace" (Salmans 1984).

Shortly after he introduced his *Report,* tensions between Rapaport and many of the DDC's elders spilled into the broader Jewish community, with a Jewish religious court ordering Rapaport to stop publishing his price list (threatening excommunication) and Rapaport receiving death threats (including one telephoned from a matzah factory in Brooklyn). The first legal shot was fired on December 9, 1981, when "counselors for unnamed diamond dealers" petitioned the Federal Trade Commission to investigate the business conduct of the Rapaport Diamond Corporation. The complaint alleged that Rapaport, as both a diamond broker and a publisher of a weekly newsletter, was "artificially fixing prices in the diamond industry by disseminating an unsubstantiated price report."[7] The FTC staff launched an initial investigation but found no evidence of any conspiracy to manipulate diamond prices, and it closed the investigation on June 7, 1982. The staff investigation observed that the wholesale market was very unlikely to be monopolized or manipulated by Rapaport or by any other dealer, concluding that "staff did not consider it in the public interest to pursue this theory because the newsletter's gross sales amounted to only about $300,000 and because additional price reporting services have recently emerged."[8]

The dispute further intensified when Rapaport, also in December 1981, reportedly said to an industry magazine reporter about diamond investment firms, many of which were run by prominent DDC members, "diamonds, ethics, Feh! If the devil himself showed up they would sell to him" (Bernstein 1992, 139). Invoking a provision in the bylaws authorizing the DDC Board of Directors to expel any member for making "any statement, act or conduct that in the Board's sole judgment and discretion reflects adversely upon the integrity of any member of the Organization"[9] (DDC bylaws, Article VII, § 2), the board voted to expel Rapaport. Rapaport promptly sued the DDC in New York state court, demanding readmission to the DDC and seeking $55 million in damages.

These events once again invited the scrutiny of the FTC, but this time the commission's attention was directed at the DDC's exclusionary and punitive conduct against Rapaport. In February 1984, the FTC commissioners authorized an investigation into whether the DDC or its members had "entered into agreements to unreasonably restrain trade or commerce by obstructing the collection and dissemination of information concerning current diamond prices."[10] Subpoenas were issued to DDC officers and other prominent figures in New York's diamond industry, and despite the DDC's repeated claims that its dispute with Rapaport was a private matter, the commissioners found sufficient evidence of harm to competition to authorize a full-scale investigation.

The parties reached a settlement in early 1986, bringing both the FTC's investigation and Rapaport's private suit to an end. Rapaport was readmitted to the DDC, his full standing in New York's diamond community was secured, and the DDC board and members took no additional actions to disrupt the dissemination of the *Rapaport Diamond Report*. Rapaport and his *Report* have since flourished in New York's diamond community, and later in 1986, Rapaport was even elected as a DDC director.

Lisa Bernstein concludes from the incident that "the norms of the diamond industry only work when they capture information that the market values," and that the DDC's failure to expel Rapaport is attributed to the value generated by his *Report* (Bernstein 1992, 139). There are, however, less sanguine lessons to draw. Like the DDC's attack on dealers of German goods in the 1950s, the Rapaport affair illustrates how personal animus and differing business philosophies can hijack the DDC's exclusionary power to inappropriately bar innocent parties. More significantly, the incident illustrates how the industry's established powers can be hostile to nonconformists and innovative entrepreneurial mavericks (Rapaport continues to pursue innovative business practices, and he also continues to attract criticism from industry interests, including one industry insider who wrote "Martin Rapaport: One Man's Destruction of Our Industry" [Reiff 1998]). Like the temptation to harness coordinated punishments to target ideological foes, there also is the temptation to target innovative entrepreneurs and those who threaten entrenched business practices. Such temptations not only can cause the industry's reputation mechanisms to veer in inefficient directions, but they can also undermine the very foundation of mutual trust that industry advocates so often hail.

Stettner v. Twersky (N.Y. Sup. Ct. 2006)

In May 2002, Brett Stettner, a retail jeweler and rare diamond trader from Galveston, Texas, traveled to New York to purchase wholesale diamonds and to obtain expert advice on cutting a flawless 25.4-carat diamond. For both of these tasks, Stettner obtained assistance from Boruch Twersky, a DDC diamond dealer and broker. Stettner put the 25.4-carat stone, worth between $1.5 million and $2.5 million, in the possession of Twersky and also had Twersky facilitate a number of sales on Stettner's behalf.

A dispute later arose between Stettner and Twersky when Stettner asked for the diamond's return. Twersky claimed that the diamond was collateral for some $200,000 worth of diamonds that Stettner agreed to purchase from assorted dealers who used Twersky as a broker. Stettner countered that the diamond was never intended as collateral, that he instead entrusted it with Twersky so Twersky could obtain an expert opinion from a master cutter, that he received less than $82,000 of diamonds on credit from

Twersky and his associates, and that he had only received an invoice for $200,000 after suing to recover the 25.4-carat stone.

When Stettner, who was not a DDC member, brought suit in New York state court, Twersky claimed that the DDC had exclusive jurisdiction over the dispute since Stettner signed a "Non-membership Application and Agreement" that bound him to DDC arbitration. The issue before the court was whether this nonmembership agreement extended to Twersky's help in cutting the 25.4-carat stone, which in part was dependent on whether the stone was intended to serve as collateral for other credit purchases. Testifying on Twersky's behalf were Isaac Merin, the dealer for whom Twersky brokered sales to Stettner, and Jacob Banda, another diamond dealer and chairman of the DDC. Stettner had separate dealings with Banda, which had developed into a disagreement, and Stettner alleged in his complaint that Twersky told him he would only return the 25.4-carat diamond "when the separate 'dispute' with Banda had been resolved to Banda's (and his) satisfaction, and not before" (*Stettner v. Twersky*, No. 6602298 (N.Y. Sup. Ct. June 28, 2006), complaint pp. 2–3). Thus, Stettner found himself up against a team of leading DDC members, all of whom were asking the New York court to cede jurisdiction to the DDC's arbitrators.

The Stettner-Twersky dispute is a classic insider-outsider conflict, in which the outsider reasonably fears that he will receive unfair treatment from the industry arbitrators, especially when the chairman of the DDC acts as an interested party. Recent developments confirm that these outsider fears are justified, as critics of the DDC's arbitration system have expressed growing concern over the quality and impartiality of the DDC's arbitration. One suit by a diamond merchant against the DDC went as far to accuse the club of only "want[ing] to protect its members" (*Sanghvi v. Diamond Dealers Club, Inc.*, No. 7601085 (N.Y. Sup. Ct. Mar. 28, 2007)). These considerations were likely, in part, why the judge presiding over *Stettner v. Twersky* ruled that Stettner was not obligated to bring his complaint before DDC arbitrators and instead ordered Twersky to return the 25.4 carat stone.

But *Stettner v. Twersky* is more than a mere reflection of nepotism or of a danger that the DDC's arbitration system is losing credibility. It also reveals a systemic challenge in private legal systems and illustrates the flip side of many of their benefits. Arbitrators are insiders with industry expertise, so they purportedly can issue judgments with greater accuracy, flexibility, and speed than generalist judges or juries. But the same insider status also threatens the arbitrators' impartiality and objectivity. Because public courts cannot credibly enforce diamond contracts, courts rely on these arbitrators and industry reputation mechanisms to secure order in the industry, yet this very reliance on private actors only magnifies the danger of partiality. To the degree that antitrust law is asked to scrutinize concerted actions against outsiders like Stettner, it should distinguish anticompetitive efforts to extract rents from outsiders from the procompetitive boycotts that punish individuals for bad behavior.

The industry's arbitration system cannot survive, of course, without a minimal degree of credibility. If DDC arbitration rulings are perceived to be tainted by bias, arbitrariness, and ideology, then parties will turn instead to alternative instruments. Merchants might construct complex contracts that rely less on credit and more on collateral that public courts, despite their costs and deficiencies, can capably secure; the industry might see more vertical integration, despite the associated bureaucratic costs; or reputation circles might become smaller, relying less on DDC membership to signal credibility and resorting to more intimate personal exchange.

As Chapter 8 discusses, many of these developments have started taking place. Precisely because the industry's arbitration system has too frequently been accused of partiality, diamontaires now seek greater use of state courts, rely more on formal banks for sources of credit, and have engineered more vertically integrated distribution channels. Indeed, if the industry loses its comparative advantage in dispute resolution, then the DDC and its supporting social infrastructure would lose its institutional functions, the diamond industry could lose its most distinctive features, and the costs of stateless commerce would lead to its demise.

Conclusion

Because reputation mechanisms remain central to the efficiencies of the diamond industry (and remain a fixture in many other parts of the economy as well), it would be odd if the collaborations on which they rely run afoul of the antitrust laws. Indeed, a per se rule that applies only to practices that "always or almost always tend to restrict competition" should not be invoked against the procompetitive use of group boycotts in the diamond industry. Because the horizontal agreements that implement group boycotts in the diamond industry enable merchants to secure contracts that otherwise would be extremely hard to enforce, the group boycotts amount to efficient private ordering responses to the prohibitive costs of court ordering. This conclusion rests on institutional economics, which illustrates through a structured comparative assessment of alternative governance mechanisms that the industry's coordinated punishments are efficient responses to a court failure. They thus should be permissible under antitrust laws that are intended to reduce the total costs of competition.

However, those same mechanisms that enable coordinated punishments also impose substantial costs. Concerted group boycotts can impose punishments for noneconomic purposes, exclude innovators and benevolent outsiders, and enable private gain to industry insiders. An antitrust analysis should therefore evaluate when a particular group boycott is designed to achieve procompetitive multilateral private ordering and when it aims to secure anticompetitive rents.

The implication for antitrust law is that it should distinguish anticompetitive group boycotts from procompetitive joint ventures, in the diamond industry and elsewhere. Antitrust scrutiny of such boycotts requires a prolonged look, rather than a conclusion of per se illegality, that examines the purpose and effect of the boycotts. The specific prolonged look should inquire whether a particular concerted boycott is a by-product of securing industry-wide trade or whether it seeks one of the anticompetitive ills discussed here. Because these mechanisms remain common in the modern economy and periodically attract antitrust attention (for example, *Silver v. New York Stock Exchange*, 373 U.S. 341 (1963), *NW Wholesale Stationers v. Pacific Stationery*, 472 U.S. 284 (1985)), the template offered here provides broader lessons on how antitrust law can understand concerted refusals to deal. It also provides another path by which institutional economics can inform antitrust law.

In sum, an antitrust examination of the diamond industry offers both modest lessons and far-reaching implications. Although the industry presents an extreme instance of court failure, and therefore a particularly ripe occasion for a boycott that policy makers ought to deem to be efficient, it points to broader opportunities for institutional economics to generate lessons for antitrust law. Institutional economics should be useful, as is illustrated here, in helping antitrust policy makers distinguish anticompetitive group boycotts from procompetitive joint ventures to enforce contracts, and it similarly might offer insight into other self-policing industries and trade associations that alternatively strive to generate organizational efficiencies and capture collusive rents. While an institutional economic analysis of the Diamond Dealers Club, an idiosyncratic trade association within an oddly structured industry, suggests a relatively minor reform to antitrust law, it also reveals the ways in which new methodologies can broadly inform antitrust analysis.

6

Lessons from Statelessness

Economic History, Ethnic Networks, and Development Policy

W HY ARE SO many diamond dealers Jewish? Does the concentration of Jewish merchants in the trade reveal anything about the diamond industry? And does Jewish success as diamond merchants reveal anything about Jewish economic performance in other industries throughout history?

Chapter 3, describing the family and Jewish community institutions that surround and support the diamond trade, concludes, "[The] two-pronged system of family-based reputation mechanisms and community-based enforcement institutions allows New York's diamond merchants to organize reliable time-inconsistent exchange. It works because all players who are entrusted with another's diamonds belong to one of the two categories and thus are subject to one of the two punishment devices. The system embodies what Yoram Ben-Porath (1980) called 'the F-connection,' where trade networks organized around families and friends (that is, community members) can execute implicit contracts that enjoy efficiencies unavailable to formal, arm's-length transactions." These diamond dealers, because of the community in which they live, are able to make credible promises that others cannot, and their credibility translates into the opportunity to obtain valuable credit for diamond purchases. In short, their community gives them a comparative advantage over other would-be dealers, and their community institutions appear to be necessary features for enabling community members to excel in the diamond industry.

This chapter explores some of the outer boundaries of this phenomenon. The success of Jewish diamond merchants reveals just one instance of how the interplay of industry and community institutions, of information mechanisms and power relations in insular communities, of industry rules and community standards, can influence economic outcomes. There is nothing exclusively Jewish about the institutional features described in Chapter 3—surely other communities offer noneconomic rewards for cooperative conduct and issue noneconomic sanctions to punish harmful behavior. Reciprocally, community enforcement mechanisms and social sanctions that induce community members to keep their promises can be economically beneficial in many industries outside the diamond trade. Understanding the community features that assist Jewish merchants in the diamond industry might inform broader questions about the institutional foundations of economic growth.

This chapter explores both sides of the complementarities that connect Jewish community institutions and diamond merchants. It investigates Jewish economic performance beyond the diamond industry, and it explores ethnic performance in the diamond industry beyond the Jewish community. It then explores whether these historical lessons have implications for modern development policy.

Jewish Economic Performance over History

Jewish economic history has been a fertile area of scholarship. There is general agreement on the beginnings of that history: In 70 C.E., at the time the Jewish Temple was destroyed by the Roman Empire, Jews were an agrarian people living mostly in Israel and Mesopotamia. But the Temple's destruction marked the end of whatever political sovereignty Jews had retained under Roman rule and began Judaism's transformation from a religion of sacrifices to a religion of Rabbinics. This redesign of Jewish practice enabled communities to sustain rituals and rites in locations far from Jerusalem and throughout the world, and Jewish religious practice subsequently coadapted with geopolitical changes, following the Jewish world as it became an urban diaspora.

As Judaism as a religion changed, so did the Jewish people. Despite their agrarian origins, Jews, for most of the two millennia following the Temple's destruction, were a population of skilled craftsmen, physicians, shopkeepers, traders, bankers, and moneylenders.[1] But the causal mechanisms explaining why Jews were attracted to, and thrived in, these professions are debated, and economic historians and other scholars offer several intriguing and not necessarily mutually exclusive explanations for Jewish economic performance over time.

The most common account attributes Jews' attraction to urban skilled trades to the laws and prohibitions of the nations in which they lived. For much of the Middle Ages, many nation-states prohibited Jews from owning land, ousted them from merchant guilds, and excluded them from traditional brands of handicrafts. Jews thus were forced into becoming suppliers of finished goods and extenders of credit. Several prominent historians, including Israel Abrahams (1896) and Cecil Roth (1938, 1961) have accordingly argued that Jewish occupational selection was a product of the many state restrictions on Jewish economic activity. In addition, Jewish communities suffered a history of expulsions and forced emigrations by Christian rulers, and were similarly vulnerable in many Middle Eastern and North African countries. The constant threat of dislocation drew them to professions with small fixed investments and easily portable inventories (Arkin 1975) and induced them to invest in occupations relying on portable human capital rather than physical capital (for example, Brenner and Kiefer 1981; Ayal and Chiswick 1983).[2]

While this account could explain why Jewish merchants were drawn to urban occupations, such as trade in gems, currencies, and other portable goods, and also why Jews distanced themselves from farming and other occupations that required fixed assets, it does not explain why Jews excelled in those trades. Early Jewish predominance in certain industries suggests not just that urban trades were a last resort, but that Jewish merchants enjoyed a comparative advantage.

A related explanation posits that Jewish tradesmen acted cooperatively to secure a stranglehold over a particular segment of commerce (Krueger 1963). In this "ethnic cartel" model, merchants in an insular community pledge to charge competitive prices only to the community's own members and to sell goods only at oligopoly prices to nonmembers. As a result, outsiders are at a disadvantage in entering a supply chain and in competing against insiders. This theory also probably has some merit. Jewish trading and professional networks certainly had entry barriers, as language, culture, and political status separated Jewish traders from others, nurtured the community's insularity, and fostered a healthy distrust of outsiders. These community features likely inclined Jewish merchants to extend favorable treatment to their coreligionists and led to the anticompetitive effects exhibited by many cartels. The diamond industry, in particular, exhibits entry barriers that have secured a lucrative source of income for Jewish communities for many generations, so one can imagine how a community's initial attraction to a particular trade would in turn allow that community to dominate the trade over time.

A significant shortcoming of the ethnic cartel model, particularly as it is applied to the centuries-old diamond industry, is that it presumes a cartel has the ability to outlast market forces. Modern antitrust scholars are generally skeptical of the ability of most large-numbered cartels to police their own members and prolong supracompetitive prices, especially in markets (like the market for diamonds) that exhibit highly differentiable goods and unpredictable demand (Posner 1969). Yet Jewish occupational patterns persisted across time and place for centuries, and, specifically, the diamond industry's seemingly anachronistic distribution system has sustained itself for nearly one millennium.

An alternative, and oftentimes controversial, explanation rests on a theory of human capital (Becker 1993). This theory suggests that Jewish professionals, families, or institutions developed know-how that enabled Jewish merchants to excel in certain trades or occupations over time. Though this human capital explanation has been advanced by many commentators (e.g., Murray 2007), it is also part of a less attractive tradition of attempts to explain Jewish economic performance. Werner Sombart's *Jews and Modern Capitalism*, written in 1911, attributed Jewish commercial success to a "Jewish genius" that makes Jews especially well-suited for capitalism's demands for economic rationalism.[3] Intending his work as a response to Max Weber's *Protestant Ethic and the Spirit of Capitalism*, Sombart identifies a Jewish ethos—rather than Calvinism or Puritanism—as the foundation for modern capitalism, and he concludes that "the capitalistic civilization of our age is the fruit of the union between the Jews, a Southern people pushing into the North, and the Northern tribes, indigenous there" (226). This conception of Jews as a separate people who are incompatible with (or impossible to integrate into) mainstream European society reflected a larger trend among social thinkers who focused on what they labeled "the Jewish Question." To be fair, Sombart does not rest his arguments on genetics, and the portions of his book that painstakingly articulate the many forces that shaped Jewish rationalism—the Talmud and medieval codes, the history of nomadism, the influence of the desert—relies on analytical reasoning that was not dissimilar from Weber's arguments for the role of Protestantism in capitalism. And reportedly, Berlin's Jews were eager to partake in Sombart's lessons, flocking to his lectures and showing enthusiasm for his ethnic generalizations (historian Derek Penslar writes "When Sombart proclaimed that the idea of maximizing turnover and minimizing profit 'is a specifically Jewish contribution, for the Jews are the fathers of the idea of free trade,' he was greeted with lively and sustained applause" [2001, 166]). Perhaps the disastrous nexus between Sombart's thinking and the foundation of the Nazi regime is apparent only in retrospect, but that nexus did express itself and has cast a severe cloud over *Jews and Modern Capitalism* and its related schools of thought. Though Sombart began as a politically active left-wing radical and an enthusiast of Karl Marx, he—like many of Germany's left-wing thinkers—heralded National Socialism in 1934, proclaiming it as a "new spirit" that would "rule mankind" and that the "chief task" of the German people and National Socialism is to destroy the Jewish spirit in England and beyond.

Despite the uncomfortable connotations, there are elements of the human capital theory that translate well in explaining Jewish predominance in the diamond industry (Jewish Nobel laureate Milton Friedman, though showing no forgiveness for Sombart's later politics, articulated genuine appreciation for and assent with many ideas in Sombart's 1911 book in a lecture titled *Capitalism and the Jews*. In fact, Friedman went on to remark "if anything I interpret the book as philo-Semitic. I regard the violence of the reaction of Jewish intellectuals to the book as itself a manifestation of the Jewish anti-capitalist mentality" [1972/1988]). Certain traditions of Jewish socialization and education help create the communal foundations that enable Jewish merchants to organize a reliable diamond supply chain, such as the prevalence of Yiddish in certain sects, widespread preferences for religious goods, and the interconnectedness of large families in intimate communities. A tradition of adhering to legal codes and rabbinic authorities might make Jewish diamond merchants particularly amenable to resolving disputes peacefully through arbitration, which certainly is a critical feature of the industry's success. In addition, the insularity of certain Jewish sects and the intimacy of Jewish family networks, perhaps facilitated by a distinctly inward-looking religious practice, might assist the transmission of critical skills that only experts can impart, such as diamond cutting and the ability to inspect and appraise gemstones. Indeed, some concentrated centers of diamond-cutting expertise have developed much like other cottage industries of skilled labor or specialized technology, in line with strategy scholar Michael Porter's (1985, chap. 9) theories of how geographic concentration of competing businesses fosters innovation and regional growth.[4]

Maristella Botticini and Zvi Eckstein, in their recent magisterial book *The Chosen Few: How Education Shaped Jewish History, 70–1492* (2012), offer a version of a human capital theory that rests on the importance of literacy in Judaism and Jewish life. As post-Temple Judaism transformed into a religion of Rabbinics, in which the new religious leaders were scholars who abided by and studied a written legal code, Jewish communities placed growing emphasis on formal religious instruction and disseminated norms for compulsory education. While literacy rates in the ancient and medieval worlds were quite low, remaining below 10 percent in most of Western Europe as late as 1500 (Botticini and Eckstein report that no people other than the Jews had a norm requiring fathers to educate their sons), Jewish community leaders built schools to train their children to read and scrutinize religious texts. This emphasis on early literacy, Botticini and Eckstein argue, endowed Jewish professionals with a comparative advantage in urban trades.

Botticini and Eckstein's study describes itself as "a powerful new explanation of one of the most significant transformations in Jewish history while also providing fresh insights into the growing debate about the social and economic impact of religion" (back cover). It is indeed an original and ambitious work, but elements of their thesis spill over from literacy and implicate other important factors explaining Jewish history.

In fact, the Botticini and Eckstein model could be read more as an institutional model than a true human capital model, and their argument might actually attribute institutions, in contrast to education per se, as the force responsible for shaping Jewish occupational trends. In their model, literacy and a tradition of written laws enabled an extrajudicial system of rabbinic courts to flourish. These courts reliably settled disputes and allowed for the development of credible cooperation that was required for commercial enterprises to grow. They write, "In a world populated by illiterate people— as the world of the first millennium was—the ability to read and write contracts, business letters, and account books using a common alphabet gave the Jews a comparative advantage over other people. The Jews *also* developed a uniform code of law (the Talmud) and a set of institutions (the rabbinic courts, the responsa) that fostered contract enforcement, networking, and arbitrage across distant locations. High levels of literacy *and* the existence of contract-enforcement institutions became the levers of the Jewish people" (5; emphasis added). Widespread literacy and a common language enabled the development of this dispute resolution system, but it was the dispute system that was central in supporting the cooperation necessary for economic success (one might say that Botticini and Eckstein focus on how literacy developed a comprehensive body of law, forgetting also to examine how those laws were enforced). The reliable dispute system enabled Jews to credibly obtain credit to finance moneylending systems, navigate trading networks across geopolitical boundaries, secure financing to invest in advanced education or support crafts, and deal in lucrative yet portable goods. The enforcement mechanisms that sustain the diamond trade today might well have sustained Jews in multiple trades across time and geography, since (especially before reliable states developed reliable public courts) each of those trades wrestles with the common economic challenge of credibly enforcing credit agreements.

Conceptually, classical components of human capital, such as literacy, education, and intellectual assets that foster individual skills, are distinguishable from community institutional features with economic implications, such as religious rites, common language, and social organizations and norms that discipline individual behavior. The features described in Chapter 3 are more institutional and suggest that family and community institutions enable Jewish diamond merchants—as a group, not as individuals with particular cognitive skills—to manage the industry's assorted demands. Those same institutional features no doubt would have helped individuals in other medieval urban trades, especially moneylending, which relies almost exclusively on the ability to enforce credit agreements. These family and community institutions support the economic performance of community members similarly to economic historian Avner Greif's depiction of how Jewish Maghribi traders leveraged local institutions to enable distant commercial relationships in eleventh-century Mediterranean trade (1989, 1993). These institutional explanations also parallel other studies that document how social norms and civic organizations can contribute to regional and national economic growth (Dore 1983, 1989 chap. 9; Putnam 1993).

The primary criticism of Botticini and Eckstein's work accuses the authors of excessively simplifying Jewish history, of not accurately representing the economic and demographic diversity of first-millennium Jews, and of relying too heavily on a single theory. In Botticini and Eckstein's defense, no one feature could alone explain Jewish economic history over 1,500 years, and certainly a complicated combination of all of these factors—community-generated institutional advantages, family networks supporting the acquisition of specific skills and human capital, anticompetitive collusion facilitated by ethnic familiarity, and external political constraints, along with historical accidents and institutional inertia—is responsible for Jewish economic performance. My slight criticism—which is couched in enormous praise and admiration—is that they highlighted literacy without emphasizing how literacy alone could enable economic achievement. Literacy supported an effective dispute resolution system, as did a well-developed legal code. But essential as well was the community's ability to enforce the resulting rulings. As unusual as high literacy rates might have been, literacy would have done little to fuel investment and economic growth without the ability to convert literate rulings into effective judgments.

Ultimately, reading Botticini and Eckstein through the lens of institutional analysis only makes their contribution more meaningful. They offer compelling evidence that Jewish communities' traditional ability to enforce promises and thus credibly obtain credit has had a powerful influence on Jewish history. Evidently, the comparative advantage that Jewish diamond merchants enjoy over rivals to purchase diamonds on credit might be the same comparative advantage that arose from Jewish community institutions throughout history to enable Jews to succeed in urban occupations. Understanding contemporary Jewish economic performance offers a window into understanding Jewish economic history, perhaps reaching as far back as the first century.

Jewish Networks and the Institutions of Criminal Activity

Private ordering is not just a story about economic achievement, nor is it only a story about sympathetic ethnic minorities excelling in unfriendly environments. The implications of Chapter 3 extend into less desirable conduct, best illustrated by seminal research on Italian mafia networks.

In 1876, Leopoldo Franchetti, a Tuscan landowner, traveled to Sicily and wrote what remains one of the most comprehensive and coherent accounts of the Sicilian mafia (Gambetta 1988b). Franchetti's account is significant for at least two reasons. First, his observations of the nineteenth-century mafia closely resemble how experts describe the modern-day mafia. And second, he offers a compelling account of the mafia's origins, which emerged as a response to "the absence of credible or effective systems of justice and law enforcement" (162). Franchetti reported (as a young Alexis de Tocqueville did approximately fifty years earlier) that since the sixteenth century, when Spanish rulers first dominated the area with an absentee aristocracy, southern Italy suffered from lawlessness and corrupt political administration. The mafiosi "do not emerge as ordinary criminals" but instead were networks designed to establish social order, control local resources, and "enforc[e] privately that public justice the Spaniards had eroded and that nobody could trust" (163–164). In short, the mafia was a particular response to an ineffective state and the need for legal certainty.

Historically, "the *crime* most characteristic of the mafia is the use of violence to enforce the monopoly of otherwise legal goods" (Gambetta 1988, 164; emphasis in original). But violence is not the mafia's only instrument for social control and for inducing cooperative behavior. Diego Gambetta reports that "the mechanisms which motivate cooperation" among the mafiosi, in addition to attractive economic benefits, included the bonds of kin and friendship and a code of honor that offers cultural or moral reasons to comply with expected behavior (168). In other words, mafia networks dispense, in addition to economic rewards and physical sanctions, noneconomic club goods through family and community institutions to encourage cooperation.

The mafia's institutional features suggest that Jewish communities, with a similar infrastructure to dispense noneconomic rewards and sanctions, might be similarly well suited to organize criminal activity. After all, criminal networks, like most other merchants, rely on credibly extending and obtaining credit to facilitate sales. And since state-sponsored courts refuse to enforce sales contracts for illegal goods, merchants in illegal goods will seek extralegal instruments to secure credit markets.

In one strange story, ultra-Orthodox Jews were employed in an elaborate drug network, and their roles reflected many of the economic features that their brethren exhibit in the diamond industry. In October 1998, Sean Erez, a thirty-one-year-old Israeli Canadian who was also a convicted drug felon, set up a network that trafficked almost one million Ecstasy tablets from Amsterdam, where they were manufactured, to New York and Miami, where each tablet commanded twenty-five dollars in night clubs. Erez's couriers, called mules, were young Orthodox Jews from Brooklyn and Monsey who, told they were smuggling diamonds, agreed to transport the bundles of pills in plastic bags or athletic socks, often tucked under their traditional Hassidic hats or in boxes resembling prayer scrolls. The sensational story predictably turned into a 2009 book, *Chemical Cowboys,* and a 2010 major motion picture, *Holy Rollers.* (One line in *Holy Rollers* has a seasoned Jewish mule justifying to a recent recruit: "Jews have been smuggling for thousands of years.") Among the many remarkable features of the story was the recruitment of the mules. Erez relied heavily on two eighteen-year-old ultra-Orthodox Jewish students, who were paid $2,000 for each courier they enlisted. The two recruited ultra-Orthodox colleagues in their yeshiva and other neighborhood circles.

Each of Erez's couriers typically smuggled thirty thousand to forty-five thousand Ecstasy pills each trip, with a retail value of $750,000 to $1.12 million. Yet, remarkably, Erez was comfortable giving his valuable merchandise to strangers recruited by unseasoned teenagers. This is even more remarkable given that the couriers thought they were carrying diamonds, which would have been worth significantly more. A couple of years later, another network of Hassidic Jews was caught helping Colombian cocaine cartels launder $1.7 billion, with ultra-Orthodox couriers transporting up to $500,000 in Colombian cash in individual trips. The same features that make Jewish diamond merchants unlikely to flee with unpurchased diamonds make young yeshiva students unlikely to flee with unpurchased Ecstasy or ultra-Orthodox couriers unlikely to steal laundered money. And the shared institutional features of traditional Jewish communities and Sicilian mafiosi enable both to discipline community members and induce certain cooperative behavior that state courts do not support.

Neither the criminal tendencies of certain Hassidic Jews nor the business acumen of certain Jewish diamond dealers is specific to the Jewish community. Although the traditional Jewish community, both today and throughout history, might exhibit institutional and cultural features that were uncommon, communities that contain similar characteristics could, according to this theory, also support their community members in similar economic endeavors. Specifically, if Jewish merchants owe their success in the diamond trade to a comparative advantage that enables them to organize diamond transactions more efficiently than potential rivals, then non-Jewish merchants who can similarly organize efficient enforcement of diamond transactions ought to succeed as well.

Enter India

The rise and emerging dominance of Indian diamond networks since the 1980s might be the industry's most significant development since diamonds were discovered in South Africa. Indian diamond merchants have made Mumbai into perhaps the world's most important diamond market. Indian firms are now a dominant force in Antwerp's diamond center and are deeply embedded in New York's diamond market (it was big news when, in 2005, an Indian merchant was elected to the board of New York's diamond bourse). It has become an increasingly common sight along 47th Street to see Indian and South Asian diamontaires roaming the markets, staffing kiosks, and hurrying along the sidewalks with handcuffed briefcases.

India's emergence in the diamond industry has been as dramatic as it has been rapid, and both the industry's profile and the diamond pipeline have been dramatically transformed. Whereas Indian merchants constituted only a small minority of the industry as recently as 1980, Indian firms now dominate the pathway between sellers of rough stones and buyers of polished gems. Eighty-five percent of all diamonds (60 percent by value) are now polished in India, thousands of Indian cutting firms have sprouted in Gujarat Province, and Indian firms and Indian government policies move the industry. Indian diamontaires have also changed the face of the Indian economy, as diamonds constitute roughly 14 percent of India's exports and now compete with textiles and computer software as the nation's largest export industry.

What does the rise of Indian merchants reveal about the economic organization of the diamond industry? And how does it affect the argument that Jewish diamond merchants excel because of unusual features of their community structure?

One immediate lesson is that the diamond distribution network is not an entirely exclusive cartel preserved only for incumbents. Although Chapter 5 explores the diamond network's periodic tendency and lingering capacity to exclude outsiders, the rise of Indian merchants reveals that the industry does open its doors to entrants from other ethnic groups even while it retains a strong Jewish presence. Certainly entry barriers exist and entry is not common, so perhaps Indian entry is the exception that proves the rule and reveals the ingredients required to enter the industry. If—as Chapter 3 argues—community institutions bestow on Jewish merchants a valuable comparative advantage over generic merchants, then do successful Indian merchants have similar institutional supports? Do Indian diamontaires, coming from a community with geographical, cultural, religious, and historical traditions dramatically different from Jewish communities, have a similar comparative advantage? Answering these questions requires understanding the origins and foundations of India's diamond industry.

India's recent entry into modern diamond production has by no means been the country's first encounter with the diamond industry. To the contrary, the Indian subcontinent was the world's only known source of diamonds from 800 B.C., when the first diamond discoveries were recorded, until 1844, when diamonds were discovered in Brazil. During the height of India's diamond production period, in the late 1600s, approximately fifty thousand to one hundred thousand carats were extracted annually from India's deposits and were a primary driver of trade with merchants from Portugal, France, the Dutch East India Company, and the English East India Company. Trade in diamonds fueled the rise of the Golconda kingdom, along the southeastern Indian coast, in the sixteenth and seventeenth centuries. It was during this period that relations with European traders—some commercial and some more coercive—brought many of the world's most famous diamonds to European royalty. Some remain objects of fascination:

the Hope Diamond was acquired by famous French gem merchant Jean-Baptiste Tavernier in the seventeenth century and sold to King Louis XIV (it was later stolen during the French Revolution and eventually repurchased by Harry Winston, who donated it to the Smithsonian); the Regent Diamond was purchased by a captain in the East India Company, sold to the French regent Philippe II, and set in the coronation crowns for Louis XV and Louis XVI (it was later an ornament on one of Marie Antoinette's hats, stolen during the French Revolution, redeemed by Napoleon Bonaparte to adorn his sword, and eventually acquired by the Louvre with the French Royal Treasury); and the Koh-I-Noor, which was the object of tribal battles from the fourteenth through the nineteenth centuries, was appropriated by the East India Company and presented to Queen Victoria in 1850 (it later adorned the crown worn by Queens Alexandria, Mary, and Elizabeth and has been on display with the Crown Jewels in the Tower of London; India periodically renews a request for its return).

India's rich past in diamonds is also reflected in many elements of Indian culture. Early Sanskrit manuscripts contain numerous references to diamonds, including elaborate descriptions of precious gemstones and associations with mythical figures at the foundation of Hinduism, and as Hindu symbols were incorporated into Buddhism, the diamond became a Buddhist symbol of religious virtue.[5] Diamonds have also played a role in India's caste system, as the different castes were only permitted to own diamonds of a specific color—Brahmins wore white, merchants wore yellow, lower classes wore gray, and only kings could possess diamonds of all colors.

Since the discoveries in African mines in the late nineteenth century, India's production of rough diamonds has remained small compared to finds in Africa. And through the 1970s, the nation's diamontaires remained separate from the burgeoning global market dominated by De Beers and the mostly Jewish and Belgian diamond merchants that controlled the downstream distribution chain. Nonetheless, the Jains of Palanpur, who for centuries served as India's diamontaires, retained their gemstone expertise. Jainism, an offshoot of Buddhism, is the religion for 0.4 percent of Indians, and Palanpur is a parched, dusty village in northern Gujarat, the state that lies just north of Mumbai. Palanpuri Jains preserved a centuries-old tradition for diamond cutting, owning and operating small cutting workshops and maintaining the tacit skills required for cutting and polishing

Figure 6.1. Number of firms, by family background, in India's diamond industry. *Source:* Munshi 2011.

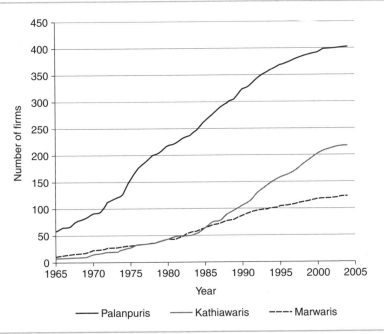

diamonds even while India's role in the industry receded. India's modern diamond era began in the 1880s when Palanpuri Jains began constructing small diamond distribution networks, and by World War II, with approximately twenty-five families settling in Antwerp in 1937, the Palanpuris had established a global presence (Hofmeester 2013, 45).

In the 1970s, some entrepreneurial Jain families sought to exploit their community's rich history and deeply rooted expertise with diamonds to lead India's reemergence in the diamond industry. This invited many more Jains to enter the industry, including some enterprising diamontaires who ventured to Europe with whatever capital they could obtain to purchase rough stones from Antwerp. They then brought these stones to their Palanpuri brethren for polishing, taking advantage of India's much lower wages, and sold the polished gems at prices against which their European competitors had trouble competing. Gradually, these new leaders asked the master craftsmen in their home villages to train new cutters and organize large-scale cutting operations. The floodgates opened when Australia's Argyle

Figure 6.2. Number of exporters, by family background, in India's diamond industry. *Source:* Munshi 2011.

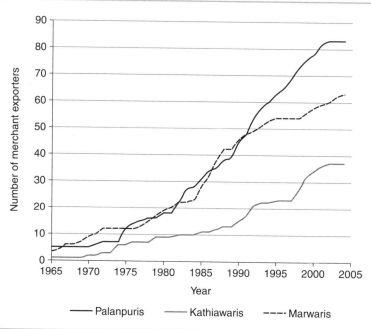

mines created a production boom in 1979, and Palanpuri family firms were poised to dramatically expand their operations (Munshi 2011). They set up thousands of cutting factories in Gujarat, employing over seven hundred thousand Indians, making it the world's diamond polishing capital and causing Jain diamond entrepreneurs to become among the nation's wealthiest. In more recent years, as is illustrated in Figures 6.1 and 6.2, Palanpuri diamontaires have been joined by other Indian ethnicities to fuel the nation's diamond sector growth.

One of India's leading business journalists remarked, "Ordinary people cannot understand how a handful of families, all belonging to one small community—Palanpuri Jains—have become so rich, so quickly" (Piramal 1996, 317). Part of the community's dramatic success is due to their leverage of low-wage labor. Prior to the Indian emergence, diamond cutting was an artisanal and rather sleepy profession dominated by individual tradesmen in Western urban centers. Indian diamond factories turned diamond cutting into a mass-production enterprise, dramatically increasing volume while paying third-world wages. The influx of new cutters also enabled Indian companies to purchase very small diamonds that previously were only commercially viable for industrial use. In recounting the early growth of India's diamond industry, Bharat Shah, among the early Palanpuri Jain diamond pioneers, boasted, "We went to the bottom end of the market, buying and cutting diamonds which the Jews had rejected" (Piramal 1996, 318) (he and his brother, Vijay, are college dropouts who now operate one of India's largest corporate empires, with interests that include construction companies and one of Bollywood's largest movie production companies). The Jains' ability to leverage low-wage labor to produce large volumes of diamonds, including many that had previously not reached the jewelry market, brought enormous wealth to these early entrepreneurs. Their success has revolutionized the diamond production process, and many diamond dealers have since opened cutting factories in low-wage countries in Eastern Europe and Southeast Asia.

But were the Palanpuri Jains, like Jewish diamontaires, uniquely advantaged to excel in the diamond trade? Ethnic and family networks certainly appear to have shaped and fueled the Indian trade. As recently as 2003, over 95 percent of the 2,400 members of India's Gem and Jewelry Export Promotion Council and the leaders of all seven of the nation's largest companies, which control 25 percent of the country's diamond exports, were Palanpuri Jain. And family and community relationships appear to be at work in India, just as they are in New York, in overcoming the transactional hazards inherent in dealing in diamonds. Family networks are evident in each Indian company, and Indian family businesses stretch from Mumbai into the world's other cutting and distribution centers. One Jain diamond merchant in Antwerp remarked, "What are my company's assets? You won't find them in the safe. They're in my family. My family has been in this business for sixty-five years, and everything my father started is still here" (interview with author, 2013). Another lamented, "This business demands personal attention and trust. Only your family can give both. I have remained a small diamond exporter because I do not have a brother whom I can send to live in Antwerp" (Piramal 1990, 8). Unsurprisingly, studies of Indian businesses identify social structures that, like those of Jewish diamontaires, rely on family, community, and cultural institutions to support their trading networks. An ethnography of Gujarati networks in Central Africa, for example, observed that "the sociologist has little difficulty in seeing how Indian culture generally is conducive to success in trade. [Indians'] culture provides them with the normative basis for effective social cooperation in small, tightly knit kinship, caste, and locality groups"[6] (Dotson and Dotson 1968, 66).

Moreover, interviews with Jain diamontaires reveal that family and ethnic networks are critical precisely because they overcome the transactional hazards so central in diamond credit sales. Like for Jewish diamontaires, family businesses create a network enabling merchants to credibly commit to pay (one Palanpuri merchant told me, "Your family is your foundation, why your business can grow and be successful. People trust you more if your family is in the business. They know that if something happens to you, there are still people to be responsible. I know I can get your brother, or your son, or your cousin to pay if you cannot."). And like Jewish merchants, Palanpuri Jain communities also dispense extralegal psychic rewards and punishments to their members that induce cooperation in the industry ("People are motivated by social peers. You don't want your community to see you as a failure, to know you went bankrupt, you don't want people not to marry your children. You want to please social peers, you want your children to be respected by social peers."). Despite the obvious differences between Jewish and Palanpuri communities, family and community institutions in each provide the transactional governance required to thrive in the diamond industry.

Manuel Gomez, a legal scholar who has studied Jain merchant communities extensively, makes a more culture-specific argument. Gomez (2013a, 2013b) suggests that certain attributes of Jainism and the Jain community are instrumental in navigating the diamond industry. Jainism's theology emphasizes asceticism, with its monks and spiritual leaders committing themselves to sometimes severe pledges of austerity. And Jain religious tradition is often described as a rejection of, and an effort historically to distinguish itself from, Hinduism's hierarchical caste system (Dundas 2002). Gomez reports that this emphasis on humility and rejection of hierarchy are reflected in Jain diamond businesses:

> What I observed during my research was remarkable but not surprising. The [Jain] community had an impressive capacity for consensus building and, unlike other ethnic groups of merchants operating in the same sector, was committed to addressing their business disputes

in a non-adversarial manner. . . . The community seems to favor consensus building and other conciliatory techniques to the arbitration that used to be the norm in the industry for many years. Even in those cases where arbitration was contractually binding, there appeared to be a significant interest within the community to attempt to conciliate first. . . . Jain merchants [also] seem to prefer relying on non-punitive measures that focus on the potential for rehabilitation, than for punishing the offender for past misdeeds. . . . From my preliminary observations, it seems that these other efficiencies have certainly played a role in the fast ascent of the Guajarati diamond merchants to the apex of the global trade, and has also contributed to strengthening their own community. (Gomez 2013a, 26)

Jainism's egalitarian and consensus-oriented values appear to be embedded within these Jain diamond companies, and perhaps Gomez is correct that these firm qualities contribute to their success.[7] They are, however, starkly different from the legalistic values—the deference to legal texts and to rabbinic authorities—that Botticini and Eckstein attribute to the success of Jewish merchants. In fact, they seem somewhat diametrically opposite: Jain success relies on consensus, whereas Jewish success relies on the acceptance of authority; Jain success relies on conciliation and rehabilitation, whereas Jewish success relies on adherence to legal codes.

The stark cultural differences between the two ethnic groups—Jews and Jains—who have succeeded most dramatically in the diamond industry should give pause to Gomez and others who might draw a causal link between cultural traditions and success as diamontaires. (In general, as the Weber-Sombart debate over cultural determinism illustrates, it is a tall order to claim that certain cultural attributes best contribute to commercial success.) The cultural dissimilarities between Jains and Jews might suggest that specific traditions or theologies are less relevant than the common structure of these tightly knit ethnic groups. What is instrumental to commercial success is the insularity and intimacy of these communities, along perhaps with their histories of being ostracized minorities, and this intimacy creates the many community linkages that interlock merchants with each other and that facilitate transactional governance. These structural linkages mobilize coordinated punishment, make flight unlikely, and induce a craving for community goods and acceptance. Community institutions arise to serve these functions regardless of the particular belief system in which those institutions operate. Perhaps we can conclude that cultural particularities are irrelevant because the cultures of those who succeed contrast so sharply, and that the institutions are important because the institutions are similar across these minority communities.

One shortcoming of discounting culture entirely is that diamontaires themselves believe it to be important. The diverse players in the diamond industry, despite their enormously different cultural backgrounds, almost uniformly link their economic success with their particular community traditions. Ultra-Orthodox Jewish diamontaires often speak of the centrality of their religious devotion when explaining both their commitment to trust and their adherence to industry and arbitration rules. They invoke principles of Jewish law when distinguishing honorable from dishonorable behavior, explaining why reputations are important, and describing how personal information ought to be shared among merchants. Jain merchants show similar community pride—and visibly highlight certain cultural features—when explaining their community's success. Are these explanations to be ignored as ex post justifications and cultural pride?

There might be a middle ground to this debate, somewhere between the "culture matters" and "culture is irrelevant" poles of debate. Perhaps culture plays an instrumental role, but different cultural attributes play different roles in different communities. In other words, cultural traditions can be instrumental through a variety of mechanisms, and therefore we observe that different combinations and expressions of cultural traditions support ethnic merchants that thrive in the diamond industry.

What is undisputed is that the diamond industry continues to exhibit enormous ethnic diversity and offers a fertile market in which ethnic networks continue to prosper. Indeed, several ethnic communities, in addition to Palanpuri Jains, have entered and thrived in India's diamond industry. One fascinating example is the *Angadias*, which in Gujarati means "one who carries valuables" or "trustworthy person" and whom a Canadian documentary called "the Icemen." Approximately two hundred Angadia firms, employing five thousand to seven thousand couriers recruited only from the Patel community in Gujarat's Mehsana district, transport diamonds and other valuables between Mumbai's diamond center and Gujarat's cutting factories. Angadias have traveled the Mumbai-Gujarat route for more than 125 years, beginning with camel caravans delivering payments from the British raj to Gujarati farmers, and they continue as trusted couriers of valuable parcels. A typical troupe of thirty Angadias—plainly dressed, unarmed, and carrying unmarked canvas sacks—will travel third class on express trains and transport $4 million in diamonds each day (one evening transport, intercepted by tax authorities, was worth an estimated $25 million) while earning salaries of less than $50 a month. Angadia networks also provide banking services, using their networks to deliver cash payments to addresses throughout Mumbai and Gujarat.

Angadias are another group that thrives in the diamond trade precisely because of their ability to impart trust and to credibly commit to refraining from stealing valuables. The Angadia community also exhibits many of the same structures as the ultra-Orthodox Jewish workers in New York's diamond industry. Ethnic, family, and community relations bind the Angadias, who come from the same Kadava Patel clan and pay homage to the same Hindu goddess, Umiya Mata. And like New York's Jewish merchants, Angadias incorporate language and rituals into their professional routines. They routinely visit the Umiya Mata Temple, asking for blessings and protection before venturing as couriers, and references to trust, honor, honesty, and kinship pervade their language. One Angadia leader told the *Wall Street Journal*, "Angadias like me will bring only persons that we know into the business because our personal honor and career is at stake" (Karp 1999), and another told a documentary film company, "The basis of our work is trust, the people who we work with trust us a lot" (Kumar 2009).

There is much more that motivates Angadias than virtue and platitudes, and, consistent with notions of calculative trust, the Angadia networks rely heavily on community institutions to support the trust they earn. The role institutions play in organizing and disciplining Angadia networks is illustrated most clearly in the deliberate process of Angadia recruitment. Although Angadia companies maintain offices in the region's transport hubs of Mumbai and Gujarat's large cities, such as Surat and Ahmedabad, their proprietors come from Gujarat's smaller rural villages, and they return to their home villages to recruit additional Angadia couriers. When a prospective courier contacts an Angadia company and requests consideration for employment, Angadia company managers ask village elders about the possible recruit and often require a village member to sponsor the applicant.

They then assign a veteran Angadia to mentor the potential recruit, and when employment begins, they are entrusted first with low-risk tasks (such as driving other Angadias between train stations). Veteran Angadias often return to their villages after serving as active couriers—the work is dangerous, and they look forward to concluding active service—and then assist in recruiting new Angadias. Accordingly, any Angadia misbehavior leads to adverse consequences for a village member's standing in the community, and, reciprocally, well-performing Angadias can expect long-standing economic and psychic benefits to continued employment, including retiring to one's village while remaining connected to the lucrative Angadia network.

Another element to Angadias' success might lie outside their trust-based networks and relates to Angadias' place in India's caste system. Angadias are predominantly from the lower Shudra castes, who traditionally occupied low social status and suffered from the deepest inequalities and stigmas (the Palanpuri Jain communities that control the diamond trade are of the higher Kshatriya and Vaishya castes). Youths from the rural villages in which Angadias are recruited enjoy few economic opportunities, and Shudras are sadly victims of frequent and unpunished violence. If India's criminal justice system fails to punish and prevent the infliction of physical punishment on Angadias, it is possible that the threat of physical violence (with little legal recourse) induces couriers to comply with their duties in part out of fear of further abuse to themselves and their family members.

In addition to Palanpuris and Angadias, India's diamond market has also seen the growth of other ethnic trading networks. In Gujarat, Jain cutting factories are now being supplanted by Kathiawari businesses, which are increasingly renowned as the dominant force of India's diamond trade (as Chapter 8 discusses, certain differences between Kathiawari and Palanpuri entrepreneurs have over time had significant consequences in the diamond trade). Kathiawaris, who are Patidars (a merchant caste) from the Kathiawar Peninsula in Gujarat, historically were farmers who migrated to Gujarat's urban and industrial centers when work became available in Jain-owned cutting factories. Gradually, Kathiawaris acquired expertise in diamond cutting and many assumed managerial, and later ownership, roles in Gujarat's polishing factories. Kathiawaris now control over 50 percent of the diamond trade in Surat, and many Kathiawari companies have become active purchasers of rough stones in Antwerp and Israel (Khanna 2008).

In sum, the emergence of India's diamond industry and its diversity of ethnic networks disposes of any suggestion that the downstream diamond market of dealers, brokers, cutters, and other middlemen is cartelized by Jewish merchants. It appears that the diamond industry is not only open but perhaps even welcoming to new entrants, so much so that the industry is sufficiently nimble to relocate production facilities and reorganize a global distribution chain when efficiencies are available. Yet entrance into the industry has sustained a distinct feel, favoring ethnic networks and family businesses, and appears to be inaccessible to would-be merchants who cannot mobilize an ethnic business network. Although the industry now reflects a dramatically different cultural and geographic profile from a half century ago, merchants have retained what appear to be the institutional features that account for success in the diamond trade. Indian merchants, like Jewish merchants, have relied on family businesses and ethnic-based trust networks, even while their communities have incubated on a different continent and carry very separate histories. And even as Indian businesses have grown while Jewish businesses have shrunk in global importance, both communities continue to compete vigorously while maintaining the networks on which they rely. In the face of global competition, these traditional community structures continue to be economic assets and not historical vestiges.

Ethnic Networks and Development Policy

The diamond industry, and the stateless elements that underlie its success, might be able to speak to broader challenges in economic policy. It is argued here that the necessary ingredient to success in the industry is the ability to enforce executory contracts. In the hierarchy of priorities for promoting economic development in emerging economies, securing contract rights is probably at the very top. No less than Nobel laureate Douglass North has advanced the strong claim that "the inability of societies to develop effective, low-cost enforcement of contracts is the most important source of both historical stagnation and contemporary underdevelopment in the Third World" (North 1990, 54).

The world has by and large listened to North's admonition. International agencies and external donors have invested heavily to promote the rule of law and legal reform in many developing countries (see, for example, Carothers 1998). Even though North cautions that no one has convincingly demonstrated how to develop state institutions that exert the requisite coercion to enforce contracts and property rights without also risking abuse of that coercive power, development strategists have followed a formal "rule of law" recipe to promote economic development. For the most part, the international community has pursued the "rule of law" strategy by aiming primarily to develop state-sponsored, third-party contract enforcement mechanisms. The classical development recipe therefore includes developing independent state-sponsored courts, accompanied by sophisticated financial intermediaries, public administrations, and other hallmarks of a first-world government.

Michael Trebilcock and his coauthors (Trebilcock and Leng 2006; Trebilcock and Mota Prado 2011) have called this strategy of pursuing legal development for economic development the "contract-formalist approach." However, as the diamond industry illustrates, state institutions are not always necessary to promote contract enforcement, and some transactions are even beyond the reach of state courts. Trebilcock observes, accordingly, that an "alternative school of thought has emerged that downplays the need for a formal third-party mechanism for contract enforcement." He calls this alternative school the "contract-informalist perspective" because it acknowledges that "extralegal, socially, or culturally determined norms can and do provide the assurance of stability and predictability necessary to induce participation in private transactions" (1523–1524). In other words, this school recognizes that informal mechanisms can—especially during a nation's early stages of economic development—serve the same roles in facilitating economic growth as conventional formal legal structures. Without diminishing the central importance of developing governmental institutions that secure property and contract rights, there appear to be informal substitutes for formal instruments of property and contract law.

Both law and society scholars and economic historians have long recognized that formal and informal mechanisms alternatively complement, crowd out, and compete with each other in securing economic transactions. Thus Trebilcock's recognition of alternative mechanisms has been similarly made by an assortment of scholars. In the context of economic development, however, Kevin Davis and Trebilcock (2008) remark that some aspects of the informalist school are associated with a "radically skeptical" view of whether legal reforms promote economic development (932). Because informalists understand that social structures can usefully facilitate commercial exchange like well-functioning courts, informalists argue that "it would be unwise for development practitioners to use the quality of a society's legal system as a benchmark for development" (933). In short, because informal mechanisms can thrive and relegate a nation's legal system to a marginal role in informal capitalism, "substantial investments in legal reform are of dubious value" (933–934).

Development practitioners debating the relationship between law and development, according to Davis and Trebilcock, can thus be divided between optimists and skeptics. Optimistic formalists believe that contract rights are advanced by building new legal institutions, and skeptical informalists believe that contract rights are secured through indigenous institutions. Although there is no disagreement over North's identification of contract enforcement as a foundational prerequisite for growth and prosperity, there is a meaningful debate over which institutions should be promoted to achieve that goal.

The diamond industry, with its reliance on indigenous enforcement and its ability—and need—to thrive without state support, has implications for this important challenge of stimulating the economies of emerging markets. It suggests not only that stateless commerce industries can thrive without relying on the state for transactional support but also that insisting on state institutions could be counterproductive. Indeed, India's emergence in the diamond industry offers a poster child for how stateless industries can thrive without first developing a comprehensive legal infrastructure. It also illustrates how valuable stateless commerce can be in bringing wealth to less developed economies.

In fact, stateless networks engineer major commercial activities in many developing economies. One such network receiving praise for its role in supporting emerging financial markets is *hawala,* a financial network that both executes international money transfers and offers a range of financial services, including money conversions, international transfers, and deposit-taking services. Emily Schaeffer (2008) describes *hawala* as a quintessential stateless network:

> *Hawala* is a set of money transfer networks in operation since ancient times, having emerged in the context where formal enforcement of internal transactions by rulers and governments was non-existent. As international trade began to emerge in South Asia in the 11th century, *hawala* networks soon became important to facilitating exchange. Moreover, these networks continue to operate today, as they did in the past, relying on reputation mechanisms and signaling to sustain coordination despite their illegality in most countries. . . . These practices represent long-standing Islamic traditions developed in various forms across the regions of the Middle East and South Asia. . . . *Hawala* first emerged to facilitate trade across geographical, political and cultural borders in a context of weak, absent or conflicting formal institutions. In many cases, individuals chose the informal services as a direct result of generally poor provision of additional banking services by the state. *Hawala* operates by transferring funds through clearing systems that minimize the costly shipment of coin and bullion. Over time, these needs led to the development of networks of lenders and businessmen that could transfer funds, often without physical currency changing hands. (96–99)

Many development experts have taken note of *hawala* as a valuable economic engine. A 2003 World Bank report praises Afghanistan's *hawaladars* for having "provided the most reliable, convenient, safe, and inexpensive means of transferring funds to far-flung regions" (Maimbo 2003, 1). *Hawaladars* provide sources of credit where the formal banking sector cannot while relying on "unwritten but nevertheless well-established codes of business practice" (5).

Both Schaeffer and the World Bank report that *hawala* networks rely on mechanisms that closely resemble those employed by diamond merchants. Schaeffer (2008) writes that "four mechanisms bind exchange: shared belief systems, repeated dealings, interconnectedness of additional business practices, and the structure of debts and credits" (105). And the World Bank reports that *hawaladors* are reliable "because of the high level of trust that makes the system viable. Dealers know that any failure to honor contracts will result in immediate blacklisting, and possible expulsion, from the market" (Maimbo 2003, 5). Indeed, financial networks often build atop social structures that can substitute for weak or inefficient state enforcement. The rise of microfinance institutions, which make small loans to entrepreneurs in poor nations (and were heralded by the 2006 Nobel Prize committee for stimulating "economic and social development from below" and working to "advance democracy and human rights"), has relied heavily on social and economic extralegal sanctions (Bond and Rai 2002). Because informal institutions play central roles in financing developing nations, reforms that disrupt indigenous financial networks could prevent capital from supporting commerce that formal financial institutions have not reached.

Yet some popular policy recommendations for developing economies can be in tension with fostering indigenous enforcement. It has become conventional wisdom, for example, that an effective competition policy is a necessary ingredient of economic development (see, for example, Kovacic 1997; UNCTAD 1998; Gray and Davis 1993; see generally Sokol, Cheng, and Lianos 2012). Advocates of enhancing antitrust enforcement emphasize the damage of local monopolies and cartels to regional economies, the utility of fostering competitive pricing in international markets, and the importance of prosecuting anticompetitive practices. However, as Chapter 5 illustrates, instituting coordinated punishments usually requires the collaboration of industry participants who normally compete with each other, and thus to an outsider appears to be a group boycott that runs afoul of competition laws. Many private ordering systems rely on mobilizing a group of affiliated merchants to direct coordinated punishments against parties who breach contracts, which in turn creates a group boycott that normally invites antitrust scrutiny. The tension between the priorities of competition law and the need for secure contracts can be put starkly: sometimes, cartels are needed to enforce contracts.

The need for reliable contract enforcement, and the necessary reliance on indigenous institutions that mobilize like cartels, offers a modest cautionary note against the call for greater antitrust—and specifically, anticartel—enforcement in the developing world. Even though certain enforcement mechanisms resemble instruments that traditionally inflict economic harm, they might be better viewed as procompetitive collaborations that are necessitated by court failures. When indigenous cartels enforce contracts that state courts cannot, there should be a general apprehension about eradicating coordinated boycotts in nations with weak contract law enforcement. Sometimes, cartel-like behavior, by enforcing value-creating contracts, promotes rather than impedes economic development.

The potential for economic growth arising from informal institutions should offer some relief to the skeptics. Not only can certain industries emerge despite the lack of formal legal institutions, but these stateless industries can be built atop a nation's indigenous institutions. To be sure, the promise of stateless commerce is limited, and many industries cannot thrive on indigenous institutions alone; legal reform and formal contract enforcement should therefore remain atop development policy priorities. But precisely because institutional development is so difficult, informalists and skeptics can nonetheless encourage the promotion of economic development atop indigenous institutions. At the very least, we should not pursue development policies that undermine those indigenous institutions and prevent their potential contributions to growth in developing economies.

Conclusion

This chapter explores the outer boundaries of lessons drawn from the diamond industry and considers whether Jewish merchants in modern New York offer insights into economic activity in different communities and in different centuries. If we understand how Jewish diamontaires secure diamond transactions without the aid of modern courts, can we also explain how Jewish merchants throughout time governed commerce before reliable state courts emerged and whether that explains Jewish economic performance for much of the past two millennia? Or how Jewish merchants manage illegal trades, where courts refuse to offer their assistance, and whether that explains the economic functions played by the Mafia or other ethnic-based illegal networks? Can we understand how the profile of the diamond industry has changed dramatically, with the entry of commercial networks organized by very different ethnic groups, and why the diamond industry has thrived so mightily in India? And might there be lessons in how we stimulate economic development in countries where courts and legal institutions remain ineffective? One should always be hesitant when extrapolating lessons learned from one industry in one place led by one distinct ethnic minority. That reticence might be especially apt if the achievements of that distinct minority group in that particular industry are the product of a confluence of unusual historical, religious, political, and economic forces. Nonetheless, if transactional governance is a prerequisite to mutually beneficial exchange, then it is useful to explore the full reach of a specific, particularly effective method of securing transactions. This is especially true when that method takes place within a context where cheating is both extraordinarily tempting and largely beyond the reach of law enforcement.

Or, put more simply, diamond merchants have constructed a self-sustaining market despite enormous practical challenges. Their success is worth understanding, and to the degree possible, their lessons are worth applying elsewhere.

7

Governing Statelessness

To the degree that legal academics are capable of romance, few theories have conjured more romantic enthusiasm than that of the law merchant, the commercial broker credited for reviving trade in medieval Europe by convening commercial fairs and forging international trade routes. Nineteenth-century German lawyer and historian Levin Goldschmidt succinctly articulates the academic adoration: "The grandeur and significance of the medieval merchant is that he creates his own laws out of his own needs and his own views" (quoted in Mitchell 1904, 10). Not only do legal scholars admire a notion of law that emerges voluntarily and organically with substantive rules tailored to address pressing problems, but policy makers—chiefly through the Uniform Commercial Code—have aimed to construct commercial law that reflects the law merchant's ideal.

Even while the entirety of the theory of the law merchant and the law merchant's law—lex mercatoria (literally, "the law of the merchant")—has come under scholarly attack (see, for example, Donahue 2004a, 2004b, 2005), enthusiasm for the law merchant has extended beyond the idealized substance of the merchant's self-made rules. The allure of the law merchant includes perceptions that law merchants also developed organic mechanisms in which they governed themselves. Some argue that what makes lex mercatoria work is that it arises from autonomous communities and not from formal political bodies. Harold Berman (1983) described the medieval law merchants as a community that formed its own mercantile courts, staffed by its own judges who implemented its own rules, to govern commerce in international fairs and markets. This historical narrative has been seized on by some libertarians (for example, Benson 1989) to suggest that merchants' capacity for self-governance obviates the purported need for state coercion to secure contract and property rights. And in a famous economic model, Paul Milgrom, Douglass North, and Barry Weingast (1990) articulate mechanisms through which private judges could enable law merchants to enforce contracts and sustain interregional cooperation through privately ordered reputation mechanisms.

Several scholars have observed, however, that medieval trade did not and could not have relied on the self-policing of merchants, and that enforcement of medieval commercial trade was not as divorced from sovereign authority as some have argued. Stephen Sachs (2006), for example, points to the thirteenth-century abbey of Saint Ives and reports that merchants invoked the coercive power of local courts to adjudicate their disputes and enforce judgments. He thus argues that the medieval merchants relied on the coercive power of the sovereign, and the security of their commercial exchange was derived from state authority. Emily Kadens (2015) similarly writes that the twelfth and thirteenth centuries' commercial fairs "owed their continued existence to their sovereign owners: kings, counts, abbeys—whatever lord had both the right to grant a charter to hold a fair and the power to ensure the protection of the contractual and property rights of buyers and sellers" (260). These recent works echo Sir Richard Atkin's foreword to *The Romance of the Law Merchant* (1923, iii), where he emphasized the reliance of law merchants on underlying sovereign authority. Atkins wrote that the law merchants "made their own rules and administered them summarily at their own courts, with the tacit or express approval of the Sovereign." According to this alternative view, the romance of self-governance veils the realpolitik of sovereign coercion.

Avner Greif (2004a, 2006a) offers a narrative of cross-border exchange that balances the roles of local sovereigns with self-governing merchant communities. Rather than giving exclusive credit to either sovereign or private coercion, Greif instead describes a symbiotic arrangement in describing a "community responsibility system." In Greif's telling, local authorities used the sovereign's coercive authority to enforce contractual claims brought by foreigners against its local citizens. In return, other sovereign authorities used their sovereign authorities to similarly enforce contracts against their own citizens. This reciprocal commitment to enforcing contracts against local citizens—and thus committing local merchants to trustworthy behavior with foreigners—enabled valuable cooperation and intercommunity trade. In other words, the gains from cooperation induced self-sustaining cooperation between merchant communities and their resident sovereigns, and the promises of collective gains motivated continued cross-sovereign collaboration. A hybrid between self-enforced law and state coercion—cooperation between local sovereigns and reputational bonds among merchant communities—forged international trade and facilitated the growth of commercial fairs in the medieval period.

The essence of the Greif model is that local polities need to reliably enforce contracts in order to enable their local merchants to commit credibly to trade with distant partners. Institutional economics has long recognized that political commitments to secure contract and property rights are foundations to attracting investment and trade (North 1990). This is especially true for mobile international merchants who can select among competing polities with various economic environments. It is also especially true for modern industries in which capital assets are highly portable, such as the diamond industry.

This mobility of trade, and in particular the symbiotic relationship such mobility induces between merchant communities and the sovereign, reveals one of the hallmarks of stateless commerce. The key feature of stateless commerce is that the state has meaningful limitations on its ability to secure transactions and govern exchange. The same features that place certain industries beyond the reach of court enforcement also make those industries unbound to any sovereign. These limitations give merchants freedoms that most commercial parties do not have, and they forge an unusual bargain—reflected in the community responsibility system—between merchants of stateless commerce and their hosting polities. These freedoms have important implications for governing stateless commerce and reveal some of the central limitations to state power.

This chapter first explores the relationship between stateless commercial activity and its host polities by reviewing the history of the diamond industry's commercial centers. Because these commercial centers were so mobile and could relocate away from unfriendly hosts to more hospitable polities, local authorities were either locked into favorable policies or saw the local diamond industry relocate. The chapter then relates this mobility to central features of the modern globalized economy and to the political and regulatory challenges that such globalization pose to traditional policymakers.

Diamond Centers and the Challenge of Mobility

The diamond trade has always been a mobile industry. In the late medieval and early modern periods, many of the Jewish merchants organizing diamond and gemstone trading networks in Europe were based in the Spanish empire's port towns. When Catholic governments in Spain and Portugal expelled large numbers of Jews and conversos in the fifteenth and sixteenth centuries, many found refuge in the tolerant Netherlands and brought their diamond trades to Amsterdam. Amsterdam remained hospitable to Jews and the industry for the next several centuries, with Jews helping to finance the Dutch East India Company and controlling much of the import of India's diamonds to Europe, and it remained the trade's global center through the nineteenth century.

In the early twentieth century, though the Netherlands remained a bastion of religious tolerance, Amsterdam's high taxes and rising wages induced many diamond merchants to set up cutting factories elsewhere. At around the same time, Antwerp, which had its own history as a diamond trading hub, became the major embarkation point for the thousands of Eastern European Jews immigrating to the United States. Many, instead of continuing their journey across the Atlantic, found work in Jewish diamond businesses and remained. Antwerp's surge in inexpensive and eager labor coincided with diamond discoveries in South Africa, thus increasing demand for diamond cutting and other labor. By the late 1930s, the diamond center's move from Amsterdam to Antwerp was nearly complete.

Another interesting chapter in the diamond industry's mobility was prompted by the tragic events of World War II. In 1939, the year before the Nazis invaded the Low Countries, Antwerp diamond exports constituted 81 percent of all imports to the United States and Amsterdam exports constituted an additional 9 percent. When Nazi edicts in 1940 started requiring registration of Jewish Dutch and Belgian businesses, Jewish diamantaires began escaping Europe. Many sought refuge in the United States and Palestine, but because immigration was restricted at both destinations, most Jewish diamond merchants were forced to relocate elsewhere across the globe: England, Mexico, Brazil, South Africa, and, most remarkably, Cuba. In each new home, Jewish diamantaires set up cutting factories and continued production (Cuba, which had no history as a diamond center, exported more polished diamonds in 1944 than London; approximately one-third of Cuba's six thousand Jewish refugees worked in makeshift diamond factories alongside native Cuban workers, aided by the Cuban government and Jewish refugee charities). Despite the dramatic global dislocation of Antwerp's diamond dealers, imports of polished diamonds into the United States were never meaningfully disrupted.

After World War II, the outflows of diamontaires from Europe quickly reversed direction. Belgium's in-exile government had maintained close contacts with Jewish diamond dealers scattered throughout the globe, and when the war ended, Belgium's leaders actively recruited those dealers to return. By 1946, most leading Jewish diamontaires were again in Antwerp, leading that city to regain its status as the global diamond center, and by 1947, there was virtually no diamond trade left in Cuba.

Today's diamond industry remains sensitive to geopolitical and economic dynamics, and the same forces that led to Antwerp's ascension are now leading to its decline. India's emergence as a diamond center is due not just to its pioneering diamontaires but also to its low labor costs and supportive government policies, and Gujarati cutting factories can polish and sort diamonds at a fraction of the cost that Antwerp's cutters can. Although Antwerp remains an important locale for trading large quantities of rough diamonds, its ancillary industries have vanished. Whereas Antwerp in the 1970s boasted a skilled diamond-processing labor force of between 25,000 and 30,000, the city now has fewer than 1,000. In contrast, Surat employs some 450,000 cutters, brokers, and couriers.

Economic Globalization

The diamond industry's long history of mobility has made it a global citizen, sensitive to geopolitical and economic forces and adaptive to assorted environments. But the industry also reveals insights into the nature of economic globalization itself.

Perhaps the most salient feature of economic globalization is the ability for firms to capitalize on the availability of low-wage labor in distant countries, and certainly the diamond industry's moves from Amsterdam to Antwerp and later from Antwerp to Gujarat were motivated by these traditional economic forces (India's success in diamond cutting has fueled further globalization, as many diamond dealers have opened cutting factories in low-wage countries in Eastern Europe and Southeast Asia). But another interesting feature of globalization motivated this most recent relocation of the industry's epicenter. The leaders of India's industry, the Jains from Palanpur, showed how a globalized economy can heighten the value of particular skills that are in short supply. Palanpur's Jains had long harbored tacit skills of gem masters, and the democratization of global trade offered a ready international market. Just as the software engineers in Bangalore have been able to collaborate with Western high-tech companies and contribute to the value chain in information technology industries, Palanpuri Jain diamontaires have assembled a global production network. In other words, the rise of India's diamontaires reveals not just the portability of the industry but also how the global distribution chain easily connects skilled Palanpuri cutters to lucrative luxury goods markets in affluent nations. In this respect, India's Palanpuri diamond cutters are globalization's paradigmatic success story—a small community in a remote location that is able to exploit its unique skills to reap fortunes in the global marketplace.

The inevitable flip side is paradigmatic of globalization as well, and the Palanpuris' success has come at the expense of higher-wage cutters in the West. In fact, the Palanpuri cost advantages are so significant, and their entry into the market has been so large, that they have both disrupted the entire global distribution network and have transformed the face of the industry. Following them have been Marwari and Kathiawari family enterprises from other regions of Gujarat, and Antwerp's, New York's, and Tel Aviv's diamond centers are now homes to substantial Indian communities. The look and feel of the diamond industry has transformed. Although diamontaires have always reflected the demands of international commerce, never before has the industry reflected as many cultures, languages, and ethnicities, as it does today.

The diamond industry's global expanse also illustrates how it might be especially suited for the globalized economy. Among the greatest challenges of navigating a global industry are the barriers to securing reliable contract enforcement. International trade introduces both the complexity of multiple sources of law and the lack of a single enforcing polity, and the resulting contractual uncertainty pushes many transnational industries away from state-sponsored law and toward new forms of private ordering (Appelbaum,

Felstiner, and Gessner 2001; Konradi 2009). But because the diamond industry has always relied on nonstate contract enforcement and reputation mechanisms, it avoids the usual legal pitfalls of transnational commerce. Precisely because the diamond industry is stateless, its millennia-old distribution system resting on layers of personal exchange is thriving in a globalized market.

For this reason, the Palanpuris' recent success reflects the flourishing of other ethnic trading networks in the modern globalized economy. It is well documented that the wildly successful Chinese ethnic trading networks, for example, continue to capitalize on extralegal certainty to organize transnational commerce in Southeast Asia (Landa 1999). These networks excel in the uncertain legal environment of international commerce for the same reason they thrive in the diamond industry. Commercial networks that can navigate the diamond market, where routine transactions are beyond the reach of public courts and require extralegal enforcement, excel in global exchange since cross-national transactions are also routinely difficult to enforce. The Palanpuris' centuries-old experience with diamond transactions, which were always imbued with legal uncertainty, prepared them for the legal uncertainty in transnational exchange. It might be ironic that trading practices that rest on ancient family or ethnic traditions—thought to have been replaced by sophisticated government institutions—can suddenly offer an advantage in the ever-modernizing global economy. Nonetheless, these institutional capabilities are the key to the success of ethnic trading networks. Being adept at domestic extralegal commerce makes them well equipped for international extralegal commerce.

However, even with these advantages, relational exchange has limits, and continued globalization will pose a severe test to the durability of the diamond industry's ethnic networks. Since reputation-based exchange works only with familiarity, relational networks will fail when their expansions dilute the intimacy the members share. Economic history contains many illustrations of reputation-based systems of contractual enforcement that became victims of their own success—transactional credibility broke down when parties were sufficiently unfamiliar that they could (and did) misrepresent themselves as reliable, long-term commercial partners (Greif 2006a). The continued expansion of diamond networks will strain the institutional capacities of relational exchange, and diamond merchants might have to find alternative systems to organize distribution. (This challenge of expansion is addressed in Chapter 8.)

Globalization's invitation to ethnic-based exchange brings other challenges as well. As Palanpuri diamontaires and other ethnic networks find themselves capable of thriving in the international marketplace, they will encounter one of globalization's more interesting dilemmas: how members of different ethnic networks can engage in commerce—and enforce contracts—with each other. If each member is beyond the reach of public courts, and thus can only be disciplined by other members of his or her network, then extralegal methods are required to secure transactions between parties from different relational circles. Theoretically, communities will be incentivized to police their own members in trade with other groups precisely for the same reasons that medieval merchant communities developed the community responsibility system. Putting this into practice, however, will require political resolve within each community, and coordinating transactional assurance becomes harder as each trading community grows and familiarity inevitably decreases. One potential solution would model how diamond markets, such as New York, have enabled cross-ethnic trade through local bourses. Such local institutions can create an institutional framework to coordinate cross-ethnic cooperation and facilitate coordinated sanctions against parties that jeopardize the reputation of their community. Ethnic networks might be ideally suited to enter and prosper in global exchange, but their decentralized structure makes local cooperation with other ethnic trading partners difficult. Just as the community responsibility system relied on an institutional symbiosis with other enforcement mechanisms, today's ethnic networks might similarly rely on complementary institutions as globalization strains their enforcement capabilities.

Still, absent international polities that can assert jurisdiction over international trade and reliably enforce contracts between international parties, we can expect a persistence of stateless relational exchange in global commerce. This despite conventional wisdom that relational exchange is inferior to systems of arm's-length transactions and impersonal exchange, and despite the irony that ancient community customs have meaningful economic advantages in the most modern economic environment.

International Regulation and Private Global Governance

Globalization has also meant the entry of diamond merchants of a very different kind. Throughout much of the 1990s, rebel movements and warlords in war-torn African nations, such as Angola, Sierra Leone, and the Democratic Republic of Congo, exploited diamond mines in their countries to fuel bloody campaigns. The diamond's immutable qualities make it the smuggler's and guerrilla's currency of choice, and it was estimated at one point that as much as 15 percent of the global supply consisted of conflict diamonds or blood diamonds, diamonds sold to finance military insurgencies or illegal warlords (GAO 2002; Global Witness 2006).

Turning a blind eye to the unpleasant origins of a product marketed to affluent consumers in developed nations might also be a central feature of globalized commerce. Salient examples include sweatshops manufacturing designer clothing, children forgoing school to assemble athletic equipment, and natural resource exploration that pollutes natural habitats (Spar and La Mure 2003). Stark inequalities in both wages and purchasing habits between the developing and developed worlds create tremendous incentives to produce in the former and sell in the latter, which fuels the growing separation of a product's origins from its ultimate consumer (Kysar 2004; Friedman 2005).

But this separation creates a particularly acute danger for the diamond industry. Diamonds are marketed, with remarkable success, as timeless ornaments to signify important emotional events—the sort of product that would be quickly spoiled if associated with a brutal warlord. The possibility that the purchase of the engagement ring might sponsor bloody civil strife threatened the core of the industry's highly successful advertising efforts and attacked the root of a diamond's romantic appeal. It became a grave concern for the entire industry.

An easy solution was not obvious. Because the structure of the diamond industry's distribution network relies on many layers of middlemen, and because of the diamond's essential features, tracing a diamond's origins is more difficult than it is other goods, such as designer apparel manufactured by sweatshop labor. Consequently, the industry for many decades overlooked the ugly origins of much of its product. Diamond dealer networks have long operated in Africa and purchased diamonds from military warlords. Conflict diamonds were routinely funneled to Antwerp and other diamond centers and mixed in with diamonds from less controversial sources. The independence and multitude of the diamond dealers, the industry's lack of vertical integration, and the inability to trace a diamond's origins made prohibiting and policing sales of conflict diamonds extremely difficult.

But the threat to global demand was too severe to ignore, particularly as NGOs and social activists—with London-based Global Witness in the lead—organized highly effective media campaigns. The industry, led by De Beers, was compelled to develop a sweeping response, and following a United Nations General Assembly resolution, diamond-producing nations met in Kimberley, South Africa, in 2000 to develop a collective response. The end product, the Kimberley Process Certification Scheme ("Kimberley Process") was finalized in 2002 and implemented in 2003.

The core of the Kimberley Process is a vast international program that is part certification and part coordinated boycott. It requires each diamond-exporting nation to label and certify that its diamond exports do not finance entities seeking to overthrow a UN-recognized government, and it obligates each member nation (currently eighty-one countries, including all major diamond markets) to prohibit diamond trade with nonmember countries. Kimberley Process membership is granted only to conflict-free nations that can comply with its transparency, labeling, and export control requirements.

The Kimberley Process requirements are transparently designed to assure would-be diamond purchasers in affluent nations. It requires that each international shipment of rough diamonds is transported in a tamper-resistant container and accompanied by a government-verified certificate that indicates the origin of each stone. The importing state's customs must then confirm that the contents of the shipment are in accord with the certificate, and each individual who thereafter handles the stone is obligated to maintain the identity tag. In theory, it provides jewelry manufacturers—reflecting the interests of engagement ring purchasers and other romantics—proof that the diamonds they purchase come from wholesome origins. Peddlers of conflict diamonds should have much greater difficulty finding buyers, and conflict diamonds should have greater difficulty slipping into the mainstream pipeline.

For a number of reasons, De Beers was eager to cooperate with the United Nations and the global activists demanding restraints on industry leaders. One reason was that the Kimberley Process removed the specter of blood diamonds and allowed the industry to distinguish conflict diamonds from what were soon called "conflict-free diamonds." It thus removed a core threat to demand for its products. In addition, the Kimberley Process removed conflict diamonds from the global market and excluded a source of competition, giving De Beers a larger market share. The *New York Times*, reporting De Beers' embrace of the blood diamonds controversy, stated that "the company has effectively enlisted the United Nations as a policeman to do the job that dictators and mercenaries once did in keeping more desperate competitors from dumping cheaper stones onto the market." Longtime industry observer Edward Jay Epstein called it "another brilliant coup" (Cowell 2000).

De Beers' nimble handling of the conflict diamonds controversy also marked a change in the company's corporate strategy to keep pace with the new politics of globalization. The company shifted its marketing strategy from one designed to stimulate consumption of all diamonds to a branding strategy highlighting the uniqueness of De Beers' diamonds. The marketing of the company's branded "Forevermark" diamonds includes a pledge to political sensibilities: "We keep careful track of Forevermark diamonds throughout the cutting and polishing process to ensure that each Forevermark diamond is natural, untreated, and conflict-free."[1] De Beers also began emphasizing the company's effort to position itself more broadly as a socially responsible company, investing in Africa's long-term development and committing itself to sharing the wealth from diamonds with the local populations (De Beers' recent corporate maneuverings are portrayed flatteringly in a 2009 Harvard Business School case study entitled "Addressing the New Competitiveness Challenges" [Porter, Marciano, and Warhurst 2009]). The Forevermark promise now assures that they are "Responsibly Sourced," that "throughout their journey from rough to polished diamonds, particular care has been taken to ensure responsible business practices, support for the advancement of women and protection of the natural world, which is the ultimate source of our diamonds." (De Beers' changing strategies, and their impact on the global diamond market, are discussed in greater detail in Chapter 8.)

More broadly, the Kimberley Process itself illustrates a new trend in modern international governance. The lack of public governance in global exchange has prompted a rise in what some have called "private governance" (Gereffi and Mayer 2005). Private governance includes self-regulation by multinational corporations, codes of conduct promulgated by international organizations and trade associations, and consumer standards—including the famous "fair trade" movement—that impose minimum labor or production standards. It is not unprecedented, nor is it unreasonable, for for-profit corporations to join those demanding private governance and collaborate with social activists to bring reform. Such cooperation has been dubbed "the NGO-industrial complex" (Gereffi, Garcia-Johnson, and Sasser 2001).

But this sort of international scrutiny and regulation is quite new to the diamond industry even though, unlike other industries that have only recently globalized, international distribution networks had always been required to bring diamonds from mines to jewelry stores. The globalization of industries such as textiles and chemicals prompted consumer alarm, and the mobilization of international private governance emerged because the internationalization of those industries meant less legal and political oversight. The diamond industry, in contrast, was always globalized and had received relatively little scrutiny (despite brutal treatment of workers in diamond mines, poor labor relations in many cutting factories, and, of course, the prevalence of conflict diamonds). Thus, the politics of globalization has meant something very different to the diamond industry. Ironically, globalization has meant the involvement of more, not less, consumer regulation and political scrutiny. Moreover, the regulatory structures arose to create a legal certainty of a different kind: global oversight mechanisms now provide consumers with regulatory compliance certainty. They aim to solve a transactional hazard between the diamond seller and the uninformed but socially aware consumer.

There is evidence that the Kimberley Process has meaningfully limited the flow of conflict diamonds—current estimates are that less than 1 percent of the current diamond supply is sourced from insurgencies. Certainly the end of civil wars in Angola and Sierra Leone helped quell conflict supply (both countries are now members of the Kimberley Process). But the transparency of the Kimberley Process implementation, the integrity of the certifications, and the overall effectiveness of the regime remain a matter for ongoing debate. In 2011, Global Witness left the Kimberley Process as an observer, citing the process's lack of effective monitoring and accusing the regime's leadership of not seriously addressing problematic diamonds originating in Zimbabwe and the Ivory Coast. That same year, an *India Today* journalist reported watching diamond dealers in Surat trading conflict diamonds from the Ivory Coast, selling at a 30 percent discount from similar conflict-free diamonds. Moreover, there are periodic reports of how conflict diamonds fuel terrorism—al-Qaeda evidently purchased between $10 million and $20 million of conflict diamonds from Sierra Leone in the months before the September 11 attacks—and the diamond trade remains vulnerable to money laundering and other illegal industries.

One South African reporter who has worked in the diamond trade had a more damning indictment of the Kimberley Process: "In reality, blood diamonds are a giant hoax. All over Africa, tens of thousands of diggers and traders make an honest living finding and selling stones. They carry no guns and do not trade with warlords. Few of them know anything about the [Kimberley Process]. Once the stones leave Kinshasa or Luanda, the exporter simply tidies up the paperwork for the recipient in Brussels, Tel Aviv or Mumbai. It can be done in hours. Every time. Without fail. Even if the stones are sourced in conflict areas, it is guaranteed that for a small fee they can be laundered through the KPC process and end up on someone's finger in North America or Europe" (Ryan 2010). This critique of the Kimberley Process is more than just a charge that it is ineffective. It goes to the heart of the challenge of private governance. Without a governing polity to secure regulatory compliance, the global community requires cooperation among a patchwork of entities. Such a coalition can be an inadequate substitute for a reliable and politically accountable state—certainly the Kimberley Process appears to be falling short of its promises—but it might serve quite effectively as a rhetorical tool for citizens and consumers seeking assurance. Such a coalition might also function as a cartel that excludes various sorts of competition. The nature of private governance is that it can appear to be an expedient mechanism to assure consumers when in reality it is designed to secure market power.

What lessons can be drawn from the diamond industry's experience with the politics of globalization? Prior to the swell of globalization, the diamond industry seemed to avoid the scrutiny it probably deserved. Just as its transactions remained beyond the reach of public courts, the industry's practices remained largely beyond the attention of social activists and constituencies that demand regulatory oversight. These parallel trends of nesting outside the public arena are interconnected. Since the industry was forced to rely on self-governance to police transactions and enforce contracts, it assumed a self-regulatory governance structure that distrusted outsiders and demanded regulatory autonomy.

But the international politics of globalization—and growing discomfort from separating the production and consumption of globally marketed goods—brought scrutiny to multinational corporations that previously escaped regulation in the industrialized democracies. When political NGOs scrutinized the role of multinational corporations in the developing world, such scrutiny naturally included De Beers. Diamond sellers now need global private governance to assure consumers, and a private, multilateral regulatory regime replaced unsupported anonymous transactions. Perhaps the general statelessness of globalization has meant the end to lawlessness in the diamond industry, however imperfect cooperative private governance might be.

Conclusion

The diamond industry's mobility is one of its defining features, and it has played a central role in characterizing the industry's relationship with sovereign polities, just as mobility framed the interplay between medieval merchant communities and their local sovereigns. The rise of economic globalization has only accentuated the industry's unusual features. Globalization has ushered in low-wage ethnic groups that have displaced Jewish merchants that long dominated the downstream market, and the industry's epicenter has moved again. Globalization has also brought political scrutiny to an industry that previously enjoyed secrecy, autonomy, and lawlessness, and it required industry leaders to adapt to a new political landscape.

The diamond industry's engagement with globalization also yields insights into globalization itself. The lawlessness of transnational exchange means that ethnic networks that have historically employed extralegal mechanisms to enforce transactions are particularly well suited to excel in the globalized economy. The absence of public regulation to govern global commerce has led to private governance, which ironically might reach and influence secretive international networks, such as the diamond networks, more than traditional state-sponsored regulation. And the shortcomings of the diamond industry's Kimberley Process reveal the real limitations of private global governance—its enforcement deficiencies, its delegation of public policymaking to private authority, and its danger of facilitating an industrial stranglehold on markets and politics.

The diamond industry's forays in international politics also reveal that certain governance challenges have not abated since the medieval period. The mobility of assets presents a sustained challenge to the jurisdictional and mechanical limits of the sovereign. Just as the institutional constraints of both the medieval sovereign and modern government invite the emergence of privately ordered trading networks, so do the institutional constraints of geopolitical regimes invite assorted efforts at private governance.

8

The Limits of Statelessness and an Autopsy of Cooperation

> When I first entered the business, the conception was that truth and trust were simply *the* way to do business, and nobody decent would consider doing it differently. Although many transactions are still consummated on the basis of trust and truthfulness, this is done because these qualities are viewed as good for business, a way to make a profit.
>
> —*Elderly diamond dealer, quoted in Bernstein (1992)*

> It used to be like that. It's not like that anymore.
>
> —*Longtime diamond dealer to author on 47th Street, 2015*

MUTUAL TRUST has been the cornerstone of the diamond industry's narrative. A *New York Times* reporter in 1984 marveled at how diamontaires "trust each other not to walk away with the world's most valuable, easily concealed commodity" (Starr 1984). Lisa Bernstein (1992) reported that obtaining access to a supply of rough diamonds requires "maintain[ing] a reputation for scrupulous honesty" (119). And popular authors, attracted to the romance of the diamond trade, have extolled the virtues of trust among merchants, intimate family businesses, and communities built around the moral fiber of business ethics. Russell Shor (1993), a prominent diamond industry journalist, wrote, "Legal and moral accountability is the foundation for the very survival of the diamond trade" ("Even if one percent of the dealers were dishonest," a dealer tells Shor, "that trust would be destroyed and so would our industry") (12). Renée Rose Shield (2002) relates in a beautiful ethnography of 47th Street that "formal contracts are unnecessary since informal contracts are heavy with moral weight and embody certain principles: to honor commitments, to produce a good product and to stand behind it, and to preserve reputation" (102). And journalist and child of diamond dealers Alicia Otulski (2011) echoes what the New York Times observed almost thirty years earlier: "At any given moment on Forth-seventh Street a dealer may be in possession of hundreds of thousands of dollars' worth of another man's diamonds. Usually, he has not paid the owner any collateral, only his word. . . . In this business, everything works on credit, loan, and trust" (7).

When I started studying the diamond industry in 2000, I heard many of the same stories of trust reigning within the trade. Mutual trust bound diamontaires to their pledges and to each other, and such trust-based exchange served as a substitute for state-sponsored courts and conventional law. These stories illustrated how an insular merchant community could construct social networks that sustain mutually beneficial trade, despite the enormous risk posed by cheating (Richman 2004, 2006). They served not only as the backbone for academic understandings of the industry but also as proof of how arbitration, reputations, and social networks could fully supplant the state-sponsored legal system (see, for example, Bernstein 1992).

But gradually, the stories I heard changed. Consider one typical telling from a diamond dealer in Antwerp in 2013: "There are not many frauds, not many thieves. People trust and try to make deals work for both sides. But there are some people who cheat. . . . And they reenter the business, by putting the company in a relative's name, by paying with cash and getting new contacts and new trust. That's what happened to me, I was cheated and I see the cheater back on the streets here. There's nothing I can do about it." He told me this story only after repeating the familiar platitudes of trust among diamontaires, how earning and maintaining trust is necessary to succeed. But when he shared this recent and clearly painful experience, he opened up; he expressed regret for what the industry has become and conceded that he is urging his son and nephew to pursue alternative careers. The return of an undisputed cheater is difficult to reconcile with the traditions and norms of the industry in which he was raised and to which he has devoted many decades. Many other dealers share his deep disappointment in what has become of the diamond industry and agree that the deterioration of the proverbial bonds of trust marks a meaningful change in the world of diamond merchants.

My interviews over the years followed this same arc: I was told of widespread mutual trust in 2000, then heard a growing number of reports of dishonest conduct in the years that followed, and now I hear mostly laments that the industry is no longer what it was. Current interviews with dealers and revelations in industry publications report that persistent and calculative cheating is becoming almost commonplace. Dealers fail to pay for items purchased on credit and yet return to the industry. "Upgrading," which occurs when a dealer purchases gems with certain Gemological Institute of America (GIA) grades (on clarity, color, carat, and cut) and then convinces gem evaluators to give those same gems higher grades, is becoming increasingly common. A variety of laser treatments are used to enhance diamond color and clarity without necessary disclosures to subsequent buyers. And there are growing instances of synthetic diamonds, which have market values approximately 30 percent lower than corresponding natural diamonds, being mixed with and presented as natural diamonds (Rapaport 2013; Sherman 2014). The growing deceitfulness prompted one longtime industry observer to tell me succinctly, "It doesn't pay to be honest anymore. When you're honest, you're viewed as a sucker."

Trust is even breaking down within what legal scholars might call the diamond industry's crown jewel: its private arbitration system. When Bernstein brought the New York Diamond Dealers Club's (DDC) arbitration to scholars' attention in 1992, she reported that it "enables parties to resolve disputes and enforce judgments quickly, inexpensively, and secretly" (148). She further heralded the arbitration system for exhibiting expertise, accuracy, discretion, and fidelity, and other industry admirers lavished the DDC's private legal system with similar praise. Shield (2002) described the "courtly system of arbitration" as "the crowning achievement of the diamond business" and said it "is emblematic of how trust and reputation are the stellar symbols of the trade" (7).

Recent portrayals of the DDC have not been as flattering. An industry watchdog remarked, "In recent years we have witnessed a serious erosion of [mutual] trust" in the industry's arbitration system, and increasingly, there are "bourse members who believe that an Israeli arbitration panel will always decide against a New York party and that a New York arbitration panel will always go against an Israeli party in the dispute" (Even-Zohar 2008a, 1–2).

And problems of the arbitration system's integrity have been dogging the DDC. There is a growing incidence of judgments rendered in absentia, where one party, usually a nonmember of the presiding bourse, claims not to have received fair notice before a default judgment is rendered against him. DDC arbitrators have been accused of being complicit in schemes by fellow DDC members to swindle consumers with inflated and fraudulent GIA certificates. For some, the problems concerning DDC arbitration are reaching a crisis point, compelling one observer to confide in an e-mail that "the quality of [DDC] arbitration (i.e., the kind of justice that is being rendered) has so deteriorated, that people are resigning their Diamond Dealers Club membership, to avoid the chance that in a business dispute they may be forced to agree to arbitration." As a result, a leading industry expert has lamented that "the DDC, once upon a time one of the most important and prestigious bourses in the world, sees its membership declining" (Even-Zohar 2008b, 4676).

DDC leadership, rather than being a bulwark against declining trust, appears to be contributing to the credibility decline. A report commissioned in 2011 revealed that the club, from 2006 to 2009, suffered from severe financial mismanagement, a failure of leadership, and frequent accounting irregularities. An accompanying exposé reported "unapproved or unjustifiable expenses incurred by the club's president, the granting of questionable loans, and activities hidden from the board of directors" (Even-Zohar 2011, 1). These reports followed a particularly ugly internal legal battle, in which a vice president of the DDC sued the Club and its president for engineering questionable procedural maneuvers, including permitting select nonmembers to participate in a vote that awarded the then president additional terms (see *Abraham v. Diamond Dealers Club, Inc.*, 914 N.Y.S. 152 (2011)). Allegedly, the president's central motivation for maintaining his office was to bestow favors to certain colleagues, including exempting membership fees and rigging arbitration decisions. It seems that not only is trust eroding among diamontaires, but the institutions designed to sustain trust throughout the industry are losing credibility.

This concluding chapter examines the developments that have brought such stark changes to 47th Street and have led longtime industry observer Chaim Even-Zohar to remark that "the diamond industry is in the middle of a constructive upheaval" (2007, 1). Specifically, it investigates the causes of why trust is breaking down—or, in accordance with an economist's explanation, why so many diamond dealers now find short-term strategies more attractive than long-term strategies associated with investing in and preserving a good reputation. And, like the rest of this book, it aims to derive broader lessons from the diamond experience for stateless commerce. It reviews the many structural changes that have taken place in the past twenty years to each of the industry's three major market levels—diamond production, retail sales, and middleman markets—and it investigates how these changes might explain why the benefits of cooperation no longer overcome the temptations for short-term gains. Since the diamond industry has been held as the paradigmatic industry in which reputations and private ordering govern exchange, the demise of cooperation in the industry has implications for foundational scholarship that had presupposed the industry's ongoing cooperation. The article revisits some of these seminal discussions and aims to derive implications from the diamond experience for the sustainability of statelessness.

Disruption in Production and De Beers' Changing Strategy

Writing about De Beers as it approached the year 2000, a Harvard Business School case study observed, "De Beers was accustomed to chaos. The company thrived on it, and had long ago learned to master it. But the millennium posed new challenges—serious challenges with the potential to undermine De Beers's legendary power and compel a rethinking of its strategy" (Spar 2000, 2). The "chaos" is the vicissitudes of a volatile commodities market combined with the demand elasticity of luxury goods, and De Beers' success throughout the market rested on its ability to assert control over the diamond market. As is discussed in Chapter 2, De Beers enjoyed monopoly control over the sale and distribution of rough diamonds for nearly a century. It either owned or secured exclusive contracts with a majority of the world's mining interests, and through its Central Selling Organization (CSO) it deliberately distributed its supplies through handpicked sightholders. Sitting atop the diamond distribution chain, De Beers was able to control what was sold each year, and it invested in sustaining global demand through creative advertising strategies and the direction of distribution chains. Whenever additional sources of rough diamonds threatened to enter the market, De

Beers swiftly entered into exclusive purchasing arrangements with the new suppliers (Spar 2000, 5). Whenever supply began to exceed demand and threatened to dampen market prices for polished diamonds, the company would show its determination to be a buyer of last resort, stockpiling rough gems to sustain stable prices (Spar 2000, 5, 9–10).

In the late 1990s, however, this decades-old strategy started to fray, and changes to diamond supply "began to hint at a very different structure for the world's diamond market and . . . De Beers" (Spar 2000, 9). Diamond mines discovered in Australia in the 1980s and in Canada in the 1990s began resisting De Beers' control and started selling rough diamonds outside De Beers' CSO in 1996; De Beers' agreement to purchase Russia's enormous production, forged in 1990 when Russia desperately needed hard currency, expired in 1995 and, after a year of Russian diamonds "leaking" into the global market, the Russian company Alrosa began distributing Russian diamonds independently of the CSO in 1996; Lev Leviev, an Uzbekistan-born Israeli diamontaire, began developing independent diamond distribution networks from Angolan and Russian sources in 1997; and rough diamonds were trickling into the global marketplace from war-torn Angola and Sierra Leone.

De Beers first responded to these new entrants with its traditional strategy of stockpiling rough gems and controlling global supply, and its inventory expanded in the 1990s from under $3 billion to nearly $5 billion, or 100 percent of the company's annual sales. But the new sources of competition severely diminished De Beers' dominance. Whereas De Beers and its CSO controlled over 80 percent of diamond supply as recently as 1989, its market share of rough production has since declined steadily. (See Figure 8.1.) The company simply could not sustain its historic degree of control over global production, and to the degree it sustained prices by maintaining large stockpiles, it was benefitting its competitors as much as itself. De Beers' directors recognized it needed to abandon its century-old business model.

De Beers' New Strategy

In 1998, Nicky Oppenheimer—grandson of Ernest and son of Harry, the two preceding leaders of De Beers—was installed as chief executive as part of a new management team, and the new leadership retained Bain and Company

Figure 8.1. De Beers' declining market share over time. Market share includes internal production and purchases from competitors, 1987–2018. *Source:* Zimnisky 2014.

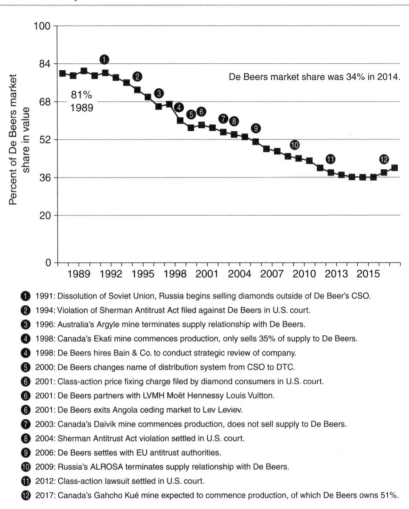

① 1991: Dissolution of Soviet Union, Russia begins selling diamonds outside of De Beer's CSO.

② 1994: Violation of Sherman Antitrust Act filed against De Beers in U.S. court.

③ 1996: Australia's Argyle mine terminates supply relationship with De Beers.

④ 1998: Canada's Ekati mine commences production, only sells 35% of supply to De Beers.

④ 1998: De Beers hires Bain & Co. to conduct strategic review of company.

⑤ 2000: De Beers changes name of distribution system from CSO to DTC.

⑥ 2001: Class-action price fixing charge filed by diamond consumers in U.S. court.

⑥ 2001: De Beers partners with LVMH Moët Hennessy Louis Vuitton.

⑥ 2001: De Beers exits Angola ceding market to Lev Leviev.

⑦ 2003: Canada's Daivik mine commences production, does not sell supply to De Beers.

⑧ 2004: Sherman Antitrust Act violation settled in U.S. court.

⑨ 2006: De Beers settles with EU antitrust authorities.

⑩ 2009: Russia's ALROSA terminates supply relationship with De Beers.

⑪ 2012: Class-action lawsuit settled in U.S. court.

⑫ 2017: Canada's Gahcho Kué mine expected to commence production, of which De Beers owns 51%.

to conduct a wide-ranging strategic review (Nicky Oppenheimer later told a Harvard Business School case writer, "For any company that is long lived, there comes a time where you have to change, and cast your skin off" [Spar 2000, 10]). The company Nicky inherited not only competed in a different competitive environment from the one in which his father's company dominated, but it also exhibited a radically different governance structure.

Before Nicky's team took over, De Beers and its sister company Anglo American were integrated through a series of complex crossholdings with both companies closely held by the Oppenheimer family (the unwieldy structure was originally designed to cushion both companies from the political hazards of cooperating with South Africa's apartheid regime, and then from the hazards of the regime's end). As the new management team took its place, the two companies spun off into separate firms. The reorganization consolidated all diamond-related industry assets and expertise into a fully integrated De Beers, with Anglo American focusing on other mining interests.

The strategic review prompted a dramatic shift in corporate strategy: rather than being the industry's buyer of last resort, De Beers would position itself as an aggressive competitor in an increasingly crowded luxury goods market. In early 2000, the company announced that it would sell off its stockpiles and would directly enter the diamond retail market. It forged a partnership with luxury goods company Moët Hennessey Louis Vuitton, developed a ring box with a logo that mimics Tiffany's high-luxury style, and established a retail store in Manhattan.[1] And it revealed a new marketing strategy to promote the De Beers brand, abandoning its wildly successful slogan "A Diamond Is Forever" for "Less than 1% of the world's diamonds are eligible to become a Forevermark diamond." The company is thus channeling its advertising might toward stimulating sales of De Beers diamonds rather than of all diamonds. Its core strategy is to make itself distinct from the rest of the industry, rather than to support the entire industry.

Consequences of Changes in Production

De Beers now produces approximately 35 percent of the world's rough diamonds by value (around 25 percent by volume), with Alrosa controlling approximately 30 percent (27 percent by volume), and three other competitors each producing between 2 and 10 percent. One might expect that because diamond production is no longer dominated by a monopolist and now involves several smaller players, diamond prices would be less stable and would sway with the vicissitudes of speculation and demand. Since the economic downturn of 2009, however, diamond prices have remained stable compared to other precious commodities. (See Figure 8.2.) This

Figure 8.2. Relative price changes in diamonds versus other commodities, 2009–2014. *Note:* Inflation is represented by U.S. Consumer Price Index; price index for polished diamonds tracks stones of different sizes. *Source:* Bain & Company 2014, 22. Used with permission from Bain & Company, www.bain.com.

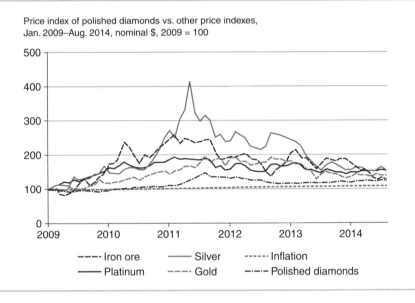

Price index of polished diamonds vs. other price indexes, Jan. 2009–Aug. 2014, nominal $, 2009 = 100

stability closely resembles the same price stability, reflected in Figure 2.2 in Chapter 2, that diamonds exhibited for much of the twentieth century.

Theory would also predict that a less concentrated market would yield lower wholesale prices and lower monopoly rents, but here too the opposite has occurred. As De Beers' market share declined after the turn of the millennium, average prices per carat, for both rough and polished diamonds, have increased (see Figure 8.3), and average operating margins among leading diamond producers have remained high, especially after the global downturn in 2009 (see Figure 8.4).

How has the diamond industry retained (and, in some cases, amplified) monopolistic features even after the decline of De Beers' notorious monopoly? Chaim Even-Zohar (2015) has suggested that the diamond oligopoly is mimicking many of the pricing behaviors of the De Beers monopoly, in part due to collusion. He notes that following each sight, detailed lists are distributed by Diamond Trading Company brokers revealing the price and composition of each purchased box of diamonds, with the intent of signaling prices for other producers. Even-Zohar further points to instances in which

Figure 8.3. Rough and polished diamond price changes, 2004–2014.
Notes: CAGR = compound annual growth rate. Polished-diamond price index,
2004 = 100; rough-diamond price index, 2004 = 100. *Source*: Bain & Company
2014, 5. Used with permission from Bain & Company, www.bain.com.

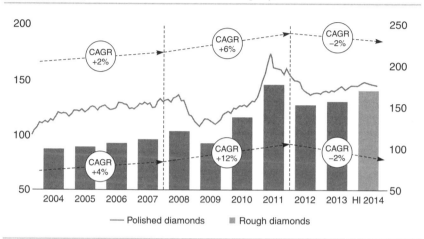

Figure 8.4. Operating margins for leading diamond producers, 2010–2014
(percent of gross earnings above costs). *Source*: Bain & Company 2014, 11. Used
with permission from Bain & Company, www.bain.com.

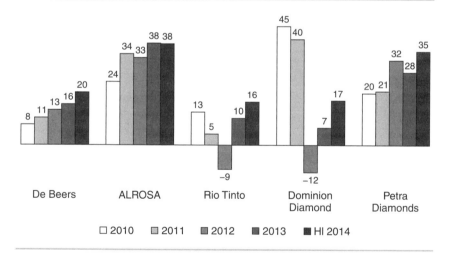

the competing oligopolist producers have devised ways to meet in private, including through the establishment in May 2015 of the Diamond Producers Association. The association, founded by the seven leading producers that are collectively responsible for about 80 percent of global production, was purportedly created to organize collective marketing efforts, sustain global demand, and counter threats of synthetic diamonds. Even-Zohar ruefully observes that, given De Beers' fraught history of antitrust violations, the company previously had "refrained from showing too close of a cooperation" but evidently is now being less cautious (2015, 4).

Even-Zohar warns, however, that the new oligopoly has departed from the monopoly in one very important respect: "The diamond producers have used their oligopolistic powers to the fullest, having successfully driven up rough prices to such an unrealistic level as to actually endanger the economic sustainability of their very own clients and other midstream and downstream levels" (2015, 4). This admonition of "unrealistic" pricing is echoed forcefully in an anonymously drafted and widely circulated e-mail from simplesightholder@gmail.com:

> dear all,
>
> As a sight holder who has suffered like all of you a few years of no profitable and even loosing [sic] boxes, I encourage you, at this difficult period not to take any box which doesn't have the value of at least 10% gross profit after polishing.
>
> Please, if your future, the future of your children and the future of your diamond business is important to you. Don't agree to take the boxes. . . .
>
> Don't be afraid to reject, nothing will really happen (unless some stupid sightholder will act stupidly and buy the boxes) they need our money, they need us and it is legitimate to expect a fair pricing which leaves also to our side some profit. If De Beers would make 300 million less a year in profit it would leave each of us (on average) with extra 3. Million dollars. What's bad and what's wrong in such a request??
>
> Let's take care of our future, brothers.
>
> I wish you all the best and I am happy to receive your comments.
> Also please forward this to other sight holders.
>
> Just a simple sightholder

Notice that Figure 8.3 supports this charge, showing that the price margin between rough and polished diamonds has narrowed since 2007.

It seems that the most consequential change stemming from De Beers' transformation is not the company's loss of market share or the market's change from a centralized monopoly to an oligopoly.[2] Rather, the most impactful change has come from De Beers' corporate reorientation. The company is no longer a diamond company run by a longtime diamond family with a mission to provide stability to an entire industry. It now sees itself as an aggressive competitor in a crowded market for luxury goods with the priority of creating and assuring value for shareholders.

De Beers' entry into the retail market reflects this new orientation and illustrates a sharp contrast to the company's longtime use of sightholders. The company now dedicates many of its rough stones to produce De Beers–branded diamonds for retail sale, aiming to be a leader in luxury goods markets and refining its product lines to meet the demands of high-end consumers. It has opted for a vertically integrated strategy in which it controls every stage of a diamond's preparation for retail sale. De Beers consequently is less reliant on seasoned diamond dealers to provide market information and direct diamonds to valuable targets and thus no longer aims to support an entire industry and its network of middlemen. To the contrary, many of these middlemen are now De Beers competitors! The diamond value chain no longer reflects the long-term collaboration between De Beers and its sightholders—between upstream suppliers and downstream distributors—and the company's relationship with these intermediaries has turned from collaboration to competition.

In fact, De Beers' vertically integrated strategies help explain some curiosities of the prior strategy. Economic theory implies that an upstream monopolist maximizes surplus when downstream markets are competitive. Yet De Beers, in contrast to theory, sold only to handpicked dealers. Moreover, and similarly in contrast to theory, diamond merchants have clamored to become sightholders atop the distribution stream, which suggests that De Beers sells diamonds to sightholders at less than the monopoly price and instead shares with them some monopoly rents. The reason for De Beers' curious distribution strategy is that it relied on these merchants to ensure that rough stones were directed to their most valuable use. It therefore selected as sightholders merchants who were sufficiently familiar with the diamond trade to know how to cut, distribute, and market diamonds to create maximum value. In short, De Beers relied on downstream merchants' market information and industry expertise, and the company implemented a pricing strategy that sustained and benefited these knowledgeable intermediaries.

The industry's longtime intermediaries—especially midsize and small operators who do not partner with leading retail chains—are both the primary victims of this new pricing strategy and the most vulnerable. Compared to the upstream production and downstream retail markets, this intermediate market for distributing and cutting rough diamonds has long offered the slimmest margins (recall Figure 2.1 in Chapter 2), and producers' new pricing strategies have caused these margins to continue to shrink. De Beers' new strategy has had major reverberations throughout the diamond distribution chain.

Innovation and Segmentation in Retail

A *Forbes* article entitled "Romance Killer" describes Mark Vadon, founder and CEO of Blue Nile, as "an unlikely party crasher in a business dominated by multigenerational family firms led by Orthodox Jews" (Murphy 2004). Blue Nile, founded in 1999 as part of the Internet retail boom, is the world's pioneer in Internet diamond sales. The company serves as an exchange between consumers and diamond dealers, in which dealers describe the attributes of each stone—carat, cut, color, and clarity (the four Cs)—in accordance with standardized GIA metrics. Each stone has a GIA certificate confirming its metrics, and consumers can compare stones by price and quality.

Blue Nile is no longer a lone force in Internet diamond retail, having been joined by Amazon, AliBaba, eBay, and other Internet sites. Internet retailers constitute 13 percent of America's total jewelry sales, and although Internet sales are not apparently growing faster than brick-and-mortar retail sales, they are having a lasting impact on the diamond value chain by introducing transparency to diamond pricing. Bringing price transparency was key to Vadon's retail strategy (*Forbes* reports that "Mark Vadon believes diamonds are just pork bellies waiting to happen" [Murphy 2004]), but it is anathema to an industry that relies on mystique, heavy markups, and careful in-person inspection.

The rise of Internet retail has had only a modest effect on large, high-end stones, and it appears that high-end diamond retail markets remain distinct

Figure 8.5. Price changes for polished diamonds by gem size and quality, in volume and value terms, 2003–2013. *Notes:* Shares in volume are estimated based on respective shares of high-quality diamonds. RDI = Rapaport Diamond Index, a price index reflecting the average price per carat for a spectrum of diamonds of various quality. D-IF = diamonds of color D (colorless) and clarity IF (internally flawless), the highest diamond grades. *Source:* Bain & Company 2014, 27. Used with permission from Bain & Company, www.bain.com.

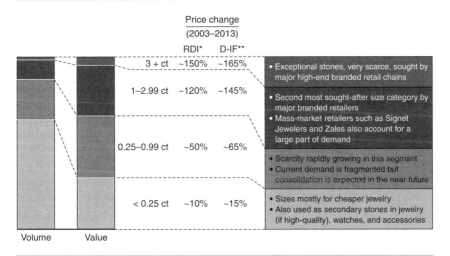

from the Internet market. This is likely because luxury retail services provide desired complementarities to high-value stones—the expertise displayed by the salesperson, the elite brand, the cozy retail space—and accordingly, very few large stones are sold by Internet retailers (Schnidman 2013). But Internet sales have put meaningful downward pressure on prices for midsize and small polished stones. While prices for large, high-quality stones rose significantly over the past decade, prices for smaller and midsize polished gems were nearly stagnant (see Figure 8.5). The new price pressures have eliminated many of the margins that diamond dealers enjoyed as intermediaries, and the gap between rough prices and polished prices (for all but the largest stones) continues to narrow.

Yet Internet retailers have done more than introduce price information and squeeze profits. They also have challenged many core foundations on which the diamond industry has traditionally relied. *Forbes,* for example, colorfully illustrates how Internet retail's emphasis on price comparisons is in tension with many forces that traditionally fueled the industry: "Vadon's success rankles many in the diamond trade. Some wholesalers won't deal with him; some retailers refuse to order from those who do. One trade group recently advised jewelers to sell their engagement rings at a loss to blunt Blue Nile's inroads.... 'We try not to sell diamonds as commodities,' adds Jonathan Bridge of the 74-store Ben Bridge jewelry chain in Seattle, which has been peddling stones for 92 years. 'Every diamond is different. There's a certain amount of romance in that.'" But Forbes is unsympathetic: "'Blue Nile is creating a race to the bottom,' complains Alan Rehs, a wholesaler and cutter in New York. 'This is bad for the industry.' He says customers walk into stores brandishing Blue Nile printouts as bargaining chips. Horrors" (Murphy 2004).

Internet sales and its ushering of transparency have introduced an even more significant disruption to the diamond distribution chain. Previously, intermediaries were relied on to direct stones to their highest value use, matching individual stones with purchasers who would pay the most. These seasoned diamontaires utilized their own market information and the information asymmetries they enjoyed over outsiders to channel stones toward purchasers who would yield additional margins. Their market information provided a key step in the value chain and secured their profitable role within it. Now, that market information is widely available. Price transparency has not just introduced new price pressures, but it has also obviated the valuable services that intermediaries historically provided.

Entry and Disruption to Diamond Intermediaries

Diamond dealers, as intermediaries between rough producers and purchasers of polished stones, have thus suffered twin pressures since 2000. Diamond producers have increasingly aimed to extract higher prices in rough diamond sales, and Internet retailers have introduced downward price pressures for many polished diamonds. Both of these developments have diminished available margins for intermediary diamontaires, and they correspondingly have diminished the incentives to sustaining strong reputations in the trade. Yet while these developments occurred in the production and retail markets, even more dramatic developments took place in the intermediate stage of sorting, cutting, and brokering diamonds.

As is discussed in Chapter 6, the emergence of Palanpuri Jain diamond merchants and the subsequent rise of India as the world's capital of diamond cutting constitutes perhaps the most significant development in the diamond industry since the discovery of South African diamond mines a century ago. Jain merchants developed networks that acquired rough diamond supply in Antwerp, orchestrated diamond cutting in Gujarat, and sold polished diamonds in New York and other retail centers (see Hofmeester 2013, 44–47). Palanpuri Jains were especially well positioned to excel in the diamond industry because of their historical roots as diamontaires, as Palanpuri family and community relationships enabled them to execute the credit purchases and distribution of diamonds that are required to thrive in the diamond market.

When India's diamond industry started expanding rapidly, Palanpuri family firms in Gujarat—joined by some Marwaris, India's traditional traders and bankers—employed mostly local Kathiawaris. Kathiawaris historically were the region's farmers, and they migrated in large numbers to Gujarat's urban and industrial centers when work became available in Jain-owned cutting factories (see Figures 6.1 and 6.2). The influx of new Indian family businesses into the web of diamond intermediaries not only transformed the profile of the diamond trade but also significantly changed the economics. The introduction of new intermediary networks made this segment of the industry more competitive and correspondingly caused margins to decline. But several aspects about the nature of this entry put additional strains on both the industry's norms for cooperation and the incentives to sustain cooperation.

In time, Kathiawaris grew from factory workers to factory owners, and Kathiawari families now control over 50 percent of the diamond trade in Surat, with many Kathiawari companies becoming active purchasers of rough stones in Antwerp and Israel. The rise of Kathiawari companies has led some to venture, in the words of an industry newsletter headline, that "Palanpuris have rivals for global diamond throne" (Shah 2008). But the Kathiawari entrepreneurs are meaningfully different from their Palanpuri and Marwari counterparts. According to a 2011 study by Cambridge economist Kaivan Munshi, Kathiawari diamond merchants were younger, had fewer years of education, were less likely to be schooled in English, and were more likely to be raised far from urban centers. More significant, especially for the diamond trade, only 35 percent of sampled Kathiawari diamontaires,

Figure 8.6. Family background of entering entrepreneurs in India's diamond industry. *Source:* Munshi 2011, 1090.

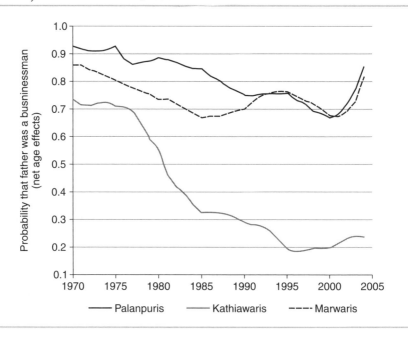

compared to 82 percent of Palanpuris and 76 percent of Marwaris, reported that their father was engaged in any type of business. In addition, the percent of Kathiawari entrepreneurs entering the diamond industry with businessmen fathers declined significantly from 1980 through 2000, whereas the percent for entering Palanpuris and Marwaris largely stayed the same (see Figure 8.6). For an industry that relies on intergenerational business to sustain long-term cooperation, the entry of Kathiawaris as first-generation merchants introduced an unfamiliar kind of entrepreneur.

Indian banking policies have further fueled the entry of nontraditional business families into the industry. To encourage exports, the Indian government requires local banks to earmark a percentage of their credit to finance exporters (Golan 2013, 106; Reserve Bank of India 2013). This financing is especially attractive because it must be offered in U.S. dollars and at a reduced rate. And since gems and jewelry are India's second-largest export and constitute approximately 14 percent of all Indian exports (and nearly 7 percent of India's GDP), Indian banks—led by the Bank of India—

found eager borrowers in the diamond sector (India Brand Equity Foundation 2016).

Although many Indian diamond firms were reliably lucrative and thus generally safe bets for banks, financing diamond operations is notoriously difficult to govern. First, because diamonds are difficult to identify individually, unlike a car or real property, diamontaires were able to take out multiple loans for a single bundle of diamonds. Second, because diamonds are difficult to value accurately, especially by nondiamontaire bankers, diamond companies were able to borrow sums that exceeded the actual value of the diamonds they used for collateral. Finally, the loan subsidies encouraged entrepreneurs with diamond companies to use subsidized loans for nondiamond purposes, or even to reloan the borrowed money at market prices. These difficulties illustrate why diamontaires historically have obtained their financing in the form of credit sales from fellow diamontaires, who understand the business, are better equipped at valuing stones, and more practiced at assessing the associated risks.

These Indian bank policies, some of which were mimicked by banks outside India, encouraged banks to overinvest in the burgeoning diamond sector. They extended generous lines of credit to diamond dealers and factory owners for the purchase of rough stones without the ability to manage the associated hazards. They also caused the Indian diamond sector to grievously overextend itself. Outstanding debt belonging to diamond intermediaries grew from $7 billion in 2002 to about $16 billion in 2013, with 40 percent of the entire global industry's banking debt now owed by Indian firms (Bain & Company 2014, 39, 43). Predictably, many are now insolvent, financing is drying up, and the spread of bad loans has destabilized the sector (Ashreena and Ananthalakshmi 2015). A former chairman of India's Gem and Jewellery Export Promotion Council recently lamented, "The rash of bankruptcies among diamond processing companies today isn't simply bad news for these companies and their creditors. It's bad news for all of us. The banks don't trust the industry any more, and today, even legitimate, well-run companies are being regarded with suspicion and are facing sharply tightened lines of credit" (Kothari 2015).

In sum, the intermediaries—the dealers, cutters, and brokers—that traditionally directed diamonds from De Beers and other producers to jewelry manufacturers have watched their industry segment transform enormously in the past thirty years. The rise of Indian merchants greatly expanded competition and reduced margins. India's longtime diamontaires, the Palan-puris, were soon joined by Kathiawaris who did not have family intergen-erational businesses and thus had fewer historical pressures to sustain a flawless reputation. And Indian banking policies encouraged financial im-proprieties and introduced new financial pressures even to scrupulous busi-nesses. These structural challenges to the intermediary segment of the value chain were well under way by 2000, when De Beers started pricing more aggressively and when Internet retail placed downward pressures on prices for polished diamonds.

The Erosion of Trust and the Rise of Vertical Integration

Chapter 3 observed that the foundations of sustained cooperation in the diamond industry lay on the motivations—or, in the language of an econ-omist, the utility functions—of the individual diamontaires. Long-term, intergenerational workers in family businesses formed the backbone of the industry, and the promise of reliable profits for foreseeable generations induced diamontaires to comply with their industry obligations and pre-serve a good reputation for themselves and their progeny. However, these diamontaires now see their expected payoffs from sustained cooperation diminishing, and simple game theory—the iterated folk theorem—illustrates why reports from industry insiders, the trade press, and 47th Street mer-chants reveal a breakdown of cooperation. In short, structural changes in the global diamond market—introduced by changes in geopolitics, industry structure, and technology—have changed the payoffs to cooperation, and this explains its industry-wide erosion.

Because the diamond industry has been held out to be the paradigm for trust-based exchange, both by the popular press and by a number of impor-tant scholars, an end to its sustained cooperation requires reassessing earlier understandings. The remainder of this chapter, aiming to derive les-sons from the autopsy of cooperation, discusses some academic debates and prevailing theories that now require revisiting.

The "Institutional Life Cycle" of Cooperation

The diamond industry clearly was, for a time, characterized by trust-based exchange. But does its erosion of trust mean that it was previously misunderstood, or is there a unifying theory that can explain how sustained cooperation breaks down? Perhaps instead of designating the diamond industry as a paradigm for cooperation and mutual trust, its rise and fall of trust-based exchange might instead fit into a broader phenomenon.

Although this erosion of cooperation pierces our accepted narrative of the diamond trade, it has some historical analogs. Economic historian Avner Greif offers several examples of what he calls the "institutional life cycle," in which institutions that emerge to sustain cooperation eventually sow the seeds of their own demise (Greif 2006, 176). Genoa, for example, was a thriving commercial center in the eleventh century primarily due to the mutual interdependence and cooperation between its ruling commercial clans; yet the success of these clans generated such wealth that control of the city offered a reward that overwhelmed the certain shared gains from continued cooperation. Once a German emperor, who had presented a common enemy to the clans, no longer posed a military threat, the clans battled for complete control of the city and abandoned productive cooperation. Similarly, the merchant guilds of the twelfth and thirteenth centuries orchestrated self-enforcing multilateral reputation mechanisms that brought wealth to both merchants and their supportive rulers, but this success led to an expansion of trade that stretched the limits of reputation mechanisms and diminished the value to the crown to protect the marginal merchant from expropriation or unfair dealing. Eventually, peripheral traders could not rely on fair dealing, and trust broke down throughout the merchant populations. And the institutions that Greif calls the "community responsibility system," which enabled impersonal intercommunity exchange in the thirteenth and fourteenth centuries, also became victims of their own success. These cooperative arrangements had local authorities commit to punishing local residents who cheated foreigners in exchange for a commitment from distant authorities to reciprocally punish their own, thus sustaining credible cross-border trade. But, Greif explains, "growth in the number of traders and communities, the locations of trade, and intercommunity interactions reduces the cost of falsifying one's community affiliation and increases the cost of verifying one's identity" (Greif 2006b, 338). Their growth also led to their demise.

It could similarly be said that diamontaires have been a victim of their own success. The lucrative opportunities as an intermediary attracted entry from ethnic networks and family businesses that were able to manage the diamond value chain. As the industry grew, it became more diverse, and the mechanisms that were historically relied upon to secure credible commitments—the prospect of bequeathing valuable reputations to the next generation—were not as effective. In a similar fashion, the industry amassed political power as it grew, enabling it to extract new and untraditional sources of financing, which inadvertently undermined the industry's historical mechanism of securing credit and punishing defaulters. When production and retail markets changed because of exogenous geopolitical and technological changes, the thinning incentives to sustain cooperation were overwhelmed.

Another feature of the industry's success has been the diamontaires' affluence and thus acceptance into mainstream society. Whereas Amsterdam's and Antwerp's diamontaires in the late nineteenth and early twentieth centuries, most of whom were Jewish, always remained isolated and distinct from the dominant cultures, Jewish, Indian, and Middle Eastern diamontaires have fully integrated into the cultural polyglots that house the twenty-first century's diamond centers. With acceptance comes acculturation, and thus greater choices and economic opportunities, and many diamond merchants—like the Antwerp merchant discussed previously—have seen their children select different occupational paths. Intergenerational businesses and the forces that sustain the value of an honest reputation are central in supporting cooperation, and the diminishing presence of children in family businesses meaningfully erodes the merchants' incentives to cooperate in the long term.

Greif's historical lessons teach that trust can break down even when only marginal merchants are not assured of being punished for wrongdoing or rewarded for cooperative behavior. It recalls what a diamond merchant told Shor (1993): "Even if one percent of the dealers were dishonest, that trust would be destroyed and so would our industry." And game theory teaches that this breakdown naturally accelerates. Once some diamontaires begin cheating, then the industry's overall credibility erodes, making it more difficult and costly for any one merchant to commit to trustworthy behavior. And once diamond merchants see dwindling profits in the future, the rewards for maintaining a trustworthy reputation decline. Indeed, a growing percentage of New York's and Antwerp's diamond merchants are seeing their children pursue careers outside the industry.

Vertical Integration and the Institutional Economics of the Diamond Chain

Unless a cooperative equilibrium is restored—and lessons from history teach that once trust is lost, it is very hard to recover—the diamond industry will undergo dramatic structural changes. The breakdown of trust-based networks, and the erosion of a reliable distribution network from producers to jewelers, will mean that jewelry manufacturers will seek alternative mechanisms to procure diamonds. It also means economists will have to reassess their understanding of the economics of the diamond chain.

The diamond chain attracted scholarly attention from some pioneering organizational economists, and their early work put De Beers' method of block booking—its practice of selling prepackaged caches of heterogeneous rough diamonds for a single take-it-or-leave-it price—within the canon of institutional economics. Recall from Chapter 2 that Yoram Barzel argued in 1977 that De Beers uses block booking to economize on measurement costs: "Had the contents of a particular bag been available for appraisal by all buyers, each probably would have spent resources to determine the properties of the diamonds. . . . The incentive for De Beers to engage in this peculiar form of trade seems to be that buyers are now in a position to spend on the actual purchase of the diamonds the amount they otherwise might have spent on collecting information" (304–305). In other words, because buyers were spared the costs of evaluating individual stones, they were willing to pay De Beers more for the average stone.

Roy Kenney and Benjamin Klein, writing in 1983, similarly observed that "a precise estimate of the value of individual rough diamonds would require costly, duplicative examination costs" (539). De Beers engages in block booking "to prevent buyers from rejecting parts of a package of products that has been averaged priced," and in return, De Beers "pays a premium to its buyers by selling diamonds at less than (costless-search) market clearing prices" (506). In short, because buyers agree to purchase the entire cache, saving De Beers the additional burden of remarketing rejected stones, De Beers is willing to charge less.

These related and contemporaneous analyses (despite the slight tension between them) stood as accepted wisdom for De Beers' distribution strategy. By remaining exclusively upstream, De Beers created and benefited from the efficiencies of avoiding the duplicative and effort-intensive measurement costs of evaluating individual stones. The block booking strategy created value both by economizing on search costs and by generating the efficiencies from a dis-integrated supply chain.

Recent organizational changes to the supply chain require rethinking these conventional explanations. Most significant of these changes is De Beers' current implementation of a vertically integrated strategy. Though it continues to sell rough stones to its sightholders, it retains many stones for itself, supervises their polishing, manages their placement in jewelry settings (and ensuring their uniformity, so as to market them as identical branded stones), and sells them through their own retail stores. It also has implemented a "Supplier of Choice" program in which it enters long-term, detailed contracts with select sightholders (see, for example, Kuryan 2015). De Beers gives these chosen distributors access to De Beers' high-quality stones and permission to market those stones as De Beers' "Forevermark" diamonds, and in exchange the sightholder invests in and implements specific production and marketing plans. This program binds certain distributors and retailers more closely to De Beers than any previous sightholder.

Other producers are pursuing vertical strategies as well. Rio Tinto, for example, teamed up with Chinese designers and jewelry manufacturers to use the company's Argyle mine stones to create products targeting the Chinese market. And Alrosa has been working with Christie's and Sotheby's to market polished diamonds directly to consumers.

Perhaps more significant, industry leaders from other segments of the distribution chain are also vertically integrating. Luxury retailer Tiffany created a wholly owned subsidiary, Laurelton Diamonds, that purchases, cuts, and polishes rough diamonds. Laurelton has also entered into long-term contracts with De Beers, Alrosa, and Rio Tinto to procure steady supplies, and it has additionally contracted with smaller producers to purchase stones from individual mines. Chinese luxury retailer Chow Tai Fook has also integrated upstream, entering long-term supply relationships with major producers and operating large cutting and processing factories. And Signet Jewelers, owners of retail chains Zales, Jared, and Kay Jewelry (plus others), now operates a polishing factory in Botswana. In addition to retailers integrating upstream, major wholesalers—in particular, the highest-volume sightholders—are integrating downward. Although the vast majority of the 5,000 firms that purchase, sort, polish, and sell wholesale diamonds are dis-integrated family firms, the largest 110 firms constitute 70 percent of the wholesale market and are increasingly integrated into polishing, jewelry manufacturing, and retail sales.

These recent organizational changes—the rise of greater vertical integration across the industry, and the corresponding end of the Barzel (1977) and Kenney and Klein (1983) models—are a direct reaction to the loss of trust-based cooperation in the industry. As retailers invest in their brands, they are increasingly vulnerable to the hazards that classically demark the diamond trade: mistakenly representing synthetic diamonds as natural diamonds, selling conflict diamonds, or selling laser-treated diamonds. Recall the model described in Chapter 4: the diamond industry relied on reputation-based exchange because it offered greater transactional security than courts while replicating the incentives of the market. But if the industry's reputation mechanisms cannot secure exchange, then the model predicts that the industry would tend toward vertical integration.

Even while this rise of vertical integration is understood as an accepted reaction to the diminishing credibility of trust-based exchange, it still presents a challenge to the explanations offered by Barzel and Kenney and Klein. Those accepted understandings of the diamond network suggested that measurement or examination costs encouraged De Beers to pursue block-booking strategies. But the loss of trust among intermediaries has no effect on measurement costs, so even if suppliers like De Beers could not trust downstream purchasers, a measurement cost explanation would mean De Beers would still resist integrating downward and assuming the resulting sorting costs.[3] It is more likely that an economizing of transaction costs induced the industry to adopt the dis-integrated chain for so many years. As Chapter 4 discusses when articulating the efficiencies of market-based organizations, value is created in the diamond chain because the network of intermediaries can swiftly match a particular stone with an optimal buyer. The diamond network is very much an open exchange, and the incentive intensity and information flows of market organizations create valuable efficiencies that vertical integration cannot. De Beers relied on the diamond network to acquire market information and to execute the matching process, but its new retail strategy of marketing branded luxury goods obviates those efficiencies; it now accumulates market information on its own. In short, the erosion of the industry's dis-integrated distribution chain reveals the true economizing forces that sustained it for many decades.

Embeddedness, Calculativeness, and the Origins of Trust

Structural changes in the diamond industry's distribution network also speak to a long-debated feud in economic sociology. As an archetype for trust-based exchange, the diamond industry fueled examinations over the very origin of trust and triggered one of the more seminal debates in both organizational science and institutional theory. The erosion of trust in the industry offers additional insight into that central debate.

In a famous exchange, Mark Granovetter and Oliver Williamson disputed whether economic relationships are embedded within social structure or whether they are responsive to economic forces. Granovetter argued that diamond transactions are "embedded in a close-knit community of diamond merchants who monitor one another's behavior closely" (1985, 492). Williamson countered that "the appearance of trust among diamond dealers is deceptive. . . . The organization of this market succeeded because it was able to provide cost-effective sanctions more efficiently than rivals" (Williamson 1993, 471–473). In short, Granovetter argued that embedded social relationships created a framework for trust-based diamond transactions, whereas Williamson argued that diamond transactions were secured only by a credible system of punishments. To Granovetter, trust was an outgrowth of social relations. To Williamson, merchants calculated the benefits and risks of engaging in particular transactions, and what looked like "trust"—what Williamson calls "calculative trust"—was a market equilibrium driven by credible sanctions. The Granovetter-Williamson debate has become a staple in many PhD field exams and starkly illustrates some core conceptual divides in the social sciences.

Recent changes in diamond relations seem to make Williamson the winner of this argument. The erosion of trust has occurred without any meaningful erosion in the associated Jewish or Indian communities. To the contrary, economic forces have reduced the benefits of trustworthy behavior and the economic rewards from a good reputation, and the loss of trust is much more a consequence of calculated self-interest. In fact, Williamson observed in 1993 that changing technologies in the diamond industry revealed that "the basis for commercial trust has become more transparently calculative" (473). He observed that advances in communication and other modernizations made the diamond exchange look increasingly like other markets, and he might have been anticipating the limits of social relations—and the centrality of efficiency considerations—in determining the industry's future.

Regardless of the forces that originally shaped the diamond industry's unique structure, there undeniably has been a concurrent loss of trust and a wave of vertical integration, and established transaction cost theory suggests that the former is driving the latter. Perhaps more significant to economic sociologists and those studying embedded social organizations, the structural changes in the diamond industry are reshaping not just its distribution network but the face of the entire industry, from the companies involved in exploration and production to the retail chains designing and selling jewelry. And, presuming that trust will be difficult to restore, one can expect more vertical integration to come. Large retailers, large mining operations, and a few elite intermediaries will likely gain greater control of the diamond value chain. They will market branded diamonds and spend little effort relying on the family-oriented diamond networks that sustained the industry for a century. One might say that 47th Street is going corporate.

There is little question that the industry's vertical integration will come with real costs, above and beyond whatever noneconomic, nostalgic losses the community and broader public might feel. As is discussed in Chapter 4, the aggressive, competitive network of diamontaires offered meaningful efficiencies to the distribution chain, which was why the value chain remained dis-integrated for so long and why DeBeers organized distribution as it did. Vertical integration cannot mimic these intensities of the market, and the industry will lose efficiencies, to say nothing of its distinct personality, as it squeezes out the diamond dealers.

Lessons from an Autopsy

Changes in the diamond industry have not gone unnoticed—there is palpable fear that growing distrust will erode the industry's foundations—and many industry insiders have called for immediate action to stem the snowballing of uncooperative behavior. Critics of New York's DDC hope that its new leadership will restore confidence in both the club's management and its arbitrators. Indian diamond business leaders have urged their brethren to use state-sponsored credit more responsibly, not just to avoid overexpansion and incipient bankruptcies but also to restore traditional mechanisms to govern credit and creditworthiness. And diamond dealers worldwide have called on De Beers and other suppliers to price at what are called more "sustainable" and "realistic" levels, to ensure the long-term viability of the intermediaries that have been the companies' historic partners. Perhaps reform among both producers and the diamond dealers will stem the attrition of trust and the collapse of the historical value chain.

But if Greif's historical analogies are apt and past is prologue, the industry's cooperation will continue to erode. This autopsy of the industry's decades of trust offers some lessons on both the economics of the diamond industry and the sustainability of trust-based exchange.

First, and most fundamentally, we have to rethink what has become the prevailing understanding of dispute resolution and cooperation in the diamond industry. Seminal works by Bernstein (1992), Shor (1993), and others, describing an industry that relied on trust alone to resolve disputes and secure exchange, that could develop its own system of arbitration and did not need the supports of state-sponsored law and courts, now appear anachronistic. Revisiting those early works through the lens of history reveals that they described only a temporary arrangement, that the cooperative frameworks they observed were dependent on a confluence of institutional and historical circumstances that did not sustain themselves in the long term. Because the industry's reliance on arbitrators, privately constructed law, and reputation mechanisms has succumbed to conventional commercial relationships and legal enforcement, the efficiencies and praise credited to those private governance mechanisms need to be reconsidered.

Second, we have to reconceptualize the economics of the diamond chain. Like Bernstein and Shor, both Barzel (1977) and Kenney and Klein (1983) offered an understanding that became prevailing wisdom but no longer conforms with reality. The distribution system they explained through the lens of measurement costs is now being abandoned for vertically integrated strategies. These structural changes are not being triggered because measuring a diamond's qualities has become less costly (there is no evidence measurement costs have declined) but instead are due to the waning reliability and growing transaction costs of the dis-integrated distribution chain. Those earlier works did not appreciate how much the distribution structure had relied on the efficiencies of a network of intermediaries, and the loss of credible reputation mechanisms along the supply chain has caused the distribution structure to change. In short, our economic understanding of the diamond industry—like our legal understanding of it—improves when historical changes pose new challenges to prior beliefs.

Third, consistent with the theory offered in Chapter 4, we observe how trust-based relationships and vertical integration are substitutes for each other, and that vertical integration takes hold when trust breaks down. In fact, given that each diamond transaction presents a significant governance challenge, and that vertical integration is deemed the most reliable mechanism to secure exchange, it is remarkable that trust-based relations— built upon family relations, homogeneous ethnic networks, and repeat interactions—were able to sustain the diamond trade for as long as they did. Much more curious than the rise of vertical integration in the diamond chain might be how the industry was able to avoid such integration for so long. To be sure, trust, social networks, and family business can sustain trade while avoiding the bureaucratic inefficiencies of vertical integration, but the organizational efficiencies of vertical integration are apparently overwhelming with the growth and modernization of the marketplace.

Fourth, and perhaps most interesting, what could be described as the rise and fall of trust illustrates both the possibilities and the fragility of trust-based exchange. The diamond industry's capacity to sustain stateless exchange into the twenty-first century and to maintain its distinctive old-world flavor, even at the center of the most modern metropolis, shows that statelessness continues to offer efficiencies and benefits that are unavailable from modern economic and legal institutions. At the same time, the gradual demise of the industry's cooperation reveals both the institutional limitations of trust-based exchange and the institutional advantages that inexorably expand the reach of corporations, state courts, and other modern institutions. Clearly, reputation mechanisms and their underlying coordinated punishments are sensitive to their institutional environment, and changes in technology, geopolitics, and culture can disrupt a cooperative equilibrium. And while a life cycle understanding of trust-based exchange suggests that success often lays the foundations of an eventual demise, the remarkable successes of stateless commerce illustrates that it will continue to thrive in the modern world so long as it incubates in the right setting.

Epilogue: The Future of Statelessness

It is unfortunate to see dishonesty imbue an industry that had become the paradigm for trust. Alternatively, it is remarkable that institutional and historical circumstances enabled such trust to thrive for so long. In a world where reputation-based cooperation is much more the exception than the rule, where coercive legal institutions are necessary to sustain cooperation and govern commerce, this one (albeit temporary) instance of trust-based exchange illustrates the richness of private institutions and the possibilities of private governance.

But even if we admire the longevity of the diamond industry's statelessness, does its demise suggest that all statelessness will eventually fade away?

As this book shows, many irresistible economic and technological forces are limiting the role of stateless commerce in the modern economy. Chapter 3 explained that sustaining a large-scale reputation mechanism in a global industry requires a rigorous set of institutions that can share information and mobilize a credible, prompt coordinated punishment. Such reputation mechanisms do not emerge by themselves and are not sustainable without the requisite institutional supports (some enthusiasts call such reputation mechanisms "spontaneous order," which I think is a misnomer). In addition, Chapters 4 and 5 identified many inefficiencies to industry-wide reputation mechanisms: entry barriers that exclude innovators, conformity pressures that can punish mavericks and unconventional thinking, and the possibility that industry-wide power can be gathered to protect its leaders at the cost of others. And finally, this chapter explains that even when certain merchant communities successfully create self-enforced cooperation, many of those cooperative systems are victims of their own success and grow beyond their capacity.

On the other hand, Chapter 6 explains that stateless commerce remains a force on many fronts. It is especially vital in lower-income nations, where formal institutions are weak, and stateless exchange can invite insular ethnic communities to partake in a global economy. Chapter 7 reminds that stateless commercial networks are especially adept at navigating certain economic and political features of continued globalization, and, more soberly, stateless exchange remains available even when geopolitics force dislocation. It can sustain merchants when national politics fail them. Perhaps most important, certain transactions remain beyond the reach of public courts, and for many of these transactions, ethnic trading networks retain the extraordinary ability to secure exchange and organize commerce where the state will fail. Stateless commercial networks will remain uniquely well positioned to meet certain economic challenges and are likely to continue finding a role in the modern economy.

For these reasons, it is likely that there will remain a role, albeit a diminished one, for stateless networks in the diamond industry. Diamond dealers might no longer trust each other, but they will continue to trust their family and close kin, and thus they will retain a network that can navigate the demands of the industry. As large retailers and mining interests expand their presence across all stages of the industry, the middlemen networks will likely become narrower and overlap or intersect with each other less regularly, and they will be unlikely to manage the collective volume that they had in years past. But even if diamontaires cannot sustain a system of impersonal exchange, they will remain able to secure personal exchange within their narrow networks of family and kin. Even if the scope of the industry's statelessness contracts, the foundation of the families and communities that enable statelessness will persist.

Perhaps this means that even as statelessness declines in the diamond industry, it retains valuable features for the global economy and might find its future scattered across many economic sectors. That brings to mind a family I met when I was in graduate school. At the time, I frequented a neighborhood dry cleaner run by a Vietnamese immigrant family, and I wondered how the family, whose parents spoke very little English, was able to run a business that clearly required coordination with suppliers, financiers, and multiple contractors. I explained to the daughter—who had the best English—that I studied family businesses (I gave her a short summary of my research on Jewish diamond businesses), and she set up a meeting with her father.

It turns out that they owned three additional dry cleaners, and I had to go to a different store to meet the dad. I asked him how he got started in the business, which I hoped was an innocuous way to inquire how he could succeed in a new country with little facility with the language. He understood my question immediately. Promptly after arriving to the United States, he connected with a network of other Vietnamese dry cleaners. His countrymen introduced him to the business and gave him a loan, which he promised to pay back in five years. "No lawyers, no contract" he said.

NOTES

REFERENCES

INDEX

Notes

Preface

1. Elements of these chapters were developed in earlier publications, and I thank the journals that published the antecedent articles for the opportunity to present my ideas. Chapter 1 was derived from "Norms and Law: Putting the Horse Before the Cart," *Duke Law Journal* 62, no. 3 (2012); Chapter 3 from "How Communities Create Economic Advantage: Jewish Diamond Merchants in New York," *Law and Social Inquiry* 31, no. 2 (Spring 2006); Chapter 4 from "Firms, Courts, and Reputation Mechanisms: Towards a Positive Theory of Private Ordering," *Columbia Law Review* 104, no. 8 (2004); Chapter 5 from "The Antitrust of Reputation Mechanisms: Institutional Economics and Concerted Refusals to Deal," *Virginia Law Review* 94, no. 2 (2009); and Chapter 8 from "An Autopsy of Cooperation: Diamond Dealers and the Limits of Trust-Based Exchange," *Journal of Legal Analysis* (in press 2017).

1. Statelessness in Context

1. A new generation of scholarship has started modeling interactions between state law and private enforcement. Eric Posner (2000) argues that social norms are behavioral patterns that, when violated, trigger social sanctions. And like law, social norms can facilitate cooperation, but often for odious purposes. Because law cannot readily supplant social norms, lawmakers cannot easily use law either to reinforce desirable cooperation or to undermine undesirable cooperation. Richard McAdams (1992, 1995, 1996, 1997) similarly models social norms as devices that can facilitate both cooperation and social waste, but he instead characterizes them as deriving from certain tastes within the utility function. McAdams warns that although law can sometimes shape social norms, the interrelationship is nuanced, and law can either correct certain dysfunctional social norms or interfere with the efficient operations of social norms. Gillian Hadfield and Barry Weingast (2012, 2013, 2015, 2016) characterize the "rule of law" as a cooperation between state and private enforcement

in which state law facilitates a coordinated equilibrium of private order by co-ordinating and incentivizing decentralized collective punishment.

All three bodies of work model interesting interactions between privately enforced norms and publicly articulated law that occur simultaneously within a very complex shadow of the law. They constitute an interesting off-shoot of a Macaulay-Coasean dynamic between private conduct and the law's shadow.

2. A Case Study in Statelessness

1. Starting in the early twenty-first century, the diamond industry has undergone significant structural changes that have reverberated throughout the diamond network. These recent changes, which offer important implications for state-lessness, are the focus of Chapter 8.

2. Note that both Barzel (1977) and Kenney and Klein (1983) acknowledge the sig-nificant costs of sorting and valuing heterogeneous diamonds, and they explain De Beers' distribution methods as a strategy to economize on these costs. But neither explanation fully acknowledges that, eventually, the diamonds need to be sorted and appraised individually, and both articles implicitly aver (without much explanation) that sorting is more efficiently done downstream, by di-amontaires, rather than by De Beers. To understand why, in fact, sorting is more efficient downstream, one must appreciate the structure of the down-stream markets (see Chapter 4).

3. Despite technological revolutions in surveying and mining diamonds, and de-spite the explosion of the modern diamond industry following the late nineteenth-century discoveries in South Africa, the technology for cutting large diamonds has changed very little over the past centuries. Cutters hold a diamond firmly in a metal grip and deliberately place it at a desired angle against a rotating grinding wheel. In earlier generations, the grinding wheel was rotated mechanically by hand cranks or foot pedals, whereas modern grinding wheels are electric and use more sophisticated grips, but the underlying process is essentially the same. The 1982 *Jewish Directory and Almanac* contains a dramatic illustration of this technological constancy: a 1850 original engraving of a diamond cutter, a 1912 picture of diamond cutters in an Antwerp attic, and a picture of a large ware-house for diamond cutting in the early twentieth century show diamond cutters similarly sitting before grinding wheels. One would see a similar sight both in small offices along 47th street in Manhattan and in huge factories in Gujarat, India.

4. I started interviewing diamontaires and diamond industry experts in the summer of 2000, beginning in New York and later in Antwerp, Israel, Hong Kong, Mumbai, and elsewhere, and my interviews have continued through the past year. The influence of those interviews is felt in each chapter, and specific quotes are scattered throughout the book. I keep quotes anonymous when I did

not explicitly obtain permission to disclose the speaker's identity, and though I have maintained personal notes from each interview, I refrain from speckling the text with individual citations.

5. Historically, diamond merchants have always had to balance capacity constraints in manufacturing with waves of supply and demand. An economic boom in 1820 Amsterdam led to the emergence of many new factories, but work was never constant and cutters were hired on a temporary basis while maintaining consistent work elsewhere. When sailing ships came into port from Brazil with rough diamonds, the factories bustled with workers cutting and polishing the new shipment. And when the consignment was polished and the dealers scurried to sell the polished stones throughout the royal courts of Western Europe, work ceased.

6. An alternative to selling diamonds on credit is for a diamond merchant to seek credit from other sources, such as banks or investors, and some banks have entered the market by extending credit to diamontaires' purchases. However, banks have never meaningfully penetrated the market, and the vast majority of credit for purchase is extended by fellow diamontaires. This is simply because diamond merchants can obtain credit from each other at a lower cost than they could from other sources. Because diamond merchants operate within close-knit trading networks, they have more information about a buyer's creditworthiness than would a bank, thus reducing adverse selection costs. In addition, as Chapter 3 illustrates, diamond networks can efficiently police borrowers who might fail to pay their obligations, thus making the extension of credit more secure.

7. Chapter 6 explores in greater detail the connection between the structure of the traditional Jewish community and Jewish economic performance over time. It also discusses the growing role of non-Jewish ethnic networks that have participated in the diamond network, evaluating whether there are common lessons from these ethnic networks with different cultural, historical, and religious traditions.

3. The Mechanics of Statelessness

1. A typical example occurred when Martin Frankel, the troubled fugitive financier whose collapsed financial schemes prompted federal prosecution, attempted to escape from U.S. authorities. Hours before his planned flight from the United States, he arranged a shadowy purchase of several million dollars of diamonds (Pollack 2002). A Google search of "diamond heists" reveals a series of similarly colorful stories.

2. While diamonds pose significant credibility challenges for credit sales, Margaret Brinig (1990) famously observed that diamonds solve a credibility problem of another sort. "Engagement rings," Brinig suggests, "were part of an extralegal contract guarantee" that bound a courting man to his pledge to

marry, and thus replaced the old cause of action for a breach of a marriage promise (213).

3. Many Jewish diamond dealers managed to escape the Nazis in the 1930s but were not permitted to enter the United States. Several found temporary refuge in Cuba, Mexico, and Brazil—and established temporary diamond centers in those countries—before returning to Europe or immigrating to the United States. Many also immigrated to Israel and started that nation's global leadership in diamond cutting and production.

4. Not all of New York's diamond dealers are Jewish, and the other significant contingent of the DDC's membership is Indians, who currently compose approximately 10 percent (and growing) of DDC members. The entry of Indian merchants into New York's diamond industry—and their substantial presence in the DDC—has been a very significant development that is changing the face of the global industry (see Chapter 6 for more discussion of the significance of Indian entry). Indian entry reveals that diamond merchants need not belong to a particular family or ethnic group to succeed in the business; merchants need only solve the commitment problem. Indian merchants and Indian diamond networks, like Jewish merchants, are also family and clan based, and business dealings are deeply intertwined with private community affairs. Thus, Indian family and community institutions serve the same economic role in enforcing contracts as their Jewish counterparts, even if the particular community rewards and punishments are different.

5. Remarkably, diamond dealers can recognize specific diamonds and differentiate one from another. Thus, when a dealer lends one of his diamonds to another for temporary inspection, he is able to confirm that the diamond that was returned was the correct one.

6. Selling diamonds on credit obviously places risks on sellers, but buyers also assume risks in many diamond sales. While diamond purchasers are able to roughly assess the value of a diamond along the Gemological Institute of America's dimensions (the four Cs—carat, cut, clarity, and color), there are certain risks that they cannot confirm. For example, diamonds can receive laser treatments that improve the stone's color, but a treated diamond is less valuable than an untreated diamond of equal color. Since only a complex laser examination can detect whether a diamond is treated, a buyer often makes a purchase based on a seller's representation. Similarly, a diamond's origins cannot be verified upon inspection. This has become increasingly relevant with the rise of "conflict diamonds," diamonds mined in some African nations (particularly Angola, Sierra Leone, and Congo) by political-military organizations determined to overthrow a recognized government. Since the conflict diamond sales fund some of the most brutal military campaigns, many consumers refuse to purchase them and many jewelers refuse to use them. They nonetheless make their way through an elaborate global network from the African mines to Antwerp for sale. De Beers estimates that conflict diamonds constitute 4 percent of the

world's market, though the U.S. and UK governments suspect that the figure is significantly higher.

7. These same qualities also make diamonds attractive to the wealthy. One diamond merchant told the *New York Times*, "It has been the same forever. Whether it was royal families in different parts of the world, or today, when people worry that their dollars are worth nothing, they want assets that will increase in value—silent assets that you can put in your pocket because tomorrow, anything can go wrong." Another added, "Billionaires everywhere in the world like to keep some of their wealth in something easily transportable" ("Following the Money, Mr. Got Rocks Goes to China," *New York Times,* June 19, 2011).

8. This means that the DDC, in modern-day New York, serves the same adjudicatory function as the private judges in the sixteenth century's Champagne Fairs described in a famous paper by Paul Milgrom, Douglass North, and Barry Weingast (1990). According to Milgrom, North, and Weingast, private judges in the medieval fairs supported cross-border trade by disseminating information on merchants' past conduct and thus supporting a reputation mechanism. Milgrom, North, and Weingast observe that the role of these private judges, "far from being substitutes for the reputation mechanism, is to make the reputation system more effective as a means of promoting honest trade" (3).

9. This calculation whether to comply with or breach a particular credit obligation can be modeled as a prisoners' dilemma problem, which is a paradigmatic illustration of how long-term repeat players can sustain mutually beneficial behavior. The classic story goes more or less as follows: Two prisoners suspected of a crime are being interrogated by authorities in separate rooms. Because the authorities have limited evidence, they offer each prisoner an opportunity to confess and testify against his accomplice in exchange for a reduced sentence. If both confess, both get moderate jail sentences; if only one confesses, he is freed while the other is convicted (in large part because of evidence offered by the confessor) and given a hefty sentence; but if both deny wrongdoing, both get only small sentences. The core idea is that regardless of how one's accomplice acts (confessing or denying), each prisoner is individually better off by confessing, yet collectively the pair are better off by both denying and presenting a united front.

10. Given the demanding conditions to sustain cooperation, some scholars are more skeptical than others about the viability of reputation-based exchange. Some of this disagreement among economists can be explained methodologically. Game theoreticians like David Kreps (1990) and Avinash Dixit (2004), for example, offer economic models that illustrate the mathematical sustainability of many reputation mechanisms. Institutional economists like Oliver Williamson (1993) focus on institutional limitations and detail both the rigorous requirements that are needed to support trust-based exchange and the many factors that could disrupt such exchange systems.

11. One famous source of industry information is the *Rapaport Diamond Report*, which collects information about participating diamond purchasers—particularly jewelry manufacturers—and assigns credit ratings. It is the Moody's of the diamond industry. The *Report* also lists market prices for diamonds of various sizes and cuts, and many transactions base their sale price on what the *Report* says (for example, a sale price for a particular gem could be "83% of the *Rapaport* reported price"). Interestingly, the DDC board initially opposed Martin Rapaport's reporting of market prices, arguing that it disclosed the club's private information. The DDC tried to expel Rapaport from the DDC and Jewish religious courts initiated excommunication proceedings against him, and Rapaport in turn triggered an antitrust investigation of the DDC. Rapaport and the board later reconciled, and Rapaport's newsletter now flourishes, but the clash reveals a common response to merchants who devise new ways of doing business (see Chapter 5 for a discussion of both the Rapaport dispute and the lessons it offers on reputation mechanisms).

12. Jewish law imposes three distinct prohibitions: making unflattering, but true, remarks about a person for no reason *(lashon harah)*, recounting to a person gossip heard about him *(rekhilut)*, and knowingly communicating false, negative statements about another *(motzi shem rah)* (Broyde 1996, 77, citing Maimonides, *Deot* 7:1–7). It is easy to imagine how the prohibitions of both *rekhilut* and *motzi shem rah* can also improve the quality of reputational information.

13. The DDC bylaws also reflect how extended family relationships extend trustworthiness. Article 3, which governs the process for gaining membership, allows easier membership requirements for spouses, widows, sons, daughters, and sons- and daughters-in-law.

14. This is best described as an equilibrium condition. If there are enough people who would transact with someone who cheated (or simply was not sufficiently dedicated to complying with contractual obligations), then the effective deterrence from breaching agreements is too dilute to induce compliance. In short, cheating and the resulting loss of trust must be accompanied by a penalty that deters cheating—a nontrivial exit cost—even if reentry into a trusting network is possible.

15. Note that in this discussion of long-term players, the role of Jewish community institutions is mostly secondary to the importance of family connections and industry rules. Jewish norms and the intimacy of the Jewish community play valuable functions in spreading information among industry players and in coordinating punishment, but the Jewish community is not alone in its ability to spread accurate information. The only irreplaceable aspect of the long-term players is their predominant tendency to be connected to intergenerational family businesses, and that feature is by no means exclusive to the Jewish community. The value of family here is paramount, and the value of the ultra-Orthodox participation is necessary only in the short-term players in the following section.

16. There should be no doubt that these workers have extreme value in their possession. Several interviews proceeded as follows:

> *Author:* So let me get this straight, brokers carry around thousands of dollars' worth of diamonds . . .
> *Interviewee [with a laugh]: Thousands???*
> *Author:* OK, tens of thousands of . . .
> *Interviewee: Tens* of thousands?? [*another laugh*]

17. This is also true for those who simply wish to lead a more secular lifestyle (without first committing theft). Individuals hoping for independence from the community's religious structures struggle to separate themselves from the community structures and navigate the modern world. Certain support networks and charities have emerged to aid those who wish to leave but feel unable.

18. Formally, a club member's utility is $U_i = U(S_i, R_i, Q)$ for $i = 1$ to N members, where S represents economic goods, R are club goods, and $Q = \Sigma_{i \neq j} R_j / (N-1)$. Additional conditions typically are $\partial U_i / \partial S_i$, $\partial U_i / \partial R_i$, $\partial U_i / \partial Q > 0$ and $U(0, \bullet, \bullet) = U(\bullet, 0, \bullet) = U(\bullet, \bullet, 0) = 0$.

   Inclusion of the Q variable in the utility function indicates that club members also derive utility from the "quality" of the group's collective club goods consumption. Q is an externality that rises with the number and average participation of the other members, so an individual's utility is increased whenever he is near community members who also consume the same club goods.

19. Even Maimonides, the Jewish twelfth-century rational philosopher who codified the modern sciences for Jewish scholars, neglected the studies of economics and other social sciences, summarily concluding in his *Treatise on Logic (Millot ha-Higgayon)* that "man's conduct is [determined] by the divine regulations."

20. Religious Jewish texts are replete with affirmation of the sanctity of verbal promises. See, for example, Proverbs 6:1–2 ("My son, if you have stood surety for your fellow, Given your hand for another, You have been trapped by the words of your mouth, Snared by the words of your mouth."). The law of misrepresentation does have notable exceptions, however, particularly for items that are hard to value.

21. Maimonides, abandoning certain sensitivities, warned, "The punishment for [incorrect] measures is more drastic than the sanction on incest, because the latter is an offense against God, while the former affects a fellow human. He who denies the law concerning measures is like one who denies the Exodus from Egypt which was the beginning of this commandment" (Yad, Genevah 7:1–3, 12; 8:1, 20, with reference to Bava Batra 89b).

22. Even though the law governing commercial conduct appears motivated by ethical precepts, economic logic probably did have a hand in the shaping of these rules over time. Salo Baron (1975, 54) notes that, as a general matter, Jewish law adapts functionally to economic and social demands, and this includes rabbinic

formulations of business rules: "[The rabbinic tradition] made it possible for scholars to read into the established texts of Bible and Talmud provisions, as well as limitations, to suit the changing needs of Jewish society. In this way the people's intellectual leaders were able to preserve a measure of continuity within a bewildering array of diverse customs and usages. . . . In many cases the communal leaders, rabbinic and lay, often personally immersed in a variety of economic enterprises and thus acquiring much practical experience, consciously made interpretive alterations to reflect genuine social needs. . . . They thus lent the Jewish economic rationales the same kind of unity within diversity that permeated the entire Jewish socioreligious outlook on life."

23. In fact, Bernstein (1992, 139n50) reported that the DDC arbitration board initiated an excommunication proceeding against Rapaport when Rapaport and the DDC leadership were in a dispute over his *Rapaport Diamond Report*. The battle between Rapaport and DDC leadership in the early 1980s is discussed in greater detail in Chapter 5.

24. Samuel Heilman (1992, 277–286) writes about the role that *shadchanim*, or matchmakers, play in arranging marriages in some communities: "In the haredi (ultra-Orthodox) community, the *shadchan* is like the college or army recruiter. He or she comes near graduation time and knows exactly where and when to find prospects" (281). The central challenge of a *shadchan* is to find a young boy and girl who enjoy (or suffer from) a comparable social status, based on their families' histories, their families' wealth, the boy's academic background and prowess, and, to a small degree, their relative attractiveness. *Shadchanim* make offers and counteroffers to the children's parents until both sets of parents agree to a match. "The marriage is kind of a *contractual* arrangement, a deal, with the couple having the right of refusal but little else. But more than that, it is also a *social* arrangement, a way to locate the couple in the community, a way of institutionalizing their passage into the next phases of their lives so that they may stay in that community" (286, emphasis in original).

25. Perhaps—although it is a stretch—another complementarity with the diamond industry is the ultra-Orthodox appreciation for the presence of the divine in the world. Diamonds have always sparked the human imagination, and the transcendent qualities that diamonds exhibit fit nicely into how many ultra-Orthodox describe the world's majesty. This idea resonated for the author when one diamond cutter was discussing his trade while polishing diamonds. Proceeding through the pile of diamonds needing polishing, he opened a small envelope with his next stone and stopped midsentence. The flawless gem was the size of a plump raspberry and projected bright facets onto the table. The cutter picked up the stone and cradled it in the back of his hand, thoroughly admiring its beauty before proceeding with the grinding wheel.

26. "In matters of taste, there can be no disputes" (literally, "About tastes, it should not be disputed"). Nobel laureates George Stigler and Gary Becker, in a famous 1977 article that co-opted the Latin phrase, echoed this same approach to under-

standing seemingly idiosyncratic or irrational behavior, arguing that economists should "treat tastes as stable over time and similar among people." They continued, "The ambitiousness of our agenda deserves emphasis: we are proposing the hypothesis that widespread and / or persistent human behavior can be explained by a generalized calculus of utility-maximizing behavior, without introducing the qualification 'tastes remaining the same.' ... We assert that this traditional approach of the economist offers guidance in tackling these problems—and that no other approach of remotely comparable generality and power is available" (76–77).

4. A Theory of Statelessness

1. Coase, in a fiftieth anniversary retrospective celebration of his famous 1937 article, said, "This statement has been called a 'tautology.' It is the criticism people make of a proposition which is clearly right" (Coase 1991, 48).
2. The example is taken from Monteverde and Teece (1982).
3. Hayek, in highlighting the economic centrality of information, emphasized that the solution requires a minimization of hierarchical control: "If we can agree that the economic problem of society is mainly one of rapid adaptation to changes in the particular circumstances of time and place, it would seem to follow that the ultimate decisions must be left to the people who are familiar with these circumstances.... We must solve it by some form of decentralization" (1945, 524).
4. Williamson attributes a firm's incapacity to mimic market incentives to "the impossibility of selective intervention" on the part of managers and the "Fundamental Transformation," in which nonspecific relationships acquire specificity when internalized within the firm (Williamson 1996b, 49–50). For a detailed discussion of the costs of bureaucracy, see Williamson (1985), chap. 6.
5. One notable exception is Cooter and Landa (1984), which identifies certain advantages in both impersonal court ordering and relational private ordering. This work stands out because it postulates an equilibrium that balances the comparative advantages of the two systems. Using a free entry equilibrium, it shows that if a group of traders surpasses an optimal size, enforcing arm's-length contracts in the public courts becomes superior to private enforcement mechanisms.
6. Richman (2004, 2343–2344) briefly discusses the interesting market for wholesale fish. Fish supplies are unpredictable, and fish, once caught, spoil quickly. As a result, wholesalers cannot plan future sales contracts, and once they purchase fish from boats that arrive in port, they must immediately sell their goods, often without securing payment or negotiating a secured contract. One fish dealer commented, "You're selling a melting ice cube. Today it's cod; tomorrow it's cat food.... [We're] selling things that ... drop[] in value by the hour. Twenty-eight cents a pound today; it's worth two cents a pound

tomorrow" ("Morning Edition: Maine Man Uses Internet to Sell Credit Information to Fish Wholesalers," National Public Radio broadcast, January 29, 1999). The short window of opportunity to execute a transaction compels sales on credit. However, enforcing those sales contracts through the public courts is costly, and it is uneconomical for merchants to pursue buyers through formal legal action. Because merchants understand this ex ante, courts cannot credibly secure ex post enforcement of credit sales.

The industry resolves the contracting problem by instituting coordinated punishments. The Internet company Seafax publicizes fish buyers who have not yet paid wholesalers, and wholesalers subsequently will refuse to sell to those publicized to be in breach. The forward-looking sanctions are enough to induce fish buyers to fulfill their credit obligations.

7. Eli Berman (2000) has shown that characterizing individual utilities along economic and club good dimensions can explain a wide variety of otherwise unusual economic and social behavior, including the pursuit of low wages and the contribution of significant time to community endeavors.

8. McMillan and Woodruff (2000) and Richard McAdams (1995) have also observed that relational contracting and closed economic networks can impose noneconomic harms as well, such as bigotry and persistent discrimination. Milhaupt and West (2000) and Gambetta (1993) similarly wrote that trust-based exchange and closed ethnic networks can also use violence to enforce compliance.

9. This argument admittedly lacks a counterfactual, as it's impossible to prove or refute that there is substantial value from undiscovered innovations, although it is quite telling that the industry has relied on a network of middlemen for centuries even as technology has radically transformed other industries. Chapter 8 documents some recent disruptions to the industry, including the replacement of the traditional network by vertically integrated firms. Even so, the technologies of examining and cutting stones have remained rather stagnant.

10. For a critique of this account of Silicon Valley, see Barnett and Sichelman (2016). In 2010, the Department of Justice sued several of the most prominent Silicon Valley companies for entering into "no cold call" agreements, claiming that these agreements were anticompetitive restraints on the labor market and violated the Sherman Act. The case settled less than a year later, with the employers agreeing to discontinue a broad prohibition against "attempting to enter into, entering into, maintaining or enforcing any agreement with any other person to in any way refrain from, requesting that any person in any way refrain from, or pressuring any person in any way to refrain from soliciting, cold calling, recruiting, or otherwise competing for employees of the other person" (*U.S. v. Adobe Systems, Inc., et al.*, final judgment, United States Department of Justice, March 17, 2011). The suit revealed that the agreements at issue were efforts by employers to restrict the mobility of their valuable employees, an

effort to counteract the engineers' professional norms that promoted open collaboration. The tension between arguably procompetitive collaboration among engineers and anticompetitive cooperation among employers illustrates how cooperative norms and agreements are not always socially desirable. See Chapter 5.

5. The Costs of Statelessness

1. This resolution followed a similar resolution at an international gathering of diamond dealers, and it was implemented by a "German Activities Investigation Committee" which was formed jointly with the Diamond Center and was assigned the responsibility of carrying out the resolutions in cooperation with like-minded international associations. Transcript of Plaintiff's Interrogatories Addressed to Defendant at 14, United States v. Diamond Dealers Club, Inc., No. 76-343 (S.D.N.Y. Sept. 1, 1954), 14.

2. It should be noted that Williamson does not blame Turner alone for ill-advised policies; rather, he blames the entire field of economics, writing, "With the benefit of hindsight, the field of industrial organization and the enforcement of antitrust were in crisis in the 1960s." In fact, Williamson credits Turner for bringing economic analysis to the forefront of antitrust policy making, appointing economists and lawyers with economic training to top positions in the Antitrust Division and upgrading the role of economists from litigation support to policy making. Williamson continues, "Tall oaks from little acorns grow. The seeds planted during the Turner administration warrant more than a passing nod" (Williamson 2003, 65).

3. The DOJ and FTC issue merger guidelines to alert parties when a merger might trigger regulatory scrutiny. There are horizontal merger guidelines and non-horizontal merger guidelines. Collectively, we can call them the *Guidelines*.

4. The DDC also argued that the boycott of German goods and merchants had no material economic impact and that it constituted political expression protected under the First Amendment. It is possible that the DDC's coordinated restraints would now be permitted under *NAACP v. Claiborne Hardware Co.*, 458 U.S. 886 (1982), in which the Supreme Court permitted black citizens to boycott white merchants in Claiborne County, Mississippi. After the white merchants sued to recover losses from the boycott, the court ruled that economic regulations cannot prohibit "a nonviolent, politically motivated boycott designed to force governmental and economic change and to effectuate rights guaranteed by the Constitution itself" (458 U.S. at 914). However, "expressive boycotts" remain scrutinized under the antitrust laws, particularly when the boycott is "conducted by business competitors who stand to profit financially from a lessening of competition in the boycotted market" (*FTC v. Superior Court Trial Lawyers Assn.*, 493 U.S. 411, 427 (1990)).

5. Immediately following this clearly insensitive remark by Judge Noonan, the DDC's attorney, Harry Torczyner, spoke up to say "I very much regret the statement just made" (6). He then spoke at length: "Now, each and every one of these people has had, each and every one—and I can name them because I know most of them personally—has had a direct experience at the hands of the Germans, or by whatever name you want to call them. Why? Because those who are not [sic] of an old age had known two invasions of Belgium. In 1914 . . . a zeppelin, if you will remember, in 1914 came over Antwerp and bombed the city. The next encounter was on May 10, 1940, when a part of these people was able to escape and to find the generous hospitality of the United States on this side of the ocean, and when the major part, the major part, were utterly and completely destroyed and annihilated by the invading Germans. The homes of these people were looted, their families were deported; practically each and every member of that center has lost somebody in World War II, if not in open combat, through the murderous activities in the concentration camps in Europe. And there are even a number of members of that center who can show you not the figures of German trade but figures imprinted on their forearm, the tattoos of the concentration camp which the Germans have inflicted on them. And that is why the Government knows the mitigating circumstances of this case" (9–10).

6. Ironically, a current complaint with the *Rapaport Diamond Report* is that the quoted prices are too high. Some complaints are motivated, in part, by criticism over Rapaport's dual role as a publisher of prices and as a dealer holding a private inventory. Charges of bias will likely continue to hound the *Rapaport Report* as long as Rapaport stands to profit personally from any manipulation of his published prices.

7. FTC Staff Request for DOJ Clearance, Matter #821-0041 (Bureau of Competition Jan. 6, 1982).

8. FTC Bureau of Competition, Government Memo, June 1, 1982, re: File No. 821-0041.

9. Although the language of the bylaws appears to give arbitrary power to the board, it also reveals the overwhelming concern for a merchant's reputation. The need to protect individual reputations, especially against inaccurate reputational information, is a good argument for empowering the board to punish those who impugn the character of a particular merchant.

10. Secretary's Matters, Open Meeting of the Fed. Trade Comm'n, Matter #821-0041, at 32 (Bureau of Competition Sept. 18, 1984).

6. Lessons from Statelessness

1. An interesting debate is swirling among Jewish historians over the significance of moneylending in Jewish economic history. The traditional narrative, the one espoused by most historians, has the Jewish moneylender as the archetype of the Jewish medieval merchant (for example, Karp 2008, Chazen 2010), and the

cultural persona typified by Shylock in *The Merchant of Venice* has sustained many unflattering Jewish stereotypes. Joseph Shatzmiller's *Shylock Reconsidered* (1990) offered one amendment to the cultural persona, arguing that Jewish money-lenders were largely respected and appreciated by their non-Jewish neighbors. Julie Mell (2016) launches a broader critique of the traditional narrative, which she calls "one of the most erroneous stories in Jewish history" (1), and argues that Jews played a very modest role in banking and moneylending in medieval Europe.

2. The Jewish people's history of marginalization feeds into the narrative that many Jewish diamond dealers invoke to describe their merchant community. Writing in the 1982 *Jewish Directory and Almanac*, the then executive director of the Diamond Dealers Club (more prominent as a diamond merchant than as an historian) wrote, "Charting the history of the Jews in the diamond industry is similar to recounting our persecuted past and our reactions as a people. Jews in general have crowded into certain trades due to reasons closely related to being Jewish. Many countries have kept us as socio-economically backward as possible due to their jealousies, fears, and outright hatreds. These national bi-ases have forced Jewish people to stay within their own districts for purposes of residence and livelihood" (Shainberg 1982).

3. Sombart not only argues that Jews were well-suited for capitalism, but in fact that capitalism would not have succeeded were it not for Jews: "Before capitalism could develop the natural man had to be changed out of all recognition, and a rationalistically minded mechanism introduced in his stead. There had to be a transvaluation of all economic values. And what was the result? The *homo capi-talisticus*, who is closely related to the *homo Judceus*, both belonging to the same species, *homines rationalistic! artificiales*" (166).

4. The *Financial Times* has said that Idar-Oberstein, a provincial town in the pictur-esque Hunsrück Mountains in Germany's Rhineland, "turns out stonecutters the way Frankfurt does bankers" (Clerizo 2004). And the *Financial Post* reports that Canada's Northwest Territories, aiming to develop its own cutting industry, has recruited thirty-three master cutters from Nor-Hajen, Armenia, a town of fewer than ten thousand people located twenty kilometers from the Armenian capital (Rubin 2001).

5. The Ratnapariksa, a sixth-century text by Buddha Bhatta, includes the following lines:

> He who, having pure body, always carries a diamond with sharp points,
>   without blemish, free from all faults;
> that one, as long as he lives, knows each day will bear some things:
>   happiness, prosperity, children, riches, grain, cows and meat.
> He who wears [such] a diamond will see dangers recede from him whether
>   he be threatened by serpents, fire, poison, sickness, thieves, flood or evil
>   spirits.

6. This same ethnography aimed to distinguish how Indian communities offer structural support to merchants' success from theories relying on ethnic-based human capital explanations: "Europeans speak of [Gujarati Indian traders] as 'born businessmen,' and Indians themselves often explain their success by reference to a presumed inherited capacity for business not shared by most other people—Jews (and perhaps Chinese) excepted. These beliefs of course represent the common tendency of people everywhere to interpret and justify a given division of labor in terms of supposedly innate racial characteristics.... [However], few of the Indians who engage in trade so successfully in Africa were actually traders in India.... In Africa itself, circumstances decreed that they exercise these talents rather than any others they might have" (Dotson and Dotson 1968, 66).

7. Gomez is consistent across his cultural studies, as he links Jewish cultural traditions with the success of Jewish diamond merchants as well. Gomez argues that Jewish historical comfort with and support for arbitration predisposed Jewish merchants to the extralegal dispute resolution that supports the diamond trade, writing, "Over the centuries, Jewish merchants have utilized arbitration almost exclusively for disputes among themselves and also for those involving non-Jewish parties, who have increasingly become familiarized with this mechanism and the substantive rules drawn from Jewish religious institutions" (Gomez 2007, 172).

7. Governing Statelessness

1. From the De Beers website, https://www.forevermark.com/en-us/our-diamonds /responsibly-sourced/.

8. The Limits of Statelessness and an Autopsy of Cooperation

1. For De Beers to create a physical presence in the United States, it first had to settle all of its outstanding antitrust convictions, including one with the U.S. Department of Justice for a 1994 price-fixing suit discussed in Chapter 5 and a series of private class actions from 2001 that accused De Beers of manipulating the price of diamonds for sixty years. De Beers decided in 2004 to plead guilty to the government charges so it could reenter the U.S. market and so its officers could travel to the United States without arrest. It similarly settled the class action in 2006, trying to—as a De Beers spokesperson said—"normalize" the company's business in America. Nicky Oppenheimer could enter into the United States without fearing arrest only after these suits were resolved.

2. The current Herfindahl-Hirschman Index, a common measure of market concentration and monopoly pricing power, currently is approximately 2,400 for diamond production, about the same as the U.S. market for breakfast cereal. When De Beers enjoyed an 82 percent market share, the index was over 6,700.

If classic economic theory were at work, the current market structure would be unable to explain the persistence of high wholesale prices.

3. In fact, the many accounts of De Beers' business practices suggest that the company, contrary to the measurement costs explanation, did indeed invest heavily in measuring, accounting, and valuing each stone sold to sightholders. Thus, these academic explanations do not square entirely with journalistic descriptions of De Beers' business practices.

References

AAA (American Arbitration Association). 2016. "About the American Arbitration Association (AAA) and the International Centre for Dispute Resolution (ICDR)." American Arbitration Association website, last accessed November 15. http://www.adr.org/aaa/faces/s/about.

Abrahams, Israel. 1896. *Jewish Life in the Middle Ages*. London: MacMillan.

Appelbaum, R. P., W. Felstiner, and V. Gessner. 2001. *Rules and Networks: The Legal Culture of Global Business Transactions*. Oxford: Hart.

Ardener, Shirley. 1964. "The Comparative Study of Rotating Credit Associations." *Journal of the Royal Anthropological Institute of Great Britain and Ireland* 94 (2): 201–229.

Arkin, Marcus. 1975. *Aspects of Jewish Economic History*. Philadelphia: Jewish Publication Society of America.

Ashreena, T., and A. Ananthalakshmi. 2015. "Fearing Defaults, Banks Rein in Credit to Jewelery Firms." *Reuters*, January 16. http://in.reuters.com/article /india-jewellers-credit-idINKBN0KP0M020150116.

Atkin, R. [1923] 1986. "Foreword." In W. A. Bewes, *The Romance of the Law Merchant*. London: Sweet and Maxwell.

Ayal, E. B., and B. R. Chiswick. 1983. "The Economics of the Diaspora Revisited." *Economic Development and Cultural Change* 31:861–875.

Bain & Company. 2014. *The Global Diamond Report 2014*, December 9. http://www .bain.com/publications/articles/global-diamond-report-2014.aspx.

Barnett, J., and T. Sichelman. 2016. "Revisiting Labor Mobility in Innovation Markets." USC Law Legal Studies Paper No. 16-15. http://ssrn.com/abstract =2758854.

Baron, S. W. 1975. *The Economic History of the Jews*. New York: Schocken Books.

Barzel, Y. 1977. "Some Fallacies in the Interpretation of Information Costs." *Journal of Law and Economics* 20:291–307.

Beawes, W. A. 1923. *The Romance of the Law Merchant*. London: Sweet and Maxwell.

Becker, Gary S. 1993. *Human Capital* (3rd ed.). Chicago: University of Chicago Press.

Behavioral Sciences Subpanel, President's Science Advisory Committee. 1962. "Strengthening the Behavioral Sciences." *Science* 136:233–241.

Benkler, Y. 2003. "Freedom in the Commons: Towards a Political Economy of Information." *Duke Law Journal* 52:1245–1276.

Ben-Porath, Y. 1980. "The F-Connection: Families, Friends, and Firms and the Organization of Exchange." *Population Development Review* 6:1–30.

Benson, B. 1989. "The Spontaneous Evolution of Commercial Law." *Southern Economic Journal* 55:644–661.

Berger, S. 2001. "Diamonds in the Rough." *Jerusalem Post,* April 6, 4B.

Berman, E. 2000. "Sect, Subsidy, and Sacrifice: An Economist's View of Ultra-Orthodox Jews." *Quarterly Journal of Economics* 115 (3): 905–953.

Berman, H. 1983. *Law and Revolution: The Formation of the Western Legal Tradition.* Cambridge, MA: Harvard University Press.

Bernstein, L. 1992. "Opting Out of the Legal System: Extralegal Contractual Relations in the Diamond Industry." *Journal of Legal Studies* 21 (1): 115–157.

———. 1996. "Merchant Law in a Merchant Court: Rethinking the Code's Search for Immanent Business Norms." *University of Pennsylvania Law Review* 144:1765–1821.

———. 2001. "Private Commercial Law in the Cotton Industry: Creating Cooperation through Rules, Norms, and Institutions." *Michigan Law Review* 99:1724–1790.

Berquem, V. 1988. "Bourses More than a Place to Sell." *Jewelry News Asia.*

Bond, P., and A. Rai. 2002. "Collateral Substitutes in Microfinance." Unpublished manuscript, https://pdfs.semanticscholar.org/0e69/a2c75d8d61f000346c5e10 5d3cfe84b1d648.pdf.

Bork, R. H. 1978. *The Antitrust Paradox: A Policy at War with Itself.* New York: Basic Books.

Botticini, M., and Z. Eckstein. 2012. *The Chosen Few: How Education Shaped Jewish History, 70–1492.* Princeton, NJ: Princeton University Press.

Brenner, R., and N. Kiefer. 1981. "The Economics of the Diaspora: Discrimination and Occupational Structure." *Economic Development and Cultural Change* 29 (3): 517–534.

Brinig, M. 1990. "Rings and Promises." *Journal of Law, Economics, and Organization* 6:203–215.

Broyde, M. 1996. *The Pursuit of Justice and Jewish Law* (2nd ed.). Brooklyn, NY: Yashar Books.

Carothers, T. 1998. "The Rule of Law Revival." *Foreign Affairs* 55:95–106.

Carr, Jack, and Janet T. Landa. 1983. "The Economics of Symbols, Clan Names, and Religion." *Journal of Legal Studies* 12 (1): 135–156.

Charny, D. 1999. "The New Formalism in Contract." *University of Chicago Law Review* 66:842–857.

Chazen, R. 2010. *Reassessing Jewish Life in Medieval Europe.* Cambridge: Cambridge University Press.

Clay, K. 1997. "Trade without Law: Private-Order Institutions in Mexican California." *Journal of Law, Economics, and Organization* 13 (1): 202–231.

Clerizo, M. 2004. "The Stone's Happy. I Am Happy Too." *Financial Times,* January 24, 15.

Coase, R. H. 1937. "The Nature of the Firm." *Economica* 4:386–405.

———. 1960. "The Problem of Social Cost." *Journal of Law and Economics* 3:1–44.

———. 1972. "Industrial Organization: A Proposal for Research." In *Economic Research: Retrospect and Prospect: Policy Issues and Research Opportunities in Industrial Organization,* edited by Victor R. Fuchs, 59–73. New York: Columbia University Press.

———. 1991. "The Nature of the Firm: Meaning." In *The Nature of the Firm,* edited by Oliver E. Williamson and Sidney G. Winter, 48–60. New York: Oxford University Press.

Coleman, James. 1990. *The Foundations of Social Theory.* Cambridge, MA: Harvard University Press.

Cooter, R. D. 1994. "Structural Adjudication and the New Law Merchant: A Model of Decentralized Law." *International Review of Law and Economics* 14:215–231.

Cooter, R. H., and J. T. Landa. 1984. "Personal versus Impersonal Trade: The Size of Trading Groups and Contract Law." *International Review of Law and Economics* 4:15–22.

Cowell, A. 2000. "Controversy Over Diamonds Made into Virtue by De Beers." *New York Times.* August 22. http://www.nytimes.com/2000/08/22/business /controversy-over-diamonds-made-into-virtue-by-de-beers.html.

Dasgupta, Partha. 1988. "Trust as a Commodity." In *Trust: Making and Breaking Cooperative Relations,* ed. Diego Gambetta, 49–72. Department of Sociology: University of Oxford.

Davis, K. E., and M. Trebilcock. 2008. "The Relationship between Law and Development: Optimists versus Skeptics." *American Journal of Comparative Law* 56:895–946.

Dixit, A. K. 2004. *Lawlessness and Economics: Alternative Modes of Governance.* Princeton, NJ: Princeton University Press.

Donahue, C. 2004a. "Equity in the Courts of Merchants." *Tijdschrift voor Rechtsgeschiedenis* 72:1–35.

———. 2004b. "Medieval and Early Modern Lex Mercatoria: An Attempt at the Probation Diabolica." *Chicago Journal of International Law* 5:21–37.

———. 2005. "Benvenuto Stracca's De Mercatura: Was There a Lex Mercatoria in Sixteenth-Century Italy?" In *From Lex Mercatoria to Commercial Law.* Comparative Studies in Anglo-American and Continental Legal History 24, edited by Vito Piergiovanni, 69–120. Berlin: Duncker and Humblot.

Dore, Ronald. 1983. "Goodwill and the Spirit of Market Capitalism." *British Journal of Sociology* 34:459–482.

———. 1989. *Taking Japan Seriously.* Palo Alto, CA: Stanford University Press.

Dotson, F., and L. O. Dotson. 1968. *The Indian Minority of Zambia, Rhodesia, and Malawi.* New Haven, CT: Yale University Press.

Dundas, P. 2002. *The Jains* (2nd ed.). New York: Routledge.

Easterbrook, F. 1984. "The Limits of Antitrust." *Texas Law Review* 63:1–40.

Ellickson, R. C. 1991. *Order without Law: How Neighbors Settle Disputes.* Cambridge, MA: Harvard University Press.

Epstein, E. J. 1982. "Have You Ever Tried to Sell a Diamond?" *Atlantic* (February Issue).

Even-Zohar, C. 2007. *From Mine to Mistress.* London: Mining Communications.

———. 2008a. "Arbitration Justice in Absentia." *Diamond Intelligence Briefs,* April 14.

———. 2008b. "Bourse Leadership, Arbitrations, and Fraudulent GIA Certificates." *Diamond Intelligence Briefs,* February 26.

———. 2011. "DDC New York: A Bourse in the Service of Its President." *Diamond Intelligence Briefing,* September 21. https://www.diamondintelligence.com/magazine/magazine.aspx?id=9862.

———. 2015. "A Splintering of the Pipeline: The Economic Threat of Synthetics on the Diamond Producers." *Diamond Intelligence Briefing,* July 20. http://www.thediamondloupe.com/depth/2015-07-20/splintering-pipeline-economic-threat-synthetics-diamond-producers.

Fafchamps, M. 1996a. "The Enforcement of Commercial Contracts in Ghana." *World Development* 24:427–448.

———. 1996b. "Sovereign Debt, Structural Adjustment, and Conditionality." *Journal of Development Economics* 50 (2): 313–335.

Friedman, M. [1972] 1988. "Capitalism and the Jews." Foundation for Economic Freedom, https://fee.org/articles/capitalism-and-the-jews/.

Friedman, T. 2005. *The World Is Flat.* New York: Farrar, Straus and Giroux.

Frontline. 1994. "The Diamond Empire." Season 12, episode 2, aired February 1.

Fukuyama, Francis. 1995. *Trust: The Social Virtues and the Creation of Prosperity.* New York: Free Press.

Galanter, M. 1981. "Justice in Many Rooms: Courts, Private Ordering, and Indigenous Law." *Journal of Legal Pluralism* 19:1–47.

Gambetta, D. 1988a. Foreword to *Trust: Making and Breaking Cooperative Relations,* ix–xii. Edited by D. Gambetta. Cambridge, MA: Basil Blackwell.

———. 1988b. "Mafia: The Price of Distrust." In *Trust: Making and Breaking Cooperative Relations,* 158–175. Edited by D. Gambetta. Cambridge, MA: Basil Blackwell.

———. 1993. *The Sicilian Mafia: The Business of Private Protection.* Cambridge, MA: Harvard University Press.

Geertz, Clifford. 1962. "The Rotating Credit Association: A 'Middle Rung' in Development." *Economic Development and Cultural Change* 10 (3): 249–254.

General Accounting Office. 2002. *International Trade: Critical Issues Remain in Deterring Conflict Diamond Trade,* report GAO-02-678. Washington, D.C.

Gereffi, G., R. Garcia-Johnson, and E. Sasser. 2001. "The NGO-Industrial Complex." *Foreign Policy* 125:56–65.

Gereffi, G., and F. Mayer. 2005. "Globalization and the Demand for Governance." In *The New Offshoring of Jobs and Global Development*, by G. Gereffi, 39–65. International Labour Organization Social Policy Lectures. Geneva: International Institute for Labour Studies.

Global Witness. 2006. *The Truth about Diamonds: Conflict and Development*. https://www .globalwitness.org/sites/default/files/import/the_truth_about_diamonds.pdf.

Goetz, C. J., and R. E. Scott. 1981. "Principles of Relational Contracts." *Virginia Law Review* 67 (6): 1089–1150.

Golan, E. 2013. "Financing in the Diamond Industry." *Idex Magazine*, October. http://edahn.com/images/Financing_in_the_Diamond_Industry-IDEX _Magazine_Oct_2013.pdf.

Goldberg, V. P. 1976. "Regulation and Administered Contracts." *Bell Journal of Economics* 7 (Autumn): 426–452.

———. 2013. "Contracts: Coordination across Firm Boundaries." Chap. 5 in *Handbook of Economic Organization*, edited by A. Grandori, 85–95. Northampton, MA: Edward Elgar.

Gomez, M. A. 2007. "Mazal U'Bracha: Dispute Processing and the Venezuelan Diamond Industry." In *All in the Family: The Influence of Social Networks on Dispute Processing (A Case Study of a Developing Economy)*, 155–185. PhD diss., Stanford University.

———. 2013a. "Gemstone Justice." *Jain Digest*, April–June, 25–26.

———. 2013b. "Precious Resolution: The Use of Intra-community Arbitration by Jain Diamond Merchants." *Belgian Review of Arbitration* 2:119–139.

Granovetter, M. 1985. "Economic Action and Social Structure: The Problem of Embeddedness." *American Journal of Sociology* 91:481–510.

Gray, C. S., and A. A. Davis. 1993. "Competition Policy in Developing Counties Undergoing Structural Adjustment." *Antitrust Bulletin* 38:425–467.

Grayzel, S. 1968. *A History of the Jews*. New York: Jewish Publication Society.

Greif, A. 1989. "Reputation and Coalitions in Medieval Trade: Evidence on the Maghribi Traders." *Journal of Economic History* 49 (4): 857–882.

———. 1993. "Contract Enforceability and Economic Institutions in Early Trade: The Maghribi Traders' Coalition." *American Economic Review* 83 (3): 525–548.

———. 2004a. "Impersonal Exchange without Impartial Law: The Community Responsibility System." *Chicago Journal of International Law* 5:109–138.

———. 2004b. "Institutions and Impersonal Exchange: The European Experience." Stanford Law and Economics Olin Working Paper No. 284. http://ssrn .com/abstract=548783.

———. 2006a. "History Lessons: The Birth of Impersonal Exchange: The Community Responsibility System and Impartial Justice." *Journal of Economic Perspectives* 20 (2): 221–236.

———. 2006b. *Institutions and the Path to the Modern Economy: Lessons from Medieval Trade*. Cambridge: Cambridge University Press.

Greif, A., and E. Kandel. 1995. "Contract Enforcement Institutions: Historical Perspective and Current Status in Russia." In *Economic Transition in Eastern Europe and Russia: Realities of Reform*, edited by E. P. Lazear, 291–321. Stanford, CA: Hoover Institution Press.

Hadfield, G., and B. Weingast. 2012. "What Is Law? A Coordination Model of the Characteristics of Legal Order." *Journal of Legal Analysis* 4 (2): 471–514.

———. 2013. "Law without the State: Legal Attributes and the Coordination of Decentralized Collective Punishment." *Journal of Law and Courts* 1 (1): 3–34.

———. 2015. "Microfoundations of the Rule of Law." *Annual Review of Political Science* 17:21–42.

———. 2016. "Is Rule of Law an Equilibrium without Private Ordering?" USC Law Legal Studies Paper No. 16-18; Stanford Law and Economics Olin Working Paper No. 493. http://ssrn.com/abstract=2785017.

HaKohen, R. Israel Meir. 1873. *Chafetz Chaim*. Jerusalem: Hebrew Books.

Hardin, Russell. 2002. *Trust and Trustworthiness*. New York: Russell Sage Foundation.

Hayek, F. A. 1945. "The Use of Knowledge in Society." *American Economic Review* 35 (4): 519–530.

———. 1973. *Rules and Order*. Vol. 1 of *Law, Legislation, and Liberty*. Chicago: University of Chicago Press.

Heilman, S. 1992. *Defenders of the Faith*. New York: Schocken.

Hofmeester, K. 2013. "Shifting Trajectories of Diamond Processing: From India to Europe and Back, from the Fifteenth Century to the Twentieth." *Journal of Global History* 8:25–49.

Holmes, O. W., Jr. 1897. "The Path of the Law." *Harvard Law Review* 10:457–478.

Hyde, A. 2003. *Working in Silicon Valley: Economic and Legal Analysis of a High-Velocity Labor Market*. Armonk, NY: M. E. Sharpe.

Iannaccone, L. R. 1992. "Sacrifice and Stigma: Reducing Free-Riding in Cults, Communes, and Other Collectives." *Journal of Political Economy* 100:271–291.

India Brand Equity Foundation, Ministry of Commerce and Industry, Government of India. 2016. "Gems and Jewelry in India." Last updated October. http://www.ibef.org/industry/gems-jewellery-india.aspx.

Joskow, P. L. 1987. "Contract Duration and Relationship-Specific Investments: Empirical Evidence from Coal Markets." *American Economic Review* 77 (1): 168–185.

———. 2002. "Transaction Cost Economics, Antitrust Rules, and Remedies." *Journal of Law, Economics, and Organization* 18:95–116.

Kadens, E. 2015. "The Medieval Law Merchant: The Tyranny of a Construct." *Journal of Legal Analysis* 8:251–289.

Kanfer, S. 1993. *The Last Empire: De Beers, Diamonds, and the World*. New York: Farrar, Straus and Giroux.

Karp, J. 1999. "Call Them the Icemen: India's Angadias Tote Diamonds in the Rough." *Wall Street Journal*, March 9, 1999, sec. A1.

————. 2008. *The Politics of Jewish Commerce: Economic Thought and Emancipation in Europe, 1638–1848*. Cambridge: Cambridge University Press.

Kenney, R. W., and B. Klein. 1983. "The Economics of Block Booking." *Journal of Law and Economics* 26 (3): 497–540.

Khanna, S. 2008. "After Years, Kathiawaris Outshine Palanpuris in India Diamond Biz." *DNA India*, March 18. http://www.dnaindia.com/india/report-after-years -kathiawaris-outshine-palanpuris-in-india-diamond-biz-1156574.

Klein, B. 1980. "Transaction Cost Determinants of 'Unfair' Contractual Arrangements." *American Economic Review* 70 (2): 356–362.

Klein, B., R. G. Crawford, and A. A. Alchian. 1978. "Vertical Integration, Appropriable Rents, and the Competitive Contracting Process." *Journal of Law and Economics* 71 (2): 297–326.

Klein, B., and K. B. Leffler. 1981. "The Role of Market Forces in Assuring Contractual Performance." *Journal of Political Economy* 89 (4): 615–641.

Konradi, V. 2009. "The Role of *Lex Mercatoria* in Supporting Globalised Transactions: An Empirical Insight into the Governance Structure of the Timber Industry." In *Contracted Certainty in International Trade*, edited by V. Gessner, 49–86. Oxford: Hart Publishing.

Kothari, S. 2015. "Crunch Time for the Global Diamond Industry." *GemKonnect*, July 2. https://gemkonnect.wordpress.com/2015/07/02/crunch-time-for-the -global-diamond-industry/.

Kovacic, W. E. 1997. "Getting Started: Creating New Competition Policy Institutions in Transition Economies." *Brooklyn Journal of International Law* 23:403–453.

Kreps, D. 1990. "Corporate Culture and Economic Theory." In *Perspectives on Positive Political Economy*, edited by J. E. Alt and K. A. Shepsle, 90–143. New York: Cambridge University Press.

Kreps, D., and R. Wilson. 1982. "Reputation and Imperfect Information." *Journal of Economic Theory* 27:253–279.

Krueger, Anne. 1963. "The Economics of Discrimination." *Journal of Political Economy* 71 (5): 481–486.

Kumar, A. (director). 2009. *The Icemen: Angadias of India*. Singapore: MediaCorp.

Kuryan, V. 2015. "De Beers Discount Deals Erode Diamond Prices, May Trigger Price War." *GemKonnect*, October 27. https://gemkonnect.wordpress.com /2015/10/27/de-beers-discount-deals-erode-diamond-prices-may-trigger -price-war/.

Kysar, D. 2004. "Preferences for Processes: The Process / Product Distinction and the Regulation of Consumer Choice." *Harvard Law Review* 118:526–642.

Landa, J. T. 1981. "A Theory of the Ethnically Homogeneous Middleman Group: An Institutional Alternative to Contract Law." *Journal of Legal Studies* 10 (2): 349–362.

————. 1999. *Trust, Ethnicity, and Identity*. Ann Arbor: University of Michigan Press.

Leeson, P. 2009. *The Invisible Hook: The Hidden Economics of Pirates*. Princeton, NJ: Princeton University Press.

Levine, R., N. Loayza, and T. Beck. 2000. "Financial Intermediation and Growth: Causality and Causes." *Journal of Monetary Economics* 16 (1): 31–77.

Libecap, G. 1989. *Contracting for Property Rights*. Cambridge: Cambridge University Press.

Lubin, A. J. 1982. *Diamond Dealers Club: A Fifty-Year History*. New York: DDC.

Lytton, T. 2013. *Kosher: Private Regulation in the Age of Industrial Food*. Cambridge, MA: Harvard University Press.

Macaulay, S. 1963. "Non-contractual Relations in Business: A Preliminary Study." *American Sociological Review* 2 (1): 55–67.

Macher, J., and B. Richman. 2008. "Transaction Cost Economics: An Assessment of Empirical Research in the Social Sciences." *Business and Politics* 10:1–63.

Machiavelli, N. ([1531] 1882). "Discourses on the First Ten Books of Titus Livius." Book 1 in *Historical, Political, and Diplomatic Writings of Niccolo Machiavelli*, translated by Christian E. Detmold, 2, 93. Boston, James R. Osgood & Co.

Macneil, I. R. 1974. "The Many Futures of Contracts." *Southern California Law Review* 47 (3): 691–816.

———. 1978. "Contracts: Adjustment of Long-Term Economic Relations under Classical, Neoclassical, and Relational Contract Law." *Northwestern University Law Review* 72:854–905.

Maimbo, S. M. 2003. "The Money Exchange Dealers of Kabul." World Bank Working Paper No. 13. Washington, D.C.: The World Bank.

Malthus0. 2011. "Friedman on Antitrust." YouTube video, 3:16. Posted March 21. https://www.youtube.com/watch?v=vMvVmlDN0nY.

McAdams, R. H. 1992. "Relative Preferences." *Yale Law Journal* 102:1–104.

———. 1995. "Cooperation and Conflict: The Economics of Group Status Production and Race Discrimination." *Harvard Law Review* 108 (5): 1003–1084.

———. 1996. "Group Norms, Gossip, and Blackmail." *University of Pennsylvania Law Review* 144:2237–2292.

———. 1997. "The Origin, Development, and Regulation of Norms." *Michigan Law Review* 96:338–433.

McMillan, J., and C. Woodruff. 1999. "Dispute Prevention without Courts in Vietnam." *Journal of Law, Economics, and Organization* 15 (3): 637–658.

———. 2000. "Private Order under Dysfunctional Public Order." *Michigan Law Review* 98:2421–2458.

———. 2002. "The Central Role of Entrepreneurs in Transition Economies." *Journal of Economic Perspectives* 16 (3): 153–170.

Mell, J. 2017. *The Myth of the Medieval Jewish Moneylender*. Basingstoke, UK: Palgrave Macmillan.

Milgrom, P. R., D. North, and B. R. Weingast. 1990. "The Role of Institutions in the Revival of Trade: The Law Merchant, Private Judges, and the Champagne Fairs." *Economics and Politics* 2 (1): 1–23.

Milgrom, P., and J. Roberts. 1982. "Predation, Reputation, and Entry Deterrence." *Journal of Economic Theory* 17:280–312.

Milhaupt, C. J., and M. D. West. 2000. "The Dark Side of Private Ordering: An Institutional and Empirical Analysis of Organized Crime." *University of Chicago Law Review* 67:41–98.

Mitchell, W. 1904. *An Essay on the Early History of the Law Merchant: Being the Yorke Prize Essay for the Year 1903*. Cambridge: Cambridge University Press.

Mnookin, R., and L. Kornhauser. 1979. "Bargaining in the Shadow of the Law: The Case of Divorce." *Yale Law Journal* 88:950–997.

Monteverde, K., and D. J. Teece. 1982. "Supplier Switching Costs and Vertical Integration in the Automobile Industry." *Bell Journal of Economics* 13 (1): 206–213.

Moore, E. W. 1985. *The Fairs of Medieval England: An Introductory Study*. Toronto: Pontifical Institute of Mediaeval Studies.

Munshi, K. 2011. "Strength in Numbers: Networks as a Solution to Occupational Traps." *Review of Economic Studies* 78:1069–1101.

Murphy, V. 2004. "Romance Killer." Forbes.com, November 29. http://www.forbes.com/global/2004/1129/016.html.

Murray, C. 2007. "Jewish Genius." *Commentary*, Apr. 1.

North, D. C. 1990. *Institutions, Institutional Change and Economic Performance*. Cambridge: Cambridge University Press.

North, D. C., and B. Weingast. 1989. "Constitution and Commitment: The Evolution of Institutional Governing Public Choice in Seventeenth-Century England." *Journal of Economic History* 49 (4): 803–832.

Oliar, D., and C. Sprigman. 2008. "There's No Free Laugh (Anymore): The Emergence of Intellectual Property Norms and the Transformation of Stand-Up Comedy." *University of Virginia Law Review* 94:1787–1867.

Ostrom, E. 1990. *Governing the Commons: The Evolution of Institutions for Collective Action*. Cambridge: Cambridge University Press.

Otulsky, A. 2011. *Precious Objects: A Story of Diamonds, Family, and a Way of Life*. New York: Scribner.

Penslar, D. 2001. *Shylock's Children: Economics and Jewish Identity in Modern Europe*. Berkeley: University of California Press.

Piramal, G. 1990. "Sparkle on Indian Diamond Market Dims." *Financial Times*, June 19, 8.

———. 1996. *Business Maharajas*. New Delhi: Viking.

Pollack, E. J. 2002. *The Pretender*. New York: Simon and Schuster.

Porter, M. 1985. *Competitive Advantage: Creating and Sustaining Superior Performance*. New York: Free Press.

Porter, M., S. Marciano, and A. Warhurst. 2009. *De Beers: Addressing New Competitiveness Challenges*, Case 9-706-501. Harvard Business School.

Posner, E. 2000. *Law and Social Norms*. Cambridge, MA: Harvard University Press.

Posner, Richard A. 1969. "Oligopoly and the Antitrust Laws: A Suggested Approach." *Stanford Law Review* 21:1562–1576.

Priest, G., and B. Klein. 1984. "The Selection of Disputes for Litigation." *Journal of Legal Studies* 13:1–55.

Putnam, Robert. 1993. *Making Democracy Work: Civic Traditions in Modern Italy*. Princeton, NJ: Princeton University Press.

Rapaport, M. 2013. "Synthetics: The Sale of Synthetic Diamonds as Natural Is Challenging the Integrity of Our Diamond Industry—What Should We Do about It?" *Rapaport*, December. http://www.diamonds.net/Docs/Synthetics /Sinthetics.pdf.

Reiff, N. 1998. "Martin Rapaport: One Man's Destruction of Our Industry." *Jewelers Circular Keystone*, July 1. http://jck.polygon.net/archives/1998/O7/jcO78-105.html.

Reserve Bank of India. 2013. "Master Circular—Rupee / Foreign Currency Export Credit and Customer Service to Exporters." July 1. https://rbi.org.in/scripts/BS _ViewMasCirculardetails.aspx?Id=8132&Mode=0.

Richman, B. D. 2004. "Firms, Courts, and Reputation Mechanisms: Towards a Positive Theory of Private Ordering." *Columbia Law Review* 104:2328–2368.

———. 2006. "How Community Institutions Create Economic Advantage: Jewish Diamond Merchants in New York." *Law and Social Inquiry* 31:383–420.

———. 2009a. "The Antitrust of Reputation Mechanisms: Institutional Economics and Concerted Refusals to Deal." *Virginia Law Review* 95:325–387.

———. 2009b. "Ethnic Networks, Extralegal Certainty, and Globalisation: Peering into the Diamond Industry." In *Contractual Certainty in International Trade: Empirical Studies and Theoretical Debates on Institutional Support for Global Economic Exchanges*, edited by V. Gessner, 31–47. Oxford: Hart Publishing.

Roberts, J. 2003. *Glitter & Greed: The Secret World of the Diamond Cartel*. New York: Disinformation Books.

Rockefeller, Edwin S. 2001. "The Enduring Nature of 'Antitrust.'" *Antitrust & Trade Regulation Reporter*. Bureau of National Affairs, vol. 81, Sept. 28, 282.

Rodrik, D. 2003. "Introduction: What Do We Learn from the Country Narratives?" In *In Search of Prosperity: Analytic Narratives on Economic Growth*, edited by D. Rodrik, 1–22. Princeton, NJ: Princeton University Press.

Roth, Cecil. 1940. *The Jewish Contribution to Civilization*. New York and London: Harper & Bros. Publishers.

———. 1961. The Economic History of the Jews. *Economic History Review* 14 (1): 131–135.

Rozhon, T. 2005. "Competition Is Forever." *New York Times*, February 9, C1.

Rubin, S. 2001. "Diamonds in the Rough." *Financial Post*, February 3, D1.

Ryan, K. 2010. "This Is a 24-Carat Disaster for Africa." *Spiked*, August 16, 2010.

Sachs, S. 2006. "From St. Ives to Cyberspace: The Modern Distortion of the Medieval 'Law Merchant.'" *American University International Law Review* 21:685–812.

Salmans, S. 1984. "A Diamond Maverick's War with the Club on 47th Street." *New York Times*, November 13, Al.

Salmond, J. W., and P. J. Fitzgerald. 1966. *Salmond on Jurisprudence*. London: Sweet and Maxwell.

Saxenian, A. 1994. *Regional Advantage: Culture and Competition in Silicon Valley and Route 128.* Cambridge, MA: Harvard University Press.

Schaeffer, E. C. 2008. "Remittances and Reputations in Hawala Money-Transfer Systems: Self-enforcing Exchange on an International Scale." *Journal of Private Enterprise* 24 (1): 95–117.

Selby, S. A., and C. Campbell. 2010. *Flawless: Inside the Largest Diamond Heist in History.* New York: Union Square Press.

Sen, A. 1999. *Development as Freedom.* New York: Alfred A. Knopf.

Shah, J. 2008. "Palanpuris Have Rivals for Global Diamond Throne." *DNA India,* October 22. http://www.dnaindia.com/india/report-palanpuris-have-rivals-for-global-diamond-throne-1200102.

Shainberg, A. M. 1982. "Jews and the Diamond Trade." In *The Jewish Directory and Almanac,* edited by Ivan Tillem, 301–311. New York: Pacific Press.

Shapiro, C. 1983. "Premiums for High Quality Products as Returns to Reputation." *Quarterly Journal of Economics* 98 (4): 659–680.

Shapiro, M. 1975. "Courts." *Handbook of Political Science* 5:321–371.

Shatzmiller, J. 1990. *Shylock Reconsidered: Jews, Moneylending, and Medieval Society.* Los Angeles: University of California Press.

Shelanski, H. A., and P. G. Klein. 1995. "Empirical Research in Transaction Cost Economics: A Review and Assessment." *Journal of Law, Economics, and Organization* 11 (2): 335–361.

Sherman, A. 2014. "Synthetic Diamonds: Opportunity or Problem?" Buyers Intelligence Group. http://www.bigjewelers.com/wp-content/uploads/2016/07/Synthetic-Diamonds_Opportunity-or-Problem-by-Abe-Sherman.pdf.

Shield, R. R. 2002. *Diamond Stories: Enduring Change on 47th Street.* Ithaca, NY: Cornell University Press.

Shnidman, R. 2013. "Online Jewelry's Growth Restraint: U.S. Jewelers Adapt to Online Challenges." *Rapaport,* February 27. http://www.diamonds.net/News/NewsItem.aspx?ArticleID=51502.

Shor, R. 1993. *Connections: A Profile of Diamond People and Their History.* Philadelphia: International Diamond Publications.

Sokol, D., T. K. Cheng, and I. Lianos. 2013. *Competition Law and Development.* Stanford, CA: Stanford University Press.

Sombart, W. [1911] 2001. *The Jews and Modern Capitalism.* Translated by M. Epstein (1913). Kitchener, Ontario: Batoche Books.

Spar, D. L. 2000. *Forever: De Beers and U.S. Antitrust Law,* Case 9-700-082. Harvard Business School.

———. 2006. "Markets: Continuity and Change in the International Diamond Market." *Journal of Economic Perspectives* 20 (3): 195–208.

Spar, D. L., and L. T. La Mure. 2003. "The Power of Activism: Assessing the Impact of NGOs on Global Business." *California Management Review* 45:78–101.

Starobin, S., and E. Weinthal. 2010. "The Search for Credible Information in Social and Environmental Global Governance: The Kosher Label." *Business and Politics* 12 (3), Art.8: 1–35.

Starr, R. 1984. "The Editorial Notebook; The Real Treasure of 47th Street." *New York Times*, March 26. http://www.nytimes.com/1984/03/26/opinion/the-editorial-notebook-the-real-treasure-of-47th-street.html.

Stigler, G. J., and G. S. Becker. 1977. "De Gustibus Non Est Disputandum." *American Economic Review* 67:76–90.

Stockum, S. 2002. "An Economist's Margin Notes: The Antitrust Writings of Timothy Muris." *Antitrust* 16:60–63.

Surowiecki, J. 2000. "The Diamond Market vs. the Free Market." *New Yorker*, July 31.

Telser, L. G. 1980. "A Theory of Self-enforcing Agreements." *Journal of Business* 53:27–44.

Trebilcock, M., and J. Leng. 2006. "The Role of Formal Contract Law and Enforcement in Economic Development." *Virginia Law Review* 92:1517–1580.

Trebilcock, M., and M. Mota Prado. 2011. *What Makes Poor Countries Poor? Institutional Determinants of Development*. Northampton, MA: Edward Elgar.

Turner, D. F. 1966. "Some Reflections on Antitrust." *New York State Bar Association Antitrust Law Symposium*, June, 1–9.

UNCTAD (United Nations Conference on Trade and Development). 1998. *Empirical Evidence on the Benefits from Applying Competition Law and Policy Principles to Economic Development in Order to Attain Greater Efficiency in International Trade and Development*. Geneva: UNCTAD Secretariat.

Velez-Ibanez, Carlos G. 1983. *Bonds of Mutual Trust: The Cultural Systems of Rotating Credit Associations Among Urban Mexicans and Chicanos*. New Brunswick, NJ: Rutgers University Press.

Weber, L. 2001. "The Diamond Game." *New York Times*, April 8. sec. 3, p. 1.

Williamson, O. E. 1975. *Markets and Hierarchies: Analysis and Antitrust Implications*. New York: Free Press.

———. 1976. "Franchise Bidding for Natural Monopolies—in General and with Respect to CATV." *Bell Journal of Economics* 7 (1): 73–104.

———. 1983. "Credible Commitments: Using Hostages to Support Exchange." *American Economic Review* 73 (4): 519–540.

———. 1985. *The Economic Institutions of Capitalism*. New York: Free Press.

———. 1993. "Calculativeness, Trust, and Economic Organization." *Journal of Law and Economics* 36:453–486.

———. 1996. *The Mechanisms of Governance*. New York: Oxford University Press.

———. 2002. "The Lens of Contract: Private Ordering." *American Economic Review* 92 (2): 438–443.

———. 2003. "Economics and Antitrust Enforcement: Transition Years." *Antitrust* 17:61–65.

————. 2007. "Transaction Cost Economics: An Introduction," Discussion Paper 2007-3, Economics E-Journal, http://www.economics-ejournal.org/economics /discussionpapers/2007-3/file.

World Bank. 2004. *World Development Report 2005: A Better Investment Climate for Everyone.* Washington, DC: World Bank.

Zimnisky, P. 2014. "De Beers Market Share to Rebound to 40% with Canada's Gahcho Kué Diamonds." PaulZimnisky.com, July 8. http://www.paulzimnisky .com/de-beers-market-share-to-rebound-to-40-with-canada-s-gahcho-kue -diamonds.

Index